EVERY-DAY LIFE ON AN OLD
HIGHLAND FARM

EVERY-DAY LIFE
ON AN
OLD HIGHLAND FARM
1769-1782

BY

I. F. GRANT

WITH A PREFACE BY

W. R. SCOTT, M.A., Phil.D.
ADAM SMITH PROFESSOR OF POLITICAL
ECONOMY IN THE UNIVERSITY OF
GLASGOW

LONGMANS, GREEN AND CO.
39 PATERNOSTER ROW, LONDON, E.C.4.
NEW YORK, TORONTO
BOMBAY, CALCUTTA AND MADRAS
1924

Made in Great Britain

PREFACE

THE manuscript, which Miss I. F. Grant has edited, in the following pages is a study which would be of great value to students of social and agrarian history in any case ; but which, in addition, has a very special importance in so far as it relates to Scotland. One reason is that, despite the efforts of the Scottish History Society, a considerable number of documents of this type is required, since it is unfortunately the case that there has been too much writing of the economic history of Scotland before it was possible to supply adequate documentation of it. Any one who has had to impose on himself the duty of verifying some statement in this field regarding events in the past often finds, as he hunts it back and back, that each writer has taken it, more or less faithfully, from some predecessor ; and it frequently turns out that the original authority may have pronounced an opinion on inadequate evidence, or that this opinion has been extended over an area the greater part of which the authority never saw, or over a period of time during which he could not have lived. More than one of such necessary corrections will be made possible by Miss Grant's work.

As regards social history—and particularly that of the Highlands—the value of the manuscript is no less, but for different reasons. Highland life, down through the ages, has been pictured in song, story, and memoirs. Quite possibly these sources are sufficient to touch the heart and to fire the imagination of those of Highland blood. But to others the whole epic must remain, to a greater or less degree, a sealed book. The way of approach of the latter is different, and something more precise and detailed is required. Here, again, Miss

Grant supplies definite quantitative details for the Davoch of Dunachton—a district on the banks of the Spey, midway between Kingussie and Aviemore— between the years 1769 and 1780.

The period and the nature of the record are both important. The time extends over the later part of the life of Adam Smith, and the data in the Account Book afford opportunities for checking his statements regarding economic conditions in the Highlands, to the extent that Dunachton may be regarded as typical of those conditions. Further, the manuscript gives a very full and exact picture of Highland farming operations in the district to which it relates at a very interesting period. It shows us the life and methods after the earlier agricultural revolution had made itself felt, but before the second revolution in northern Scotland, when sheep farming was immensely extended during the French Wars at the end of the eighteenth century.

William Mackintosh of Balnespick, the writer of the memoranda, was what was known as a 'tacksman,' a position which assumed a special form in the Highlands. A 'tack' was the Scottish term for a lease ; thus, before the Union the men who leased the collection of the Customs were 'tacksmen of the Customs.' In the Highlands the system of certain land leases was intimately connected with the original working of the clan system. The position and the power of the Chief depended on the number of clansmen he could muster, and this involved a form of what might perhaps be termed automatic recruiting. That in its turn required some method by which kinsmen of the Chief would each become responsible for providing their respective quotas of men for the total muster. One method of giving effect to this was through the Chief giving to his kinsmen or followers tacks or leases of land, and the latter, in their turn, took under-tenants, who were counted on to provide the necessary number of men for the field. Like many other customs, this one survived after the reasons which had brought it into existence had passed away. It will be one of the most interesting reflections of the reader of Miss Grant's pages to trace step by step whether the existence of William Mackintosh of Balnespick as a tacksman was a mere historical survival, or whether the old military organisation had gradually and imperceptibly assumed a new economic signification which, after fulfilling its purpose, again changed in such a manner that in time it divested itself of the tacksman altogether. The second stage, of which Balnespick may be taken in many ways as a type, is very carefully treated by Miss Grant in her introduction, and is supported by a great number of entries in the Account Book. Once the old days of cattle-lifting had passed away, the population of the Highlands had to learn to support itself on its scanty resources and very largely in isolated communities. Thus, the tacksman became the organiser, and often the financier, of his particular community. Hitherto very little indeed has been known of how and why the system worked, but Miss Grant's interpretation of Balnespick's entries gives a vast amount of light on a subject which has hitherto been most obscure. Her patient treatment of the data has the further merit of giving important indications as to how far it may be possible to generalise from this instance to other cases about the same time. As regards the position of Balnespick in relation to his ground-landlord on the one side and to his tenants on the other, it appears that the rents due from his sub-tenants nominally covered the chief rent he paid. That left him the produce of the portion of land he reserved for himself for his own maintenance. At this point there are two characteristics which may or may not be exceptional. He only received a part of the rents payable by his tenants, the remainder being irrecoverable; while, on the other hand, he was not dependent on the produce of the lands of Dunachton for his own living, since he had other sources of income. This raises the question as to how a case of a tack of land would have worked out, where the tacksman had not the latter resources. In that event there might have been some danger that the under-tenants would have suffered.

Miss Grant's readers will find her both a competent and interesting guide to the intricacies of the old Account Book. Fortunately in the eighteenth century land accounts were not standardised ; and the few who made some attempt to keep them found it necessary to add many glosses explaining their own entries. For this reason many of them are documents of very great human interest. They show as much of the working of a man's mind as of that of his property. At the same time the modern reader requires someone to make clear to him the exact environment of the writer. This Miss Grant has done in a wholly admirable manner. Her patient research has been remarkable, for she has insisted in mastering comparatively minute details of the farming practice of her ancestor, while she has the wise restraint to convey to her reader only the results. For instance, she was not satisfied till from various sources she was able to recreate the exact lay-out of each field as it had been a century and a half ago.

In another direction also, she has exercised a wise restraint. Though William Mackintosh was her ancestor, she has concentrated on matters of general interest, and the book has no trace of the usual type of family history. Indeed it might be said to belong to what seems to be the new school of a particular group of writings. People have become tired of the type of book which is produced by some member of a family in which his ancestor or ancestors are represented as having all the virtues of all ages and none of the vices of any age. Now the tendency seems to be to go rather to the other extreme ; and, lest he should be accused of partiality towards his ancestors, the modern writer is often severely critical. So we may be approaching a stage at which it will be said ' Oh that my enemy's descendant had written his biography.' Thus one forms the idea that, while judged by modern standards Balnespick's farming methods were somewhat pitiful, according to those of his own day he had considerable claims to be regarded as ' an agricultural improver.'

W. R. Scott.

FOREWORD

I HAVE to ask the reader's indulgence for a considerable variation in the spelling of the place-names, especially that of the field of Auchnabeuchin. In quoting from William Mackintosh's Account Book, or describing his times, it seems natural to use his spelling of the names he mentions. The eighteenth-century forms vary, and they differ considerably from those in use at present ; yet in dealing with modern conditions, as contrasted with those of earlier times, it would seem even stranger not to use the current spelling—in fact, it might lead to confusion about some of the localities mentioned.

I should like to express my gratitude and my indebtedness to all those who have helped and advised me, and especially to thank Colonel G. Mackintosh, C.B., C.O.B.E. (Clune), and also Canon W. L. Mackintosh of Balnespick—both direct descendants of the ' old Balnespick ' of the book—for the loan of valuable material ; Mr. Alexander McEwan, who spared time to help me in this and in very many other ways. I am especially indebted to Mr. E. Fergusson and Mr. Stuart for the practical, actual facts they so kindly gave me, and I owe very much to Mr. H. W. Malkin, C.B., C.M.G., of Corriebrough ; to Colonel Wolrige Gordon, C.M.G., of Esslemont and Hillhead ; to Miss Biscoe of Newton; to Mr. Critchley; to Miss Macbean; to the Rev. Mr. Maclean, Minister of Alvie; to Mr. Erskine Jackson, Secretary of the Scottish Land and Property Owners Federation ; to Admiral Sir Wilmot Fawkes, G.C.B., K.C.V.O., LL.D. ; and to Major H. F. McClintock.

I should like to mention how very grateful I am to Mr. W. Angus, Curator of the Historical Department, the General Register House, Edinburgh, for the kindness and learning with which he helped me in solving several difficulties, and to Mr. A. M. Mackintosh for expert advice and for access to his valuable collection of papers ; to Mr. J. M. Keynes, C.B., Editor of the *Economic Journal*, for his very kind permission to reprint part of an article that appeared in that paper ; to Mr. Hutchison, Editor of *Northern Notes and Queries*, and to those of his readers who interpreted several obsolete agricultural terms ; to Professor Rait, C.B.E., Historiographer Royal for Scotland, for kindly encouragement ; and, most of all, to Professor W. R. Scott, M.A., Phil.D., for advice and stimulus, and for sparing the time to give my book the very great advantage of having a Preface by so eminent a scholar.

I can only wish that my readers may have one-hundredth part the pleasure in reading this book that I had in writing it, for, whatever be the shortcomings of his modern chronicler, the company of an old Highland gentleman and of the countryfolk that were his neighbours is about the best that the heart of man could desire.

I. F. GRANT.

June 1924

CONTENTS

AN OLD HIGHLAND FARM

CHAPTER I

INTRODUCTORY

THE entries in this old estate and farm Account Book were jotted down between 1768 and 1782. They were made by William Mackintosh of Balnespick, the head of one of the older Mackintosh families.[1]

William Mackintosh had sold Balnespick to Macpherson of Invereshie in 1748,[2] and at the time he wrote (1769–82) in his Account Book he held a tack (*i.e.* lease) for 'Three nineteen years' from the Chief of Mackintosh of the Davoch of Dunachton and Kincraig in the parish of Alvie on the upper reaches of the Spey. He married a daughter of Grant of Clury, an old Strathspey family, and died in 1784, and it is evident, from the handwriting and briefness of the later entries in the Account Book, that he had begun to fail some years before that date.

He had three sons : Lachlan, the Lachie so often mentioned in the Account Book ; William, who afterwards became a colonel and died at Nairn ; and the 'dear Geordie' of the Account Book, whom he set up in America, and of whom nothing at all seems to be known. Lachlan, the eldest son, married a Miss Mackintosh of Mackintosh, and had two sons—William, who succeeded him, and Eneas, who died comparatively young and unmarried, after a most gallant and distinguished military career. He volunteered for the post

---

[1] Old family papers and traditions. An excellent account of the family was given in the *Northern Chronicle* of December 13 and 20, 1893.
[2] See *Mackintoshes and Clan Chattan*, by A. M. Mackintosh, p. 397.

of leader of a forlorn hope at the storming of Badajoz. His name is mentioned once in the Account Book.[1]

There is a tradition in the family that Balnespick tried to buy the estate of Raits, which marches with Dunachton, but the poet Macpherson forestalled or outbid him.

The old Account Book is tantalising reading, for a good many sheets have been torn out, so that it is difficult to trace any transaction through to its conclusion. From the number of half-finished pages scattered through it, it is evident that Balnespick jotted down at random items that happened to be associated in his mind;[2] and it would seem that some of the entries were copied out of some other book, for the records of some of the harvests are to be found early in the book, and those of the sowings for the same years towards the end. There is throughout no sort of chronological order, and many of the records are irritatingly incomplete.

Another difficulty to the present-day reader is the similarity of names and nicknames. Most of the country people about were related to each other, and the number of surnames and Christian names was very limited. The nicknames that were constantly used numbered only about four, so that it is exceedingly difficult to pick out entries relating to one individual among those referring to his quite numerous namesakes.

The book, in fact, is not the clear statement of a trained book-keeper; still less is it a record intended for the information of posterity. It is merely the scribbled private jottings of a fussy, hard-headed, conscientious old gentleman; and although in some respects the information that it contains is maddeningly inadequate, yet, as one puzzles out the scrawled, faded

---

[1] Old family papers and traditions. See also *Northern Chronicle*, December 13 and 20, 1893.

[2] Such jottings seem to have been fairly common in those days. I know of the existence of two books kept by gentlemen farmers of about the same period as Balnespick, and in each case the entries are noted down in the same disjointed style.

script on the yellowing pages, the intimate, everyday details of life in an age that is dead and gone become almost startlingly present—even though they be isolated vignettes rather than continuous records.

The historical value of the Account Book is greatly enhanced by the date at which it was written. William Mackintosh of Balnespick happened to live through the most crucial time in the whole history of the Highlands,[1] for by 1769 not only had the new system of agriculture, which wrought such great changes in even the settled rural life of England, and which we speak of as the ' Agricultural Revolution,' begun to permeate the wilder and more backward uplands of Badenoch,[2] but the whole social, political and mental life of the people was being rapidly changed, owing to the systematic policy of the Government of opening up the Highlands after the Risings of '15 and '45.

Nor is the interest of the old Account Book merely antiquarian. A sense of history, and of the vital connection of the past and the present, seems to cling about arable land more strongly than about anything else. Just as old Balnespick and his sub-tenants cultivated the soil, with all the weeds and enrichment that had come to it through the labours of the chain of long-dead husbandmen who had tilled it in succession from time immemorial, so have succeeding cultivators continued the work down to the present day—machinery is flung on to the scrap heap, but the brown earth serves mankind from generation to generation. The connection between the conditions of the past and the problems of the present must surely be closer in rural social life than in urban districts, and in the records of their economic history must lie a very special interest and value.

[1] Although the date of his birth is not known, he certainly lived through the '45. He was infeft into Balnespick in 1743. See *The Mackintoshes and Clan Chattan*, by A. M. Mackintosh, p. 397.

[2] Most contemporary writers describe the Agricultural Revolution as just beginning to affect Badenoch at this time; see, for example, *First Statistical Account for Alvie Parish*, vol. xiii. No. 26, p. 375.

CHAPTER II

THE PSYCHOLOGICAL ATMOSPHERE

BEFORE trying to reconstruct the daily life of the people, so much harder, and more poverty stricken and circumscribed than that of their descendants, it is surely worth while considering how incomparably richer was the atmosphere of tradition and association that surrounded them, and which has long since faded from the ken of all but the oldest people.

Even yet a dim, faint memory survives of the ceillidhs [1] that were held of an evening in the huddled, turf-built cottages, where neighbours gathered round the fire and the only light was the glow of the peat and the flicker of the fir candles [2] glimmering through the smoke-wreaths ; and when the fitful drone of the women's spinning-wheels made a background and accompaniment to the strange old songs and stories that were the mental heritage of the clachan. Here and there a story or a tradition has survived, preserved, like some museum specimen, for its antiquarian interest, and such fragments throw a valuable light on the mental outlook of a people that took delight in them and to whom they were intensely vivid and real.

Mrs. Grant of Laggan [3] was stating a fact when

[1] Ceillidh.—Informal gathering for songs, stories, and mutual entertainment; pronounced Caily.

[2] Fir candles.—A splinter of firwood, preferably from a tree preserved in a peat moss, was the usual means of lighting employed by the country people (Sir Eneas Mackintosh of Mackintosh, *Notes on Strathdearn*, 1774–83, p. 35).

[3] Mrs. Grant of Laggan.—The wife of the minister of Laggan, a parish further up the Spey in Badenoch. Her *Letters from the Mountains* (1773) are written in a pedantic style, but give a vivid picture of the everyday life of the district.

she wrote : ' In every cottage there is a musician and every hamlet a poet.' [1] The Rev. Dr. Sinton, in his ' Poetry of Badenoch,' has collected and preserved 500 closely written pages of local poems and their translations. Expression is given to every varying mood and incident of life—there are laments and love songs, satires and humorous rhymes, songs for the ploughman and the reaper, and a large number of devotional pieces. In reading them one is not only struck by their literary merit but by the fact that they are so strongly native to the locality. Many of the place-names that are mentioned also occur in the old Account Book—thus there is a reaping song from Ballachroan, a lament for a member of the Borlum family ; and a pathetically beautiful love song to the ' Fair Haired Youth of Ballourne ' refers to the little farm that bordered Balnespick's tack on the east, and that he constantly mentioned under its other name of Pitchurn. One of the later and more florid pieces is a lament on the death of William Mackintosh of Balnespick, grandson to the writer of the Account Book.[2]

The Highlanders were also intensely musical. Miss Grant of Rothiemurchus wrote that in her day every tenth Highlander at least could play tolerably well on some kind of musical instrument,[3] and Mrs. Grant

[1] *Letters from the Mountains*, p. 73.

[2] It extends to two pages ; the following verses are a sample :
' Like am I to Ossian who would be telling how it happened to the Feinns, who would be talking about Oscar ; who would be sighing over the deeds of the valiant men,
' 'Tis what hath intensified my misfortune—the swiftness with which William son of Lachlan hath gone to death—a young man of high spirit—the topmost branch of all the Mackintoshes.
' Little wonder that thou shouldst be haughty, and the many great roots out of which thy body hath grown ; the blood of King Fingal with coating a living lining to your clay.'

[3] *Memoirs of a Highland Lady*, p. 35, by Mrs. Smith, *née* Miss Grant of Rothiemurchus, a property a few miles down the Spey on the opposite side of the river from Dunachton.

of Laggan also describes the charming playing of the
country people. In the old Account Book two professional fiddlers are mentioned. But it was the inter-
mingling of singing with the daily work of the people
that was one of the most distinctive and charming
features of old Highland life. Every task had its
special tunes.[1] Thus Burt, in his 'Letters from the
North of Scotland,' 1754, vol. ii. p. 87, describes the
women harvesting in time to their singing ; and bend-
ing, rising, and turning with the precision of a company
of soldiers. Even still, in the old Scotch songs, one
can trace the jerk of the loom, the swing of the scythe,
the intermittent cadence of the old muckle wheel, and
some of the other working rhythms that long-dead folk
put into their music to help them through their daily
toil. Perhaps we are coming back to something of the
old idea through the more prosaic channel of ' scientific
management.'

The old Highlanders had a deep and intense love of
nature. It is evident in such fragments of the Ossianic
poetry as have come down to us. They had many
curious half-beliefs and ceremonies. General Stuart
of Garth, in his ' Sketch of the Manners and Character
of the Highlanders of Scotland,' written in 1825,
describes ' superstitious rites and ceremonies' that
' were common thirty years ago, but they have now
disappeared even among children ' (p. 9).

' The anniversary of Bel (in Gaelic Bealdin) was
celebrated by children and shepherds with a feast of
milk, eggs, butter, cheese, etc. These remains of
ancient superstitions were accompanied with many
ceremonies and offerings for the protection of their
flocks from storms, eagles and foxes. This festival
was held on May Day. When all was ready, a boy

---

[1] Examples of singing at work are given in Dr. Ross's introduction
to *Home Industries*, a publication of the Scottish Home Industries
Association. *Songs of the North* have a few examples of working songs,
but the largest number are to be found in Mrs. Kennedy Fraser's collection
of Hebridean songs.

stood up, holding in his left hand a piece of bread, covered with a kind of hasty pudding, or custard of eggs, milk, and butter ; and with his face turned towards the East, he threw a piece over his left shoulder, and cried, " This to you, O Mists and Storms, that ye be favourable to our corns and pasture : This to thee, O eagle, that thou mayest spare our lambs and kids : This to Thee, O Raven," etc. . . . Similar to this festival was the Samhuin, or Fire of Peace, the origin of which tradition ascribes to the Druids or Daoni-Si, who assembled the people in the open air for the purpose of administering justice. In many parts of the country are seen the small conical hills on which these courts were held, and which are called Tomvoide, *i.e.* the Court Hill. . . . The anniversary of these meetings was celebrated on the first of November, the Hallow-e'en of the Lowlands. Immediately after dark, large fires were kindled in conspicuous places in every hamlet. The inhabitants at the same time assembled, and the night was passed in dancing, and the observance of numberless ceremonies and superstitions, the principal object of which was to discover occult events and to pry into the future.'

A little knoll below the present Dunachtonmore is named Tom-void. Balnespick wrote of it as Tomwode, and mentions it constantly in the Account Book.

Life was made more terrifying, but infinitely more picturesque and interesting, to the old Highlanders by their strong belief in witches, fairies, ghosts, etc. Much has been done to collect the old lore of the witches' malevolences and of the sinister doings of the Little Folk and their thefts of children and even of grown-up people. Doctor William Mackay, in ' Glen-moriston and Glenurquhart,' chap. xx. p. 417, gives a most interesting account of the strange ritual of bunches of rowan berries, runes, and other precautions that were taken against these supernatural foes. Not only were such things believed in, in general, but Badenoch, like most other Highland districts, had a

number of well-authenticated local stories.[1]   It is easy
to realise how far more stimulating to the imagination
were oral traditions of events that were said to have
happened in familiar places than any mere story-book
fairy tale.   Thus the Witch of Laggan is said to have
lived at Lynchat, only three miles off, and the way she
took in her desperate attempt to escape her fate was
probably much the same as would be followed by
anyone crossing the bleak Monaliadh Hills between
Dunachton and Clune, in the parish of Dalarossie,
which Lachlan, Balnespick's son, had bought.   There
was evidently a good deal of coming and going between
Clune and Dunachton, and surely the younger Balnespick and his servants must often have thought, as they
went, of the wild story of the witch-woman.   She had
taken the form of a gigantic cat and had tried to kill
a man who was hunting in the Cairngorm Hills, but
by some form of white magic he wounded her mortally,
and she fled back to her cottage in Lynchat and, re-
suming her natural form, died in the presence of some
horrified neighbours.   About the hour of her death
some herds were walking from Dalarossie—the churchyard of which is so holy that all magic and witchcraft
lose their power within its boundaries.   As they went
a woman passed them, running towards Dalarossie,
wounded in breast and throat as the witch-woman had
been, and struggling on in desperate haste.   Soon afterwards a black man, mounted on a black horse and
accompanied by two black hounds, rode by, following
hard on the woman's tracks.   Later on the black man
overtook them, riding back the way he had come,
with the body of the woman across his saddle-bow and
the two hounds with their teeth set fast in her body.
By this the good folk of Badenoch knew that the soul
of the witch had sought sanctuary in Dalarossie Kirkyard, but that the devil had overtaken her before she
reached it and had carried her off to his own place.

[1] A good selection of local stories is scattered through *Lectures on
the Mountains*, by an anonymous writer.

This story is only a specimen of many wild tales, most of them without the traditional happy ending and all with a strongly localised setting.

Of a more cheerful type of fairy were the two brownies attached to the Rothiemurchus family, who threshed and reaped and performed superhuman feats of work in return for a little milk and a few bannocks left in the kitchen overnight. Sometimes one of the brownies, or another spirit attached to the family, would even lean over the Laird of Rothiemurchus' shoulder as he sat playing at the dambrod and advise his next move.[1]

Dunachton itself had a 'bogle' in the cellar, but nothing seems to be known of its habits and disposition.

The passing of the fairies from Badenoch is recorded in an official document, for in the 'Second Statistical Account for the Parish of Alvie' (1845) (p. 82 in the edition published by Blackwood) the minister of the parish states that :

'The ignorant country people, particularly the old, who are strongly wedded to the absurd superstitions of their venerated ancestors, consider the whirlwind as indicative of a procession of the imaginary beings called fairies. This superstition, however, is wearing fast away : and it is probable that in less than half a century not a trace of it will remain, providing the progress of education shall not be obstructed by the failure of adequate means of support to the schools at present so extensively in operation. The Venerable Principal Baird, whose labours of love will long be remembered with heartfelt gratitude in the Highlands of Scotland, has contributed, by his benevolent exertions, in an eminent degree to the expulsion of fairies from the Highland Hills.'

It is a less picturesque narrative than Kipling's charming ' Dymchurch Flit ' in ' Puck of Pook's Hill.'

Besides ghost and fairy stories, there were the old Ossianic legends to repeat. Macpherson, the

---

[1] Rothiemurchus is several times mentioned in the Account Book. It lies a few miles east, on the other side of the river.

'translator,' was born at Kingussie[1] and spent his youth there, and, whatever were the fragments on which he based his earlier pieces, they must have been heard locally.

General David Stuart of Garth, in 'Sketches of the Character and Manners of the Highlanders of Scotland,' published in 1825 (see p. 114), says that when he was a boy he often used to listen to the older people reciting long epic poems. In older times, he says, 'when a stranger appeared, after the usual introductory compliments, the first question was, " Bheil dad agad air na Fheinn?" ("Can you speak of the days of Fingal?") If the answer was in the affirmative the whole hamlet was convened, and midnight was usually the hour of separation. At these meetings the women regularly attended, and were, besides, in the habit of assembling alternately in each other's houses, with their distaffs or spinning-wheels, when the best singer, or the most amusing reciter, always bore away the palm.'

In addition there was an almost incredible store of clan traditions and stories to draw upon—some of them as legendary as the Ossianic epics, others with a strong historical basis, but all intensely interesting to the old Highlanders ; for the disintegration of the clan spirit had only begun, and the story of his ancestors and of his own descent was one of the main preoccupations of a clansman. Where the tie of kinship was not present, it was always assumed. Even among the meanest of them 'almost everyone was a genealogist.'[2]

It would be impossible to indicate even one-half of the picturesque details in which the turbulent histories of the Mackintoshes and Grants abound. But it may be worth indicating some of the stories that are attached to the immediate neighbourhood. Balnespick, William Mackintosh's original property, which lies just across the valley from Dunachton, means the ' Field of the Bishop.' It was originally in the possession of the

[1] Kingussie is about five miles from Dunachton.
[2] Burt's *Letters from the North of Scotland*, 1754, vol. vi. p. 126.

Bishop of Moray, and the story ran that a notable villain, John du Garve of Knockandow (this place-name is mentioned in the Account Book, p. 63), wished to be revenged on a Grant of Achernick. Overhearing a quarrel between Achernick and the priest of Duthil, he murdered the latter so that Achernick should be accused of the deed. The Bishop of Moray had Grant of Achernick seized and thrown into his prison at Spynie (on the Morayshire coast), where he lay in chains for months and finally died. Soon afterwards Du Garve was executed for theft and confessed the murder, and the Chief of Grant pursued the Bishop for injury to his kinsman, and received as compensation the Church's holdings in Strathspey. The story does not relate that any amend was made to the family of the luckless Achernick himself![1]

Kincraig (part of the land rented by Balnespick and constantly mentioned in the Account Book), South Kinrara, and Dalnavert were known as the 'Davochs of the Head,' and were part of the satisfaction made for the wrongful beheading of William, 15th Laird of Mackintosh, by the Marquis of Huntly in 1556. The main facts are historical,[2] but the more picturesque tradition tells that the Chief of the Mackintoshes, having quarrelled with the head of the Gordons, feared that the latter would be too strong for him and that his clan would be defeated. He therefore decided to make his peace, and set forth almost unattended, choosing a time when he knew that Huntly would not be at home, in the hopes of finding his lady more merciful. It happened to be the season of Martinmas, and he found the lady in the kitchen, superintending the cutting up of the meat for salting for winter use. The Chief pleaded that Huntly's

---

[1] This story is told in *Lectures on the Mountains*, vol. ii. p. 129. The transference of Balnespick from the Bishop of Moray to the Chief of Grant at this time is historically correct: see *Northern Chronicle*, December 13, 1893.

[2] See *The Mackintoshes and Clan Chattan*, by A. M. Mackintosh.

wrath should not be visited upon his clan, and offered his head as forfeit. The lady briefly ordered him, if he were as good as his word, to lay it on the block upon which the carcasses of the beeves were being dismembered, and the Chief having done so, she signed to one of the cooks to cut it off with his chopper.

Although there is no historical foundation for the story, the country people used to point out a white streak of late-lying snow in a corry of the Cairngorms that was known as the ' Kist Maratt ' (*i.e.* the kist or coffin of Margaret). An unfortunate lady, whose sweetheart had been murdered by one of the chiefs of Mackintosh, is said to have laid a curse upon the family that the chiefship should never descend from father to son, and to have wandered into the hills and perished. Months after she had disappeared it was reported that her dead body was found in this drift of snow. The story of the murder and the curse is entirely legendary.

The country people still point out the cave of the nine robbers of Raits. The robbers preyed upon Clan Macpherson, hiding, in between their raids, in a cave excavated under a cottage. Their food was passed to them through a hole in the floor masked by a cupboard, and for a long time their retreat was not discovered. Finally, a man named John Macewan went to the cottage disguised as a wayfarer and demanded a night's shelter, according to the old custom ; and he discovered the trick. The robbers were attacked and killed, but, according to the story, John Macewan and his descendants were all liable to an internal complaint—showing the Highland hatred for an informer.

Invernahaven, mentioned in the Account Book, and now absorbed into the neighbouring estate of Belleville, was the scene of a great clan battle in the fourteenth century between the Mackintoshes and the Camerons ; and Garten Beg, also mentioned, was where a Lachlan, Laird of Mackintosh, was said to have

died on his way home from the Court of James I and
VI. He was the victim of slow poison, administered
by rival gallants, who were jealous of his feats of skill
and strength, and of the praises of the ladies of the
Court for the beauty of his white skin—at least, so runs
the old story.

Dunachton itself was for many years the residence
of the Chief and the centre of the clan life. In 1688
Coll Macdonald, nominally a supporter of Dundee,
took occasion to settle private scores with Mackintosh,
and ' did most barbarously in contempt of the present
Government burn his house in Dunachton, haill furniture and office houses belonging thereto, and did harrie
and robb his haille lands in Badzenoch, Strathnairn
and Strathdearn, thereby exposing the petr. to a vast
loss and his tenants to beggarie, whereby his whole
lands are laid waste and will so continue until the petr.
be in a condition to replenish them.' Coll had carried
away ' all portable goods thereupon worth at least
40,000 merks, so that the whole tenants and possessors
thereof were forced to flee, and are now with their wives
and children begging their bread and living upon
charity, not daring for fear of their lives to return to
their ground.'[1] It is only fair to state that Dundee was
very angry with Coll for his unauthorised raid.

Besides clan fights, the people of Dunachton must
have had a rich inheritance of stories and traditions
of the cattle rieving that went on more or less continuously down to the '45. Graham of Gartmore, writing
but shortly before the Rising, says :

' It may be safely affirmed that the horses, cows,
sheep and goats yearly stolen in that country ' [i.e. the
Highlands] ' are in value equal to £5000 and that the
expenses lost in the fruitless endeavours to recover them
will not be less than £2000. That the extraordinary
expense of keeping herds and servants to look more

[1] Quotations from two petitions to the Scots Parliament, sent up by
Mackintosh in 1790. They are reprinted in *The Mackintoshes and Clan
Chattan*, by A. M. Mackintosh, p. 285.

narrowly after cattle on account of stealing, otherwise not necessary, is £10,000. There is yearly paid in blackmail or watch money, openly or privately, £5000. . . .' Even allowing an ample margin for exaggeration in this calculation, when it is remembered that the average price of cattle was about £3 a head, and for goats and sheep much lower, it is easy to realise that the amount of raiding must have been very considerable. A goodly proportion of such raiding was carried on close to Dunachton, for, besides local enterprises, the upper valley of the Spey and that of its tributary, the Dulnan—where Balnespick had his summer shielings—formed a convenient corridor along which the wild Highlanders of the West came and went on their periodic spreaghs into the fertile 'Moray lands where all men taken their prey.'[1]

The East Coast lairds were glad to subsidise the Laird of Kyllachy and Cluny Macpherson to maintain watches in Strathdearn and Laggan, and an exceedingly business-like receipt of Ewan Macpherson for Sir Robert Gordon of Gordonstone's contribution has been published in C. Fraser Mackintosh's 'Letters of Two Centuries.'

It is this acceptance of wild forays and fierce pursuit as everyday business transactions that amazes one in reading such old letters referring to cattle raids as have been preserved to us,[2] and which was doubt-

---

[1] *Northern Rural Life in the Eighteenth Century*, p. 67.

The moon was known as 'Lochiel's Lantern,' and there was a saying that 'Highland lairds counted their daughters' tochers by the light of the Martinmas moon.' At Martinmas the cattle were in good condition from their summer feeding and the great droving trysts were held about then ; it was therefore the favourite time for cattle lifting. Burt, in his *Letters from the North of Scotland*, published in 1754 but written earlier, states (p. 242) that cattle raiding was Macdonald of Keppoch's main source of livelihood.

[2] Captain E. Dunbar, in *Social Life in Former Days* (p. 292), prints a letter from Cluny Macpherson, dated 1676, in which he says it is 'very probabile' that some stolen cattle are in the 'Braes of Moray' (mentioned in the Account Book), 'or els whir at this tym,' as the watch was dissolved

less the attitude of the country people at Dunachton, although the story of the exploits of one or two raiders and members of the watch became local sagas. Such were the deeds of John Beg Macandrew, *i.e.* Little John Macandrew, who lived at Dalnahatnich, on the Dulnan, about 1670. He was a member of the watch, and many stories are still told of his wonderful prowess with the crossbow. Precautions were taken to keep the names of the members of the watch secret, to protect them from the vengeance of the raiders, but John Beg became well known, and he made a platform in

for the year. He advised that a careful 'waitch' be kept on the remaining cattle lest 'you should come to miss a pairt of them.' See also C. Fraser Mackintosh's *Letters of Two Centuries*, pp. 117 and 126. The latter is not of especial interest, but it happens to be addressed to the grandfather of the Balnespick who wrote the Account Book, and is therefore perhaps worth reproducing.

'Inchs, *3rd September* 1687.

'Sir and Loving Cousin,—These are showing you that upon Sabbath was eight days, the 25th of August last, their was stolen out of my field seven head of cattle, of which there was one gotten back that straggled from the thieves, which my men took home, who were in pursuit of them. The other six I am informed, were carried to Badenoch, to the Davoch of Laggan. There was but three in company, as I am informed took them away, viz. two men and one boy. The men's names as I am informed were Sorle Dow Vic Finlay Vic Allister, in Laggan, John Dow Vic Sorle Vic Ian Mor, the boy's name I got not. These men dined in Altuaslanack on Sabbath day with Mackintosh his bowman and the said Sabbath day by ten o'clock at night as I am informed, carried away the said oxen and cows. Their colours and marks are as follows, viz.: one dun ox and one dun bull, one black ox and one brown young ox, with a white ball in his forehead. One gaired or sprainged cow, red and black, two horns little and cross, and one large black. I entreat you make all search ye can, to know if they come to Badenoch, and acquaint me thereof, how soon ye can, and send me your advice what to do thereanent, which is all at present from, sir,

'Your affectionate cousin and servant,

(Signed) 'W. ROBERTSON.

'Let this present my service to your bedfellow and children.'

Addressed: 'For his much respect and affectionate cousin Lachlan Mackintosh of Balnespick, these.'

a tree to which he retired at night if he had reason to
suspect that the caterans were in the neighbourhood.
One evening he was surprised in his house by seven
fully armed men, but his wife began to rate him as a
neglectful herd, and he slipped out, as if going to water
the cattle.   He climbed into his tree, and picked off
every one of his would-be assassins with his bow and
arrows before they were able to rush him.   After that
he was left undisturbed.[1]   It is hard to believe that
such episodes were of everyday occurrence in the
neighbourhood only one hundred years before the
very matter-of-fact Account Book came to be written.

Nor were the local people's exploits entirely on the
side of law and order.   In 1690 some Grants were
concerned in a raid on the cattle of Gordon of Gordonstone.   Gordon dispatched a messenger with a Letter
of Citation against the Laird of Grant as answerable
for his clan.   In Abernethy Forest—about eight miles
down the Spey from Dunachton as the crow flies—the
messenger, who had an escort of three armed men,
relates that he was ' seized upon be a pearty of armed
men, who most maisterfully and violently struck me
with their gunnes, gave me a stob with a durk in my
shoulder, and a stroak of my owen sword, robbed me
of my money, my linnens, some cloaths, my sword
and provision, and of the principal Council letters
many coppies thereof, and uther papers ; then bound
me and my compeny, and allways threatened me with
present death for executing the foresaid letters.'[2]   The
story of this assault seems to have been widely known
at one time.

In another cattle raid of 1692, record of which
has happened to come down to us, three of the
participants were said to be Macdonald of Keppoch's
' countrymen, who lives upon the Duke's land under
Borlum, in ane brae room upon the Water Tullnan

[1] C. Fraser Mackintosh, in *Antiquarian Notes* (Series II. p. 423),
gives two stories of John Beg McAndrew.
[2] *Social Life in Former Days*, by E. Dunbar of Dunbar.

very near marching with Strathspey, who has a hand in the Strathspey Watch as soldiers for their own benefit.' Borlum's property of Raits marched with Dunachton, and, as the country people generally remained in the same districts, some of Balnespick's sub-tenants of the name of Macdonald may well have been descendants of these ' soldiers.'

After the '45, organised cattle-lifting was put down, but even at the time of the Account Book the country was far from settled. Sheriff Fraser of Farraline, writing in 1799,[1] says : ' You will probably recollect the state of the County of Inverness at the period I came into office, when a number of armed desperadoes infested some parts of it, and that thievous practices very much prevailed in the district contiguous to Fort Augustus ' (probably including the wild regions of upper Badenoch). The Sheriff suggests the establishment of fourteen armed posts at strategic points in the Highlands. Three of these posts—at Dalwhinnie,[2] on the Tromie, and at the Ferry of Invereshie—were respectively within 20, 6, and 2 miles of Dunachton.

Even now, stories of the Risings in '15 and '45 seem to strike a far more responsive note from the average Highlander than the old fairy stories and clan traditions. At the time of the Account Book they must have been far more vivid—many of them being personal experiences told at first or second hand.

Numbers of Dunachton folk must have been among the 600 clansmen and tenants whom Mackintosh called out in 1715, or among the 700 who responded to the summons of Lady Anne Mackintosh in 1745, and who fled back, past the gates of Moy, after Culloden, ' in their shirt sleeves and in a bloody condition and panting for want of refreshment.'[3] A younger brother to the Balnespick of the day was ' out ' in the '15, and

[1] C. Fraser Mackintosh, *Letters of Two Centuries*, p. 337.
[2] This was on the high ground towards Drummochter Pass, not the farm near Raits that is mentioned in the Account Book.
[3] Sir Eneas Mackintosh, *Historical Notes*, p. 8.

was captured at Preston.   He was condemned to death,
but the sentence was commuted to one of transportation
to Virginia, whence he returned with broken health
and fortunes.[1]   A far more prominent figure in the
'15 Rising was Brigadier Mackintosh, Jun., of Borlum,
whose home was at Raits, the property adjoining
Dunachton, to which he returned again and again
in intervals between his Jacobite intrigues.   Thus in
1711 he wrote from Raits to his brother : ' Forget not
to get me a bag full of ashe and siccomore seeds, which
I believe hang yet on the trees ; also an ounce of
spinnage, and half an ounce of garden cresses seeds.'
As soon as Mar unfurled the Stuart Standard in 1715

[1] C. Fraser Mackintosh, in *Letters of Two Centuries*, has printed a
note of James Mackintosh of Balnespick's losses due to the rising of
1715, ' being two years abroad, one year in prison and another in
Virginia.'   The total amounted to £1162 9s. Scots.   He also printed
a copy of the indenture for transportation : ' The Indenture of a person
transported for rebellion against our Most Gracious Sovereign Lord King
George which upon the humble petition of the rebel herein mentioned,
was most mercifully granted by His Imperial Majesty, upon condition
of serving seven years and other conditions as follows, viz. :

   ' This indenture made the twenty-eighth day of June, anno
   Regni Regis Georgii Magn Brittan etc.   Secundo Annoque
   Domini One thousand seven hundred and sixteen Between James
   Mackintosh of Kinrara in the Parish of Alvie in the County of
   Inverness, gentleman, on the one part and Henry Trafford of
   Liverpool in the County of Lancaster, merchant, on the other,
   witnesseth that the said James Mackintosh doth hereby covenant
   and agree to, and with the said Henry Trafford, his executors and
   assigns, to serve him, the said Henry Trafford and his assigns from
   the day of the date of these present until the first and next arrival
   at Virginia, or any other of his Majesty's plantations, and after, for,
   and during and unto the full end and term of seven years from
   thence next ensuing, fully to be complete and ended, there to
   serve in such service and employment as he, the said Henry
   Trafford, or his assigns shall employ him in, according to the
   custom of the country in like kind.   In consideration the said
   Henry Trafford doth covenant and agree to pay for his passage, and
   to find for him and allow him meat, drink, apparel, and lodging,
   with other necessaries, according to the custom of the country.'
   The Mayor of Liverpool signed the document as well as the contracting
parties.

the Brigadier took an active part in stimulating the
Chief to call out Clan Mackintosh and to capture
Inverness. He was then given high rank in Mar's
army, and entrusted with an important expedition to
raise the borders. He seems to have been one of the
ablest leaders in the quarrelsome, distracted march to
Preston.

After the surrender the old Brigadier was still an
outstanding figure, for when the prisoners were marching to London ' Brigadier Mackintosh, remarkable for
the grim ferocity of his scarred face, attracted in the
captive procession glances which, through the influence
of his formidable presence, had in them more respect
than ridicule, even from the exulting crowd.'[1]

An indictment for high treason was found against
him, but he escaped from Newgate Prison with several
companions ' in an unexpected and indeed unexampled
manner, viz., mainly by plain force, over the bellies
of both keepers and soldiers who they knocked down
and opened the doors.'[2]

A reward of £1000 was set on his head, but he
escaped to France in safety, and still devoted body and
soul to the Stuart cause, ventured back again and again
on the affairs of his Royal master.

In 1724 he was stated to be ' up and down the
country, but chiefly resided at the house of his son,
Shaw Mackintosh '—i.e. at Raits, where he passed as a
cousin visiting his relations.[3] The officer command-
ing the soldiers at Ruthven Castle (about seven or eight
miles from Dunachton), having his suspicions of the
identity of this ' cousin,' marched to Raits with six soldiers
very early one morning, ostensibly on a friendly visit, and
surprised the Brigadier in his dressing-gown and slippers.
The Brigadier was arrested, but the country people

[1] Quotation from Burton, in *Brigadier Mackintosh of Borlum*, by
A. M. Mackintosh, p. 33.
[2] Quotation from *Annals of King George*, in *Brigadier Mackintosh
of Borlum*, by A. M. Mackintosh, p. 35.
[3] *Ibid.*, p. 42.

round collected in large crowds to rescue him, and broke into the house, and in the scuffle that followed the Brigadier made good his escape, only to be recaptured four years later.

Shaw Mackintosh was arrested in his place and taken to London, and had great difficulty in securing his own release. His name occurs several times in the old Account Book. On page 171 of Account Book he wishes to examine the marches, and on page 22 victual is supplied for his funeral.

The Clan of Mackintosh took a notable part in the '45. The Balnespick who wrote the Account Book was ' out,' and many of the sub-tenants on Dunachton must have been among the clansmen whom ' Colonel Anne ' called out to follow Prince Charlie. The Chief of Mackintosh was a Hanoverian, but his wife, Anne Farquharson of Invercauld, was a strong Jacobite, and the old story was that she upset the great pot of kail that was simmering on the fire over Mackintosh's legs in order to put him out of action while she raised the clan.

The people of Dunachton were no doubt too far off to take part in the ' Rout of Moy,' but the exploit must have been dear to every member of Clan Mackintosh and its allied septs. Two nights before Culloden the Prince's army camped at Moy—the residence of the Chief of Clan Mackintosh—and Lord Loudon, with 1500 men, was dispatched from the Hanoverian head-quarters, then at Inverness, to surprise him. A Jacobite lady in Inverness—some of the stories have it that it was the maid waiting at table on some of the English officers—smuggled through a warning just in time, and the blacksmith of Moy hastily collected a handful of old men and lads (the main fighting force of the clan was already under arms with the Prince), and took up his position at the ' Pass of the Threshold.' As the English toiled up the steep narrow pass, the black-smith's men stationed themselves behind hillocks and peat stacks, and whistled and called to each other ;

and the English, mistaking them, in the darkness, for a great army, beat a hasty retreat.[1]

After Culloden, Moy was ransacked by the Hanoverians, and the Lady of Mackintosh was only saved from actual violence at their hands by an officer, Sir Everet Falconer, who had been one of her admirers before her marriage. She was taken to Inverness and imprisoned for six weeks under conditions of great severity. This old lady died at an advanced age, and brought up her husband's niece, Anne Mackintosh of Mackintosh, who married Lachlan, old Balnespick's son. How intimately must Lachie's children have known the brave old stories !

Mr. William Gordon, the minister of Alvie, gave generous help to the fugitives from the broken Stuart army, and Cumberland, having heard a report of it, had him arrested and taken to Inverness. The little country minister, who, according to the old nurse who told me the story, was a small, portly man, addressed the Royal Duke with perfect calmness : ' May it please your Royal Highness, I am exceedingly straitened between two contrary commands, both coming from high authority. My Heavenly King's Son commands me to feed the hungry, to clothe the naked, to give meat and drink to my very enemies, and to relieve to the utmost of my power all objects in distress, indiscriminately, that come my way. My earthly king's son commands me to drive the houseless wanderer from my door, to shut my bowels of compassion against the needy, and to withhold from my fellow-mortals in distress the relief which it is in my power to afford. Pray, which of these commands am I to obey ? ' The Duke of Cumberland answered quite mildly that the minister must of course obey the command of his Heavenly King, and allowed him to go home in

[1] Sir Eneas Mackintosh, in his *Historical Notes* (p. 27), gives a short account of this exploit. The blacksmith continued to ply his trade at Corrybrough, a few miles from Moy, and no one molested him. His tombstone can be seen in Moy Churchyard.

peace.[1]   Mr. Gordon was still minister of Alvie at the time of the Account Book.   Once or twice sales of grain and pease to him are recorded (see p. 156).

The adventures of Cluny Macpherson must also have been of great interest to the Badenoch people, for his estates and many of his refuges, including one at Ovie, a place-name mentioned in the Account Book, were within the district.[2]   At the time the Account Book was being written the Cluny estates were still forfeit to the Crown, for they were not restored until 1786.[3]

The '45 left memories that linger to the present day, but it bequeathed no bitterness.   The husband of ' Colonel ' Anne Mackintosh was succeeded as Chief by a staunch Hanoverian, who, in 1754, raised 500 men of his tenants and followers for the 42nd Highlanders— the Black Watch.

The number of men in His Majesty's Forces who were drawn from the Central Highlands is amazing.   In ' Lectures from the Mountains,' Series II, chap. ii., it is calculated that between 1793 and 1815 forty battalions of the line and seven of militia were raised in the Highlands—i.e. 37,600 men—and, in addition, there were volunteer regiments.   Of the regulars 10,000 men came from Strathdearn, Badenoch, Strathspey, and part of Lochaber.

According to the ' Statistical Account ' the people of Alvie were somewhat backward in offering themselves for recruits, but in such an intensely military district this backwardness was probably only relative, especially when one remembers the large number of local lairds and gentlemen farmers with the prefix ' Captain ' to their names, who are mentioned in the Account Book— Balnespick's brother, William and Lachie his sons,

---

[1] *The Second Statistical Account for Alvie Parish* (p. 85) tells the story, but hearing it from my nurse is one of my earliest recollections. Locally it now seems to be nearly forgotten.

[2] Alex. Macpherson (*Church and Social Life in the Highlands*, p. 419) gives a full description of them.

[3] C. Fraser Mackintosh, *Dunachton Past and Present*, p. 29.

Lachie's son, Captain Shaw of Ovie, etc.—for it was then generally the custom for a Highland gentleman to obtain a commission by bringing a quota of recruits to his regiment.[1]   In the old Account Book the name of ' Sandy the Soldier,' son of old Macphadruck, appears once or twice, and there are two ' Chelsamen ' or more (*i.e.* men in receipt of a pension from Chelsea Hospital), so that one cannot doubt that there were many lads from Dunachton serving on the Continent and the Indies, and anxious hearts at home.

In reading through Balnespick's prosaic statement of accounts, one cannot but speculate on the welter of conflicting thoughts and ideals that must have surged through his mind and those of his humbler neighbours. The outside world was invading the isolation of the Highlands.   Old social relationships were breaking down ; new standards of living were being introduced ; the people were losing their own individual local life, and much that was unspeakably precious was lost with it.   On the other hand, the world was thrown open to the Highlanders.

The study of the development of agriculture in the Highlands is so fascinating, not because one merely learns of fields that have doubled their yield, or the sweetening of sour and boggy soil by deep drainage, but because of its effect upon the whole rural life of the people, and because it bore an important part in the actions and reactions of an extraordinarily interesting time in Scotch history, when mediævalism and modernism actually touched, and which has left good and evil effects which are still vital factors in the rural life and the politics of the present day.

.   .   .   .   .   .

Perhaps some explanation and apology are needed for the inclusion of fairy stories and old wives' legends

[1] Osgood Mackenzie, in *A Hundred Years in the Highlands* (p. 62), quotes an extreme example of such recruiting.   C. Fraser Mackintosh, in *Letters of Two Centuries,* quotes another example in the letter given for 1749.

in the preface of what would fain attempt to be a serious study of eighteenth-century agriculture in the Highlands. I have deliberately introduced them as the most important part in the general picture. Not only was the crowding of the rural population mainly due to the warlike times of the past, as I shall hope to indicate later on, but because, in dealing with a people so full of character and so intellectual as the Scotch, it would be grossly misleading to describe the hardness and narrowness of their material economic conditions, which might be common to any starveling, down-trodden peasantry, without indicating the pride and courage, fervent imagination and intellectual energy of the race, that has sent them forth from their rocky hills, not merely to subsist in the wider world, but to dominate it.

It is also more and more important, with our steadily rising present-day standards of comfort, to remember how much of poetry and romance and love of nature, of old clan ideals and old working songs, of the sense of history, and of the pride of birth, have passed away from the Highlands with the simpler and incomparably harder way of life of the folk that went before us.

Note

Local Characters

In considering the strongly marked character of the people, it is rather striking to find how many local individuals there were in Badenoch, about the time that Balnespick wrote his diary, who were sufficiently outstanding to be remembered even down to the present day.

Mr. Gordon, the minister of Alvie, I have already mentioned in connection with the '45. I have also alluded to the distinguished career of Brigadier Mackintosh of Borlum, another near neighbour. The old Brigadier was captured in 1727 and imprisoned in Edinburgh Castle, where he died in 1743, and in his old age and captivity his thoughts evidently turned to the planting and agricultural reforms he had begun at Raits thirty years earlier. He wrote a valuable book on agriculture under the title of ' A Lover of his Country,' and in the Introduction he says : ' Fourteen years and more in this place has made me incapable of rendering all that time any personal service to my country ; and I will say had I more years been in the world, some thousands of acres had been this day enclosed, planted and carrying some profitable vegetable that now (and I doubt not ever will) bear only the heath, moss or water, Noah's flood left upon them.' [1]

There can be little doubt that, had the Brigadier cared to acknowledge the Hanoverian dynasty, he would have obtained a pardon, but he remained loyal to the Stuarts to the end, and one of his last acts was said to be the writing on the wall of his room of an invocation of God's blessing on James VIII.

Unfortunately, the Brigadier's successors distinguished themselves in quite other ways. His eldest son having died in America, survived by two little girls, his second son, Shaw Mackintosh, went over to try to kidnap them. The attempt was frustrated, and Shaw was nearly lynched in Boston. This Shaw is mentioned two or three times in the Account Book. Shaw's son Edward became a highway robber. The Pass of Slochd Muick, on the high road to Inverness, was one of his favourite haunts, and a pool between Belleville and Dunachton is pointed out as the scene of a murder committed by him. He finally fled the country in 1773, but his widow survived him for many years and lived at Kingussie. Edward had his following of a few wild lads, but robbery, apart from cattle rieving, was most repugnant to the Highlanders ; and my mother can well remember in her young days the disgust with which the elder people spoke of his doings.

Another man of note who was connected with Raits

[1] A. M. Mackintosh, in *Brigadier Mackintosh of Borlum* (p. 49), quotes from this book.

was James Macpherson, the poet and translator of
Ossian.[1]   He was of humble origin, and began his
career as schoolmaster at Kingussie.   At the time the
Account Book was being written he was in London
enjoying the 'Universal Deluge of approbation,'[2] and
the sharp reaction therefrom, that his 'Translations'
produced, and he only bought Raits and renamed it
'Belleville' in 1784, the year of Balnespick's death.
Probably local opinion was more taken up with his
personal character, which Charles Fraser Mackintosh
deals with mercilessly,[3] than with his poetic productions which so deeply influenced the literary life of
his age.

Balnespick does not mention Captain John Macpherson—a person of considerable notoriety who went
under the name of the Black Officer—although he sold
corn to two of his sub-tenants at Ballachroan.   The
Black Officer was employed as local recruiting officer,
and it was popularly said that he was in league with the
devil, and all sorts of stories were current of the guile,
force, and supernatural powers he employed in in-
ducing men to take the King's Shilling.[4]   These
rumours seemed to receive a terrible confirmation when
he was lost in an avalanche in the Forest of Gaik—a
well-known haunt of witches and demons—and even
yet the country people will speak of the supposed nature
of his end with some detail ; but, as he long survived
Balnespick, it scarcely comes within the scope of the
present book.   His name is mentioned several times
in papers left by Lachlan Mackintosh, Balnespick's
son.

Lord Adam Gordon, son of the second Duke of
Gordon, was a person of some distinction, for he was

---

[1] D. Gray Graham, *Scottish Men of Letters*, p. 226.

[2] *Ibid.*, p. 231.

[3] See, for instance, *Antiquarian Notes*, vol. ii. p. 404.

[4] Alex. Macpherson, in *Church and Social Life in the Highlands*
(p. 147), gives one example and also a vindication of the Captain's
character

General and Commander-in-Chief of the Forces in Scotland. He has a certain territorial connection with the district, for his House has great possessions there ; his name appears in the Account Book as debtor to Balnespick for a considerable sum.[1] (See Account Book, p. 267.)

That one remote Highland district should have been able, in so short a time, to produce men of such outstanding, diverse, and noteworthy characters is surely not merely chance, but is an indication of the vigour of the race that inhabited it. The old Account Book emphasises how essentially local—one might say parochial—were Balnespick's interests and circle ; but it is rather important to remember that in this narrow sphere he met men whose personalities and actions—good or bad—were so outstanding that their memory survives down to the present day.

[1] Information kindly supplied by A. M. Mackintosh. It was about twenty years later that the lady who is still spoken of in the north as ' the ' Duchess of Gordon came to live at Kinrara close to Dunachton. The Balnespick family received much friendliness and kindness from her, but she can hardly be included among old Captain Williams's contemporaries.

CHAPTER III

GENERAL APPEARANCE AND CONDITIONS OF THE COUNTRYSIDE

DUNACHTON lies among the natural birch and oak woods on the lower slopes of the Monadliadh Hills. The River Spey runs along the valley, widening out into Loch Inch immediately below the farm. General Wade's old military road passed between the house and the loch, and the modern high road and the railway line now run parallel to it. At the end of the loch and on each side of the river there are wide marshy meadows. The opposite side of the Strath is bounded by steep foothills, rising to the great mountain masses of the Cairngorm Range. Older people say that the birchwoods round Dunachton have grown very much within their memory.

The exceptional beauty of its mountain setting is deeply appreciated by the country people of the district, but it also has a very considerable effect upon their economic conditions. In the eighteenth century the Highland hills still formed an important barrier shutting out the rest of the world. In the twentieth century they are the main attraction to the country.

It was probably not a mere chance that, beyond one or two allusions to 'the Glen,' Balnespick does not mention the scenery or hills at all. Quite possibly he did not admire them, for the influence of the 'romantic school' was but beginning, and only a few years earlier Burt had described the beauties of the Scottish hills as follows : ' The summits of the highest are mostly destitute of earth, and the huge naked rocks, being just above the heath, produce the disagreeable appearance of a scabbed head, especially when they appear

to the view in a conical figure. . . . To the East, if
one casts one's eye from an eminence toward a group
of them, they appear still one above another, fainter
and fainter, according to the aerial perspective, and the
whole of a dismal gloomy brown, drawing upon a dirty
purple ; and most of all disagreeable when the heath
is in bloom. . . . Of all the views, I think the most
horrid is to look at the hills from East to West, or
vice versa, for then the eye penetrates far among them,
and sees more particularly their stupendous bulk,
frightful irregularity, and horrid gloom, made yet more
sombrous by the shades and faint reflections they
communicate one to another.'[1]   He gives detailed
descriptions of several ' horrible ' views.

Even Miss Grant of Rothiemurchus, writing of
1812, is not very complimentary to Dunachton and its
surroundings : ' A little further on rose Belleville,[2]
a great hospitable looking place, protruding from young
plantations and staring down on the rugged meadow
land now so fine a farm.   The birchwoods began to
show a little after this, but deserted the banks about
that frightful Kincraig where begun the long moor
over which we were glad to look across the Spey to
Invereshie. . . . On we went over the weary moor
of Alvie to the Loch of the same name.'[3]

James Robertson, D.D., in his ' General View of
the Agriculture in the County of Inverness ' (1808),
gives an idea of the appearance of the country from
a farmer's point of outlook.   He describes the large
hay-meadows that covered the bottom of the strath [4]
and the comparative prosperity of the farming that
climbed the steep slopes above the course of the river ;

[1] Burt's *Letters from the Highlands*, vol. i. p. 282.

[2] Belleville House was built by James Macpherson, the poet, on the
old Borlum property of Raits.   This, of course, took place after the
Account Book was written, for the property did not change hands till
1784.

[3] Mrs. Smith, *Memoirs of a Highland Lady*, p. 159.

[4] James Robertson, D.D., *General View of the Agriculture in the
County of Inverness*, p. 178.

'houghs abound almost without interruption on both sides of the river' throughout Badenoch.[1]

Dunachton lies in Lower Badenoch, and the conditions were probably more like those obtaining farther down the Spey than those of the more pastoral part of the district. Robertson writes : 'From Castle Grant to Aviemore, along the side of the Spey, the face of the country is very much diversified. In some places the ancient mode of occupying the ground remains in full force : cottages crowded into hamlets, the farmers living in clusters and in one place, their land open and in alternate ridges. But in other places the land is enclosed and a neat steading set down for a substantial tenant, and where the people are less affluent, the land is divided into separate lots of fewer or more acres, according to the ability of the occupants, where every tenant is set down upon his own lot.'[2]

At the time when Balnespick wrote his Account Book the enclosure alluded to by Robertson had barely begun. In fact, Robertson's book shows how rapid was the advance made in agriculture between Balnespick's time and forty years later. For instance, Robertson writes that the cultivation of rye had been almost given up by even the poorer tenants, whereas we know, from the Account Book, that Balnespick regularly grew it.[3] Yet the foregoing description describes features of rural life which were almost universal a hundred and fifty years ago,[4] and which have long since passed away : i.e. the existence of a considerable number of small lairds and principal tenants, who farmed professionally and were mainly responsible for the introduction of agricultural improvements ; open field farming ; the presence of a dense population of cultivators on a

---

[1] James Robertson, D.D., *General View of the Agriculture in the County of Inverness*, p. 16.

[2] *Ibid.*, p. viii.

[3] *Ibid.*, p. 167.

[4] *Ibid.*, p. 404. See also *First Statistical Account for Alvie Parish*, vol. xiii. No. 26, p. 379.

very small scale, a ' load of tenantry,' as Marshall calls them.[1]

The organisation of the rural population of the Highlands in the eighteenth century was the direct outcome of the clan system and of the warlike conditions of the past, when the prosperity and even the survival of the people in a locality depended upon their military strength. The old Account Book throws interesting light on the manner of life and economic position both of the tacksmen and of the joint-tenants and crofters in one stage of their evolution, and in this book I shall hope to deal more fully with these facts under separate headings ; but in this chapter of generalisings it may be worth while to compare the legal position of the Highland runrig farmers with that of the English cultivators on the open fields.

In England, as is well known, there were considerable common rights attaching to definite lands. Professor Gonner, in ' Common Land and Enclosure,' has dealt with the subject exhaustively (see p. 8 and onwards), and has given a list of the six methods by which such lands can be subdivided and individual portions of it freed from common rights. The most usual method, during the eighteenth century, was by Private Acts and other Parliamentary powers.

It is true that in Scotland an Act was passed in 1695 ' anent lands lying runrig ' to enable ' any heritor to apply to the Sheriff, to the Steward or Lord of the Regality or to the Justices of the Peace to the effect that these lands may be divided according to their respective interests.' But although actions under this statute have occurred there has not been the same large number of legal proceedings regarding the subdivision of open field such as took place in England, and private Acts were never required. There was a considerable extent of land on the hills and moors of Scotland that was so valueless that the proprietors did not trouble to

---

[1] Mr. Marshall, *General View of the Agriculture of the Central Highlands of Scotland*, p. 25.

define their exact marches, and most of the 'Commonties' seem to have been more like this land with undelimited marches, than like the English 'champion,' with its network of carefully defined and well-established rights.   Two examples of such commonties are mentioned in C. Fraser Mackintosh's 'Letters of Two Centuries' for the years 1790 and 1702.[1] There were also 'servitudes' upon certain lands in Scotland. Erskine defines a servitude as 'a burden affecting lands or other heritable subjects, by which the proprietor is either restrained from full use of his property, or is obliged to suffer another to do certain acts upon it, which, were it not for that burden, would be competent solely to the owner.'[2] A common example of servitude would be the right of pasturage.   Yet although these two forms of joint ownership existed in Scotland, it seems to be clear that the open field in that country was mainly a personal arrangement between the joint tenants and the landlord.

The 'inferior tenantry' of Scotland were mainly tenants or sub-tenants, at will or on very short leases. The farms were merely let to a group of tenants instead of to a single one, and, so long as the term of years specified in the lease was not infringed, no legal formality had to be gone through by a laird or tacksman who wished to consolidate his farms or take land under his own management.   Sir John Sinclair, in his description of Scotch unfenced farms, clearly brings out the fact that the common grazing was merely a matter of preference among the individual cultivators : 'The tenantry in general, according to the commonty rule, have their lands intermixed with their neighbours, in

[1] In Green's *Encyclopædia of Scots Law* commonty is described as 'a peculiar sort of common property in land, of great antiquity, . . . There is still ground for dispute whether it rose out of provisions for the cultivation and use of the Barony and manor, or whether these were superimposed on it.   In historical times it appears as common property in moorland or outfield land, held by persons owning neighbouring lands in severalty, as accessory to the land so held.'

[2] Erskine, ii. 9, 1.

what is called run-ridges ; they have no enclosures, and prefer during the winter months, an universal commonty of each others lands for pasture, rather than be at the expense of herding, otherwise than by precarious attention of their numerous families of children ' (' General View of the Agriculture of the Northern Counties of Scotland,' p. 11).

The difference between the two countries is brought out clearly by the meanings that were attached to the words ' enclosure' and ' to enclose ' in England and in Scotland respectively. In England, when it is used in connection with rural history, the word has a technical meaning and is applied to a definite division of common land. In Scotland the word constantly occurs in old letters written during the eighteenth and early nineteenth century, but it invariably means only the construction of walls or fences round portions of land. Thus in the 'Second Statistical Account for the Parish of Moy,' compiled in 1846, the farms are spoken of as ' unenclosed,' although it is extremely unlikely that there was the least survival of the practice of runrig in the district at that time. The writer meant that there was very little fencing on the farms, as is indeed the case on some of them down to the present day. (C. Fraser Mackintosh, in his ' Letters of Two Centuries,' quotes many examples that clearly show the meaning of the word, as, for instance, in the examples given for 1775 and 1803.)

The hill-sides above Dunachton seem to have been considered as little good for grazing, for there is an old saying that one of the three curses of Badenoch was that the pasture grounds were so far away from the arable ground. Those of Dunachton and Raits lay on the upper waters of the Dulnan, seven or eight miles distant. Before the introduction of sheep farming on modern lines, the moorland in many parts of Scotland was probably far more barren, and with less grass upon it, than at present. The heathery hill-tops must have been almost quite useless ; in fact, they were

D

detrimental to the neighbouring farmers, because they
provided a harbourage for foxes and other vermin.
The depredations of such creatures among the sheep
and lambs was a serious matter before game was preserved.   In most districts the people had to club
together to employ a fox-killer, and in the parish of
Moy such a man is said to have killed eighty foxes in
one winter.

In Balnespick's time shooting had not become a
popular recreation among the lairds—still less the
principal source of revenue of very many proprietors.   It
is said that in some families a servant was employed to
do the stalking and to supply the household with veni-
son.[1]   In the rambling statements of the Account
Book, Balnespick does not once allude to game or sport ;
nor is there any mention of it among the many old family
letters and papers relating to this time that I have been
allowed to read.   At the present day, among men of
Balnespick's position, such an omission would be most
unusual.

In the County Valuation Roll the arable land,
farmhouses, cottages, etc., upon Dunachton and Kincraig are set down at less than £200, whereas the
shootings and lodge are estimated at £1432.[2]   The
shootings thus represent a very important asset to the
proprietor ; they are also a source of employment and
revenue to the countryside.

Besides men who are employed as keepers, gardeners,
etc., for the shooting tenant, a shooting brings a considerable amount of less continuous work into a district
for ghillies and beaters.   In 1923 the usual rate for
a beater was 6s. 6d. per diem, and £1 for a man and a
horse.   Money is also brought into the country by the
sale of dairy produce to the shooting tenants.

There is a widespread opinion that grouse moors

---

[1] Among papers left by Lachlan, Balnespick's son, there is an entry
stating that Donald Forbes, Dunachton Beg, had paid a debt due to
Captain Lachlan by killing a deer and giving him the skin.

[2] Inverness-shire Valuation Roll.

have encroached on arable land and caused much of the rural depopulation. On Dunachton none of the land mentioned in the Account Book as under cultivation seems to have gone back to heather, with the exception of the small and unproductive piece known as the Priline, which Balnespick does not seem to have cultivated after the first year of the Account Book, and perhaps a part of the very low-rented croft of the Cluanach. On the other hand, the introduction of extensive sheep farming may have influenced the abandonment of the less productive holdings of Craigandhu, Carit and others. The changes took place after the days of old Balnespick, and it is always exceedingly difficult to disentangle the direct and indirect effects of four definite causes for the abandonment of arable land in the Highlands. After many talks and discussions with people closely connected with the soil of the Highlands, the present writer would put these four causes of depopulation in the following order of importance, as a matter of mere personal opinion :

1. The rising standard of living, and increased openings in the southern manufacturing towns and overseas, which rendered the old existence on very small, poor holdings insufficiently attractive to the sub-tenants, and opened opportunities to them of improving their position. These causes of migration and emigration had begun to lead to depopulation in Badenoch before either preserving or large-scale sheep farming was introduced (see Colonel Thornton's ' Sporting Tour,' p. 78, written in 1786).

2. The rising cost of farming, due to higher wages, heavier rates, etc. ; the lower returns and prices caused by foreign competition ; the higher standard of produce that is demanded, for the old starveling cattle, natural hay, very light grain, and inferior butter would no longer find a market.

3. The need for sheltered feeding for the sheep during the autumn and spring, without which the higher pasture would be useless.

4. The increased need for low ground pasture, owing to the stricter preserving of the grouse moors, which generally would only mean a few weeks' less pasturage on the hills in the autumn and a stricter 'souming' (*i.e.* the number of animals to which a tenant is limited in his lease of the pasturage).

Whatever the exact ratio of losses and gains, there can be little doubt that the letting of shootings is, on the whole, advantageous to the Highlands.

The modern appreciation of mountain scenery has also brought considerable prosperity to Strathspey out of the pockets of the 'summer visitors' who flock there, especially in July and August. They are to be found in hotels, villas, and among the cottage folk, and their payments must, both directly and indirectly, very appreciably add to the wealth of the district.

The coming of the summer visitors is intimately connected with the opening up of the Highlands by roads and railways. Until 1814 the mails from the south went round by Aberdeen to Inverness, and back from thence to Grantown by runner. In that year a coach began to ply between Inverness and Perth.[1] At the time of the Account Book the life of a Highland strath must have been virtually a self-contained unit both socially and economically. Balnespick and his sub-tenants were primarily 'subsistence farmers,' and lived upon the produce of their farms. Even where surplus products were sold, with the important exception of the cattle trade, the market was entirely local. Thus the total sales of corn recorded in the Account Book amounted to 375 bolls, of which 300 bolls were sold locally in small quantities, 249 bolls being sold to people actually living on the Davoch itself.

The Account Book gives ample evidence of the hardship that dependence on local grain supplies inflicted on the inhabitants of a country with a treacherous climate like that of the Highlands of Scotland. In six years, out of the ten covered by the Account Book,

---

[1] Mrs. Smith, *Memoirs of a Highland Lady*, p. 222.

many of the smaller holdings must have been unable to yield a sufficient return for the maintenance of the cultivator himself and his family, and on three occasions corn had to be procured from Perthshire and the coast lands of Morayshire, at considerable expense, to supplement local harvests. The local price of corn fluctuated considerably, being low when the cultivator could sell and high when he was obliged to buy.

The Account Book gives little information with regard to the advantages and disadvantages of localised rural industries, but, from the vivid picture of the times that it calls up, it is easy to guess at probabilities.

The 'First Statistical Account' of the parish is not flattering to the quality of the work of the rural craft workers[1] : it gives a list of the craftsmen in the parish—2 smiths, 6 weavers, 4 tailors, 2 brog-makers—and adds, ' These hand craftsmen are fit only for the coarsest work.'

When the lowness of the price of the finished article and the cumbrousness of the old-fashioned methods are remembered, it is obvious that only an exceedingly low standard of living could make such productions possible. Servants' shoes had to be replaced twice a year, and cost 1s. 6d. to 2s. the pair. The whole of the implements required on a farm cost only about £1 5s. 5d.—less than half as much as a modern plough—but they had to be renewed every two years.[2] Sheets and blankets were more durable, but they were coarse in texture and had to have a seam down the middle, as the fly-shuttle had not been introduced so far north. A great deal of the handicraft work was cheaper, but less good, than our bulk-produced modern goods, and the work-people who made them must have been very considerably worse off.

On the other hand, the rural industries flourished under far more favourable conditions than at present.

[1] *First Statistical Account*, vol. xiii. No. 26, p. 375.
[2] Sir John Sinclair, *View of the Northern Counties*, p. 76 and onwards.

The workers' markets were at their very doors, for
they were producing goods for the use of folk in their
own class and living in their own district, instead ot
articles of ornament and luxury subject to the fluctua-
tions of fashion and for people whose ways of life were
very different from their own.   The old-fashioned system
of agriculture, with its seasons of business and slack-
ness, tended to foster the carrying on of subsidiary
trades, and the isolation from industrial centres ensured
a regular local demand.

Another general feature that is noticeable in the
Account Book is the extraordinary shortage of currency.[1]
Instances abound of round-about exchanges—one can
hardly call them sales—such as those recorded on pp. 168
and 176, and they form a convincing illustration of the
leisureliness of the times, and of the parochial scope
of most of the transactions.   They also indicate the
extreme poverty of Scotland and the money shortage ;
but Adam Smith shows that there was another and more
interesting reason, for he considered that the cause of
the small use that was made of gold and silver in ' the
greater part of the domestic transactions in Scotland '
was, ' not the poverty, but the enterprising and project-
ing spirit of the people, and their desire for employing
all the capital which they can get as active and productive
stock.' [2]

---

[1] Adam Smith, in *Wealth of Nations* (p. 281 in Methuen's edition,
edited by Professor Cannan), estimates the currency at half a million.
Charles Fraser Mackintosh, in his *Letters of Two Centuries*, gives
a curious illustration of the shortage of money in the Highlands, in the
letter he quotes for 1745 (p. 212).   It described a lawsuit that arose
from the alleged tampering with a £10 note.   The plaintiff was at
Ruthven Fair—the most considerable local market—and wished to cash
the note.   The defendant offered to try to arrange it for him, but
returned saying that he had tried everywhere and had failed to do so.
This statement the plaintiff apparently accepted as quite natural.

[2] Adam Smith, *Wealth of Nations*, p. 281 in Methuen's edition,
edited by Professor Cannan.

CHAPTER IV

FARMING AT DUNACHTON IN THE EIGHTEENTH CENTURY

THE upper valley of the Spey has always been pastoral rather than agricultural.[1] Even in Abernethy, about eight or nine miles farther down the river than Dunachton, the total amount of grain raised in the parish was calculated to be at the rate of $1\frac{1}{2}$ bolls per head of the inhabitants (6 bolls being the yearly allowance for a farm servant),[2] and there can be little doubt that from time immemorial the most important source of support of the cultivators of Badenoch, taking bad years with good, was by their beasts rather than their grain. This is still generally the case at the present day, although on most farms sheep are now the more lucrative kind of live stock, rather than cattle.

The old place-names for different parts of the land that Balnespick farmed have, very many of them, come down to the present day, and the boundaries of his arable land, to a large extent, are unmistakable, formed as they are by the loch and river, moorland and broken ground, or the march line of old-established holdings. It is therefore possible to compare results given by the old methods and the present-day ones, and to visualise unusually clearly what the eighteenth-century farming was really like, and the curious general lay-out of an old-fashioned farm.

---

[1] *Lectures from the Mountains*, Series II, Sections I and II.

[2] See Sir John Sinclair, *General View of the Agriculture of the Northern Counties*, 1795, p. 76, for the allowance. The calculation for Badenoch is included in the foregoing reference.

From constant references in the Account Book to the ' Cross Dyke,' it is evident that Balnespick's land at Dunachton was arranged somewhat in the fashion common at that time. The head dykes were very ancient and ran along the sides of the valleys, dividing the arable land from the open moor. The cross dykes ran down from the head dykes at right angles, dividing the farm's cultivated land in half.[1] All other boundaries were made of sod. Above the head dyke portions of land were gradually reclaimed from bare moorland and used for corn for two or three consecutive years, and then as pasture until the ground was sufficiently rested to bear corn again. At Dunachton itself no trace of the head dyke or cross dyke remains—the permanent arable has probably gradually extended above the former—but in many Highland glens the line of the head dyke along the hill-sides can be easily followed. Thus in parts of Glen Lyon it is unmistakable. The walls are about twenty yards or more above the present limit of the arable land, and the heathery ground below shows obvious signs of having been under cultivation.

It was usual to divide farm land into ' infield ' and ' outfield.' Practically all writers on eighteenth-century Scotch farming have described the treatment accorded to these two kinds of arable land.[2] The infield was constantly under oats and barley, the whole manure of the farmyard being spread raw on it. The outfield, which was generally on less productive land, or on some that was more distant from the cultivator's house, was fertilised by ' tathing ' (see p. 254), i.e. folding the animals at pasture in an enclosure of sod walls every

[1] James Robertson, *General View of the Agriculture in the County of Inverness*, 1808, p. 109; Mr. Marshall, *General View of the Agriculture of the Central Highlands*, p. 16.

[2] D. Gray Graham (*Social Life in Scotland in the 18th Century*) and Alexander (*Northern Rural Life*, in the chapters on Agriculture) quote freely from old references. Sir John Sinclair (*View of the Northern Counties*, p. 9) gives a good abstract. The *Second Statistical Account for Alvie* (p. 92) gives a vivid description of local conditions.

night for eight or ten nights, and then moving the enclosure a little farther on, till all the outfield had received
some enrichment.[1] It was then ploughed up and bore
crops of oats or barley for about three consecutive
years, until the soil was so exhausted that the last crop
was known as ' rush ' oats (see p. 161), and was only
fit for feeding to the cattle unthreshed.[2] The soil
then lay derelict for seven or eight years, when the process was repeated. The land was entirely useless during
the first two years of its fallowing, and the grass had
only begun to grow on it by the time it was again
ploughed up.[3]

The agricultural improvers readily pointed out the
two most serious weaknesses of such a system—that
the provision of winter feeding was quite inadequate
(which must have been an especially serious disadvantage
in a stock-raising country such as Badenoch), and that
the ground was never properly cleaned.

The proportion of infield and outfield on a farm
appears to have varied considerably, but Balnespick
was evidently somewhat exceptional in having the
greater part of his land as outfield. This was not due
to the poverty of the soil, for Dunachton is on unusually

[1] James Robertson, in *General View of the Agriculture in the County
of Inverness*, pp. 74 and 110.

[2] Alexander (*Northern Rural Life*, p. 22) describes rush corn. The
word is not often met with, but Balnespick uses it constantly.

[3] Sir John Sinclair, *General View of the Agriculture of the Northern
Counties and Islands of Scotland*, 1795, p. 9 : ' The farmers or tenants
never think of artificial grasses, have their lands under constant crops of
oats, of that often three crops following three barley and sometimes a
little pease and potatoes. Their only pasture arises from some rigs or
ridges of hay, so over-cropped that they can yield no more oats and
therefore must be rested for want of manure, having no other mode of
recovering their fertility. These hay ridges are almost the only pasture
they have for their horses or for a milk cow or two, miserable pasture
it generally is, consisting chiefly of weeds of all descriptions.'

A reference quoted by the author of *Northern Rural Life in the
Eighteenth Century* describes the outfields as being ' allowed to remain
in a state of absolute sterility, producing little else than thistles and
other weeds.'

fertile land, and one can only assume, either that Balnespick rented more land than he could cultivate fully,
or that he tried it as an experiment in keeping the land
clean and in good heart.

The arrangement of Balnespick's farm was extraordinarily different from that of a modern one. To
the east it extended over land that now forms part of
the policies of the shooting lodge : it covered the
upper and middle parts of the present farm of Dunachton-
more, and extended to various small patches of more
level ground scattered through the wood that are not
now considered worth cultivating. Certain westerly
fields of the present farm—Cuilintuie and Auchnabeuchin—were then let off to groups of sub-tenants,
but the amazing difference between the old and the new
farming was the presence of small sub-tenants whose
holdings were more or less mixed up with Balnespick's
land.

Thus Balnespick held certain strips of land in the
township of Dunachton-more, which was cultivated
jointly by six sub-tenants ; the ' crofts at the Gate '
were tiny holdings, which were grouped along the
King's Road between the House of Dunachton and
the twenty-acre tract of alluvial soil at the mouth of the
burn, then known as the Chapel Park, which seems to
have been one of Balnespick's most esteemed portions
of the farm ; the croft in the Red Park cut into the field
of that name and lay immediately to the west of the house
and between it and the infield of Dunachton-more.
One can well imagine that this arrangement was made
to secure a good supply of joint labour for the toilsome
agricultural processes of the times, for the inconvenience—especially when it is remembered that the
fields were unfenced—must have been considerable.[1]   In
the Account Book there are several instances of payments for ' Skaith ' or damage done to the corn by

---

[1] Among Lachlan's papers there is a letter from a farmer complaining
of the difficulty of working his farm because ' the tenants in the two
towns have made ways for themselves and left me in the lurch.'

cattle.[1]   It was also perhaps an illustration of the casual,
careless methods of the times that several of the tenants
had their little patches of land broken up : thus the
smith—probably a personage of some standing by
virtue of his calling—had an oxengate on Drumstank,
one of the joint groups of sub-tenancies, and two oxengates on another named Achnabeuchin ; and as it can
be seen, by comparing the yearly rent roll, that there
were vacancies on both these holdings at the time, it is
difficult to account for such an inconvenient arrangement.   To quote Andrew Wright [2] in his description
of Perthshire in 1778 : 'The farms are all interwoven.'

The appearance of the arable land must have been
strangely irregular and patchy.   Fencing and the
division of land [3] into fields was unthought of at that
time in such a remote district, and it was customary
to work the land up into ridges, partly as the result
of unskilful ploughing and partly in the attempt to
provide drainage.   The good soil constantly tended
to accumulate on the crown of the ridges, leaving
a stony trough between them.[4]   In the case of
Laganamer and the corner of Chapel Park that is now
cut off by the railway line, and also in the abandoned
sub-tenants' holdings of Carit and Craigandhu, the wavy
irregular line where cultivation ended can still be distinguished, and the grass is striped with irregular

---

[1] In a statement drawn up by Captain Lachlan's trustees, in one of
the usual complicated accounts of claims and counter-claims between the
tacksman and his sub-tenants, there are two entries relating to damage
by animals : ' That some time after Balnespick's milk cows had been in
Forbes corn and the Damage was comprized to be 8 pecks Small Oats,
and that at that time the Small Oats was at 10/– the Boll—A year thereafter Forbes Horses were in Balnespick's Corn, and the loss comprized
at 3½ pecks small oats—.'   It is only typical of the times that Forbes
paid for the difference by giving Balnespick a deer that he had killed
' on South Side Spey.'

[2] Andrew Wright, *Present State of Husbandry in Scotland*, 1778,
p. 34.

[3] See *Second Statistical Account for Alvie Parish.*

[4] Alexander's *Northern Rural Life*, p. 19.   Many other writers
describe these ridges.

ridges and hollows as if by some vast subterranean Atlantic swell.

The patches of arable land were yet further diversified by wet places and clumps of rushes. The farm of Dunachton is unusually lucky in lying on fairly steep gravelly slopes, so that it probably owes far less than most parts of the country to the introduction of pipe drainage. Yet even on Dunachton the present farmer has estimated that a considerable amount of land has been made productive by this means—perhaps the total gain in improved bearing would be about one-quarter of the whole crop, but this would vary considerably according to the shift, and according to what fields were under oats or grazing.[1]

Towards the end of the eighteenth century the improvers were beginning to consider the problem of drainage, and many items in Balnespick's Account Book refer to the making of a 'dutch' (see p. 216)— it was some years before he learnt the proper spelling— beside the ruined chapel in the Chapel Park. He paid the man who made it 6*d.* a day, or gave him the equivalent value in meal. Chapel Park went out of cultivation, but was taken in again lately, and Balnespick's ditch was discovered and cleaned out. It was beautifully constructed of flattish stones fitted together, and closely resembled the ditches that Sir John Sinclair describes in his 'View of the Northern Counties' (p. 39) as the latest word in fashionable farm improvements in the late eighteenth century.

The ancient implements of the Highlanders were almost entirely constructed of wood. The harrows

---

[1] In the old days very much of the best land was merely unproductive marsh for want of draining (see Paper on *The Making of Aberdeenshire*, by W. Alexander, read before the Aberdeen Philosophical Society in 1888). Drainage is described by the minister of Gamrie (*Second Statistical Account*, vol. xiii. p. 288) as ' our greatest modern improvement.' Deep drainage was introduced in 1834 by Mr. Smith of Dunston, and ' has ever since been practised to such an extent as to have changed the very appearance and character of whole districts of Scotland ' (see Report by the Royal Scottish Agricultural Society issued in 1884).

were 'little better than rakes'; the old plough, 'that very singular and feeble instrument,'[1] was of very clumsy construction.   It was drawn by twelve oxen, with four or five men to guide it and its team, 'and if the whole party managed to overturn one ridge at a yoking the husbandman's hopes were realised.'[2]

Dr. James Anderson wrote : ' The plough itself is beyond description bad ; and it is of so little conse- quence to perpetuate the memory of what can never be imitated elsewhere, that I shall omit the description of it.   I shall only observe that it made rather a tri- angular rut in the ground than a furrow, leaving the soil for the most part equally fast on both sides of it, so that if all the loosened earth were stripped from a ploughed field, it would remain nearly in this form $\wedge \wedge \wedge$ only it would sometimes happen that a gap would be made in these protuberances.'   In ' Northern Rural Life,' chap. vi., the implement is fully described ; it was made of pieces of wood, pinned together by wooden pins, the only iron parts being the ' coulter ' and ' sock.' ' An expert wright could make three ploughs in a day, working diligently ; and he was paid eight pence to a shilling for each.'   The material cost about 8*s.*

In many parts of the country the ground had to be ploughed over twice, or the furrows had to be pre- pared with the restle—a horse-drawn implement ; or else the work of the plough had to be supplemented by digging with the càs chrom—a clumsy kind of wooden foot-spade, examples of which can be seen in Glasgow Museum.   The anonymous writer of ' Lectures from the Mountains ' says that it was customary to encourage the oxen by whistling or singing, and that the animals stopped if the music ceased.   Burt also alludes to the practice, but calls it ' a hideous Irish noise.'—So much for the point of view.

Sir John Sinclair, in his ' View of the Northern

---

[1] Mr. Walker, *On the Hebrides*, vol. i. p. 122.

[2] *Lectures from the Mountains*, Series I, p. 26.   The fullest account is in *Northern Rural Life*, chap. iv.

Counties,' p. 76, gives the following list of farm implements required by a small farmer :

	£	s.	d.	
A plough mounted . .		5	0	[Plough and am-bles, £4 4s.]
2 pairs harrows, 3/- each .		6	0	[Harrows, £1 10s.] [Chain harrows, £2.]
1 spade		2	6	
4 wooden shovels, iron shod, 8d. each . .		2	8	
2 cabbies, or small half-side mattocks . .		2	6	[1 grubber, £4.]
4 kellacles or carts, 2/6 each		10	0	[2 carts, £16.]
4 ditto with rungs or rails for carting corn, 2/6 each		10	0	
4 horse collars of straw, 1d. each		0	4	
4 hair halters, 2½d. each .		0	10	
4 crook saddles, 6d. each .		2	0	
4 hair or hempen ropes for traces . . .		2	6	
3 yokes and wooden bows, 4d. each . . .		1	0	
2 flails, 2d. each . .		0	4	[Barn fanner, £3 10s.]
2 sieves, 1/- each . .		2	0	
2 fans, 4d. each . .		0	8	
3 riddles, 4d. each . .		1	0	
6 sheaving hooks, 5d. each		2	6	[Reaper, £14. This sum would not include a binder, and would only pay for an old-fashioned, very simple machine, such as only a small farmer would now have.]

	£	s.	d.				
2 flaughter or turf spades, 6d. each		I	O				
2 corn forks, 2d. each		O	4				
Iron chain or soam, for the oxen plough		6	O				
Sundries, exclusive		3	6	[Small imple-ments, £5.]			

	£	s.	d.		£	s.
	£3	2	8	[Scuffler.	I	9]
				[Roller .	I	10]
				[Turnip sower.	5	o]

He adds, three pages later, that the wear and tear on these wooden implements was so great that they required renewal every two years. I have added in brackets the value of implements required on a small farm at the present day. They would, of course, last for very many years, and would require infinitely less labour to use.

Balnespick does not mention his implements. He almost certainly used an improved iron plough, for the 'First Statistical Account' for the parish mentions that ' the Gentlemen use the English plough from which they derive great benefit'[1]; but the wooden plough was in general use among the inferior tenantry some time after his death.

He was backward with his ploughings, compared to the custom of the district at the present day, and he gives no details of his methods. Fortunately some of the old writers give much fuller information. Thus an old ' Treatise on the Proper Fallowing,' by a Lover of his Country, recommends three or four ploughings to prepare the ground for every grain crop, and there are copious quotations from the early transactions of Farmers' Societies in the more modern books to show that such treatment was quite common. As Heron says :

---

[1] *First Statistical Account for Alvie,* vol. xiii. p. 375.

'Here everything is done by rude strength and perseverance.'[1]

The crops that Balnespick and his tenants reared were oats, bear, barley, rye, peas, and potatoes. Two kinds of oats were sown, white oats and small oats, the latter a very inferior grain that had almost deteriorated to the original black, hairy oat that was so light that it required twice as large a measure as good oats to make a boll of meal.[2] Bear, or bigg, was a very indifferent variety of barley. Balnespick, during the time that he kept the Account Book, gradually increased the proportion of barley and reduced that of bear in his sowings, and sold a good many very small quantities of barley seed to his sub-tenants. Peas also were probably in the nature of an experiment. Potatoes are not mentioned till 1774, and were only grown in one small patch. Rye was sown in small but very varying quantities. The most important crops were bear or barley and oats. In Sir John Sinclair's tables in his 'View of the Northern Counties,' the proportion of barley and bear seed sown was about one-third the quantity of oat seed. Balnespick's sowings were very variable, but more or less in proportion. It is difficult to explain the variations from year to year in Balnespick's sowings. The productiveness of the preceding harvests do not seem to have much bearing on it. Probably it was partly caused by the condition of the ground and by the needs of the household, for Balnespick was mainly a 'subsistence' farmer and most of his produce was actually consumed on the farm. Some connection between the amount of malt made in one year and the barley sowing of the next spring can be traced.

The quality of the grain was probably not very good. Adam Smith wrote in his 'Wealth of Nations' (p. 77 in the edition published by Messrs. Methuen and

[1] Robert Heron, *General View of the Natural Circumstances of the Hebrides*, 1794, p. 89.
[2] Personal reminiscences of an old crofter; see also *Lectures from the Mountains*, Series I, p. 22.

edited by Professor Cannan) that 'the quality of grain depends chiefly upon the quality of flour or meal which it yields at the mill, and in this respect English grain is so much superior to the Scotch that, though often dearer in appearance, yet in proportion to its bulk it is generally cheaper in reality, or in proportion to its quality, or even to the measure of its weight.'

SOWINGS.

Year.	Total Amount of Seed Sown.	Rye.	White Oats.	Small Oats.	Bear and Barley.	Peas.	Mixed.
	b. f. p.	b. f. p.	b. f. p.	b. f. p.	b. f. p.	b. f. p.	b. f. p.
1771	34–0–0	1–2–0	3–1–0	25–3–2	2–1–0	1–0–2	Nil
1772	27–2–0	1–0–1½	2–0–0	18–1–0½	3–0–2	Nil	3–0–0
1773	20–2–2	1–0–2	3–2–2	12–2–2	3–1–0	Nil	Nil
1774	29–0–2	1–1–0	4–2–2½	14–2–2	6–1–3½	Nil	2–0–2
1775	25–1–0	1–0–1	0–3–2	17–1–1	5–1–3	0–2–1	Nil
1776	40–2–2	6–0–0¹	3–1–2	25–0–1	4–3–1	Nil	1–1–2
1777	41–3–2	1–1–2	5–0–3	28–0–2	2–0–2	Nil	5–0–1
1778	33–1–2	0–3–1	6–0–0	20–2–0	2–3–2	Nil	3–0–3
1779	21–0–1	0–1–1	3–3–1	9–2–0	2–1–1	Nil	5–0–2

In addition, much of the seed that was sown was actually defective. Some of the grain was 'kiln dried' (see p. 243), either as the old-fashioned cure for 'smut'[2] or merely to dry it. Corn that was 'brocked' or damaged was also sown (see p. 244). Crofters still living can remember hearing that in their fathers' days the lightest grain was sown in order to save the best for food.

Rye, bear, small oats, and peas (as a field crop) are no longer sown in Badenoch—the five-shift course of barley, hay, grass, oats, and turnips being followed.

The arrangement of the crop appears to us even

[1] Rye was generally the first crop Balnespick took off newly broken ground. That year new 'lymed' and tathed ground is mentioned, which probably accounts for the unusually high proportion of rye that was sown. Some of the 'new ground' was down by the loch and has evidently reverted to swamp.

[2] This remedy is still used in the Outer Isles. I have been told by someone who had seen it in operation there that it is a very difficult and risky operation. If grain is heated above what is necessary, its fertility is liable to be affected.

stranger than the varieties that were sown. In some
seasons Balnespick sowed a mixture of grain—a practice
that is now quite obsolete. He does not seem to have
done so especially in bad seasons, and it was probably
a kind of experiment. Rye and bear grind more
economically than oats, and old people have told me that
in their fathers' days, on smaller holdings, in times of
poverty, the practice of mixing grain was extensively
carried on as a form of economy. The resulting mixture
must have been very like our much-abused ' war bread.'[1]

It is more difficult to explain why the separate kinds
of grain were sown in such very small quantities. A
peck or so of rye, bear and white and small oats would
be sown on the same ' row ' or ridge, or in one plot, as
was done on Balnespick's share of Drumstank in 1774
(see p. 208). As they were sowed and ripened at different
times it must have been a most inconvenient arrangement.
Perhaps, as seasons were hazardous, and the ground was
extremely variable in richness, dryness, etc., Balnespick
was anxious to give them all as equal a chance as possible.

There were no fixed shifts for crops, and the number
of consecutive grain crops raised on different parts of
the ground varied very considerably. The infield of
Dunachton-more—now the three fields immediately
surrounding the present farmhouse—where Balnespick
held some strips of land, was under constant crops,
and from the mention of the ' Barley row,' etc., even the
kind of grain sown on particular parts of that land
does not seem to have varied. The ' Gardners Croft,'
which cannot now be identified, also bore an almost
uninterrupted succession of cereal crops. The accom-
panying table gives some idea of the apparently erratic
culture of the rest of the farm.

The sowing of the oat seed was generally begun
about a week later than at the present time, rye being
sown first. The whole of the sowing lasted about two

---

[1] Mixed grains—usually oats and barley—are extensively sowed in
England under the name of 'Dredge Corn.' The crop is used for
feeding stock and poultry.

	1769.	1770.	1771.	1772.	1773.	1774.	1775.	1776.	1777.	1778.	1779.
Below Prosnapoil	White Oats										
East of Cross Dyke	White Oats										
West of Cross Dyke	Small Oats										
The Prilline (very poor ground, now moor)	Bear										
The Cleckersnach	Small Oats										
Hill of the Stack	Small Oats										
The Kerth	Small Oats										
The Yard	Small Oats								Bear		
Faiscalloch	Barley / Small Oats	White Oats	White Oats						Barley / Small Oats	White Oats	White Oats
Laganamer (3 to 4 acres, fertile land now out of cultivation because such a small patch with difficult access is not worth cultivating)											
This Side of Gate Park (now covered by a 30- or 40-acre field that used to be known as the Red Park)		White Oats / Small Oats	Rye / Small Oats	White Oats / Rye	Rye	Barley	Barley	Rye			Small Oats / White Oats / Barley
Gartan Gowr		White Oats	White Oats	White Oats							
Croft na Core			White Oats	Barley							
Next Kitchen			Small Oats	Rye							
West Park			Peas	Peas							
Above Ditch (very steep back, now covered with scrub)				White Oats							
Dolinloch				Small Oats	Small Oats	Small Oats / White Oats	Small Oats / Rye	Small Oats			
Drumstank (now covered by a field of the same name of about 15 acres)					Small Oats / Barley / Rye	Small Oats / Barley / Rye / White Oats	Small Oats / Barley / Bear	Bear / Small Oats			
Behind the Barn						Barley / Bear	Bear	Bear / White Oats / Small Oats			
Chapel Park (land on each side of the Burn)								White Oats		Rye / White Oats	Bear
Tom Votch (now covered by a field of that name, 9 acres)									White Oats / Rye / Small Oats	White Oats / Rye	White Oats / Small Oats / Rye
Drummore (now covered by a field of that name, 12 acres)							Bear		White Oats / Small Oats	White Oats / Small Oats	White Oats / Small Oats

weeks longer, as a rule, than it generally does on the farm at present.

Unfortunately, there is no record of what treatment the sprouting crop received. It would be interesting to know if Balnespick's attitude to the weeds on his land was passive like that of the old-fashioned farmer who ' expressed great gratitude to Providence for raising such a quantity of thistles ; as otherwise how could we, in this district, where we cannot allow our good corn land to be in pasture, find summer food for our working horses ? '[1]; or if he adopted the heroic measures for cleaning his land that the earlier improvers advocated. ' Northern Rural Life,' in chap. v. p. 24, quotes from an early treatise upon the suppression of ' yarrs, skellacles, gules,' and other weeds, which ' advance with incredible celerity, and unless they be crushed—soon overtop the brier, and maintain the victory.' Harrowing the growing corn was advised, ' and if, after all, the weeds happen to prevail, it may be eaten up with beasts betwixt the beginning and middle of May,' in the hope that the young corn would then grow more quickly than the weeds. Even though the earlier weeds were by these means vanquished, the wild corn threatened to do ' very notable mischief ' to the cultivated corn, and the farmer was admonished to strike them down with a rod.

Marshall says : ' Taking one year with another, the quantity of weed seeds must be nearly equal to that of the grain produced. In some of the oat crops of 1793 the proportion of produce must have been greatly on the side of the weeds.'[2] The harvest usually began about the third week in September and the cutting and stooking lasted nearly a month ; the stooked corn often stood in the fields a month longer. The dates of beginning, duration, and ending are more variable than at present.

[1] D. Stuart of Garth, *Sketch of the Manners and Character of the Highlanders of Scotland*, 1825, p. 174.

[2] Mr. Marshall, *General View of the Central Highlands*, 1794, p. 40.

In Lower Badenoch, under modern conditions, the harvest usually begins early in September, and the time required to gather the crop on Dunachton is about four weeks. It is difficult to draw an exact comparison between the old and new methods, owing to lack of sufficiently exact information ; but even though it is evident that the acreage under cereals in any given year was rather smaller in Balnespick's time—judging by the quantities sown it was between 20 and 40 acres, compared with over 40 on the present farm—and although one extra hired servant was employed in the old days, it is rather surprising that the difference in the time it took to gather the harvest was not greater. Balnespick's patches of cultivation were smaller, his carts had less capacity, and cutting, binding, and stooking were done by hand. The rapidity of the work was probably caused by the labour-dues of the sub-tenants.

Balnespick always mentions the number of 'thraves' that were harvested. The 'thrave' is an obsolete term for two stooks of twelve sheaves each. The sheaves were smaller than modern ones, for they were supposed to fill the space between the prongs of a fork that were five inches apart. (A local farmer remembers seeing such a fork in his youth. The 'birleyman,' or 'proofman,'[1] an arbitrator elected by the tacksmen and sub-tenants, had charge of the implement, and was responsible for the sheaves being of the correct size. The workers were supposed to bind a certain quota of sheaves, and were apt to scamp work by making them unduly small.) The proportion of thraves to the amount of seed sown would give an indication of the quality of the straw rather than of the grain, but in a given harvest it does help to show the extraordinary variability of the soil. Thus, in 1769—a very good year—white oats in some places yielded three thraves for every peck of seed sown, and in others only three-quarter thraves for the same amount of seed (see p. 160).

---

[1] *Aberdeen Journal*, 'Notes and Queries,' vol. vii. p. 82, defines 'birley-man' as 'chosen by common consent'— 'byrlaw man.'

The small oats in 1775 show an even greater disparity (see p. 246). On the modern farm the poorer land has either been improved so that it has become as productive as the better land, or it has gone out of cultivation as not worth the labour required by it. Even as early as 1724 the cultivation of inferior land in Scotland was attributed to the presence of an over-abundant supply of cheap inefficient labour. 'A Lover of his Country' writes : 'For we in this country being in use to labour our grounds at a much smaller charge, with less industry than they do in England, are content with a very small return, so that we continue to labour our grounds for corn, till it be reduced to a state of almost absolute sterility, which may be said of ground when it does render three-fold . . . whereas in our neighbouring country of England, grounds are looked upon as unfit to be continued longer in tillage when they render less than five-fold.'[1]

By comparing the meal account, the list of sales and the sowings of the following spring for each year, it is possible to work out a rough estimate of the amount of meal and grain produced in the preceding harvest, though unfortunately not the total amount of grain, for the yield of meal per boll of grain must of course vary with its quality. According to this rough-and-ready calculation the returns for each boll of seed sown would be :

1769	.	.	Oats 3·26	Bear and barley 6·74
1770	.	.	,, 0·5	,, ,, (?)
1771	.	.	,, 1·12	,, ,, 3·68
1772	.	.	,, 1·88	,, ,, 4·64
1773	.	.	,, 3·16	,, ,, 5·17
1774	.	.	,, 2·45	,, ,, 2·37
1775	.	.	,, 3·86	,, ,, 4·8
1776	.	.	Both together 2·53	
1777	.	.	Oats 2·13	Bear and barley 3·14
1778	.	.	,, 2·66	,, ,, 1·33

[1] *A Treatise Concerning the Manner of Fallowing the Ground*, p. 35.

These harvests are considerably better than Sinclair's average returns, which give practically the same figures, and are for grain only ; but the present returns on Dunachton, which average nearly eight-fold, are also much higher than those of the surrounding district, which would probably be under six-fold, taking good and bad years.[1] This gain is not clear profit, for, besides the cumulative effect of draining, liming, etc., in the past, the land receives 5 bushels of fertiliser per acre every fifth year, when it is laid down to turnips, in addition, of course, to the farmyard manure, of which there is a far larger supply than in Balnespick's time, and which is now properly fomented.

Balnespick produced mainly for home consumption. No bread or wheaten flour ever seems to have been bought for the use of his family ; and their allowance of 6 bolls of meal a head was the most important item in the farm servant's wages. The following table summarises the position. It throws rather a curious light on the inability of the north of Scotland to support a large population entirely on home produce. The

—	Total Crop in Bolls.	Used at Home.	Sold of Home Crop.	Bought.
1769	172	83	89	None.
1770	Not noted. Almost total failure	Not stated	None	50 bolls. 25 for the use of the household.
1771	41	81	None	77 bolls. 40 for the use of the household.
1772	36	79	None	170 bolls. 43 for the use of the household.
1773	80	88	6	21 bolls. Used 14.
1774	67	67	None	54 bolls, all sold locally.
1775	79	74	10	5 bolls, for change of seed.
1776	96½	Not stated	Not stated	3 bolls, for seed.
1777	82	76	15	9 bolls, for seed.
1778	66	62½	11½	7½ bolls, for seed.

[1] In an old paper of accounts, dated 1769, Dunachton was said to be ' the greatest pennyworth in the Lordship of Badenoch.'

plight of the people in bad harvests in earlier days, when the Highlands were closed and there were no roads, must have been terrible.

After the corn was carried it was put in stacks—sheaves of the different grains being put in the same stack, apparently quite without method (see p. 219). Threshing with the flack or flail then seems to have begun at once, and the grain was ground in the old water-mill that stood somewhere below the present farm.

The price of meal was variable : in good years, when Balnespick and his tenants were able to sell, it fell below 16s. ; in the worst years, when they were obliged to buy, it rose to over 20s. a boll. The price of oatmeal was 28s. a boll (10 stone) in 1923.

Balnespick was fortunate in having an unusually large proportion of hay-meadow and grazing, both on the swampy ground that lies on each side of the Spey, which now gives summer pasture to a few cows, and in the clearings in the woodland. Before turnips were grown, hay was the only winter feeding that could be preserved for the live stock, and was therefore extremely valuable. Before hay grasses and clover were sown with the barley crop, the stubbles and ley fields can have provided very little sustenance even for grazing, and the only hay available was that from the native grasses on permanent meadows, which, especially in the Highlands, is unsuitable for such a purpose.

The Account Book has an entry that mentions hay being cut ' among the bushes.' Marshall's vivid description of a Perthshire hay-making would therefore probably give a pretty good picture of Balnespick's methods.[1] He describes the only hay ground as actual bog land, and meadow ground whose ' present state is merely that in which Nature left them ; encumbered with stones and bushes, so that scarcely a rood of free surface, for the sithe to pass over, can be

[1] Mr. Marshall's *General View of the Agriculture in the Central Highlands of Scotland*, p. 41.

found in a town ship. . . . After the sithe has gone
over the free patches, the sicle is used to hook out
the remainder from among bushes, and to clear round
and between stones, and to shave the sides of hollow
ways, etc., until every handful of green herbage be
collected, and every part be pared to the quick.' He
goes on to describe how grass in woods was cut and
carried out to the open ground and spread on bushes
to dry. The Account Book also describes how in one
year the hay harvest was interrupted by the rising of
the river (see p. 186). From the appearance of the
marshy meadows along its banks, flooding must be a
frequent occurrence, and they are exactly what an
anonymous tourist through Scotland in 1702 described
when he wrote : ' The hay meadow was a marsh where
rank natural grasses grew, mixed with rushes and other
aquatic plants.' [1]

Hay sold at 5d. a stone. In 1768 Balnespick sold
431 stone, and in the following year 239 stone. There
is no further mention of hay sales on a large scale till
1778, when he sold £1 0s. 10d. worth of hay at 5d. a
stone ; but scattered through the Account Book there
are a good many entries of sales of small quantities to
sub-tenants, although in some cases there is no date.
In 1778 he spent a few shillings in wages to hay-makers ;
probably he had a bumper crop, and the usual labour
dues did not suffice for its gathering.

Harvests are obviously largely dependent on the
weather, and the most pessimistic modern grumbler
could hardly complain that present-day conditions were
worse than in Balnespick's time. In 1769 ' the season
was so rainy ' that the corn stood in the fields till the
end of November.

In 1770 there was snow on the ground till the middle
of April, the 16th being ' the coarsest day ever seen,'
and the cold lasted into May. In 1771 rain, snow, and
frost delayed the harvest. There followed a real old-
fashioned winter : frost and snow were ' very intense,'

[1] Quoted in *Northern Rural Life*, p. 19.

and continued from December 23 till April 4. The spring was cold and windy.

The late spring of 1774 was fine, but before that there was ' snow and frost closs from the 15th December till the 22nd March.' That summer there was ' hardly one day without wind and rain,' with the exception of ' four days very hot,' and the hay ' midow ' was flooded. In 1775 Loch Inch was partly frozen, and the spring was ' stormie ' ; the following spring sowing was delayed because the season was ' cold, with snow and rain and frosty wind from the North,' and the harvest weather was bad : ' Since we begun shearing till we had done got but five days from morning till night—there being rain, fogs and frost.' In 1777 one is relieved to hear of several periods of ' tolerable weather,' but the spring of 1778 was ' very cold with frost and high winds '—as Balnespick truly remarks, ' most disagreeable weather.' Fortunately 1779 was kinder ; of the spring he writes : ' Never did see finer season,' and the harvest weather was good on the whole. The winter that followed was so unusually stormy that the cattle were housed. From ' the 11th November till the end of ffebry Loch Inch was close frozen, then it only broke, we had yn a thaw with rain and wind for four days so that the river was different times near the Chapel.' Snow lay on the ground till the end of February, with ' many days most violent drift,' and the weather continued to be stormy until April.

Unfortunately, in 1782–83, the weather must have been even worse, for the harvest failed almost entirely, and the memory of the terrible shortage survived among the country people almost to our own times.

Balnespick kept cattle, sheep, and horses—pigs and goats are not mentioned at all in the Account Book, although in the preceding century, according to the Gordon rent roll, goat keeping must have been considerable in the district, for kids formed part of the rents in kind. (See ' Miscellany of the Spalding Club,' vol. iv., p. 165 onwards).

Cattle raising was the Highland farmer's greatest source of revenue.[1] Not only did the cattle provide milk, butter and cheese, which were important items in a Highlander's dietary,[2] leather for brogues and harness, and horn for spoons—the ' payment of the rents depended almost entirely upon the sale of the black cattle.'[3] The beasts were sold to the south-country drovers in the autumn, and were driven to England for winter fattening. Towards the end of the eighteenth century the trade was a very considerable one, and Adam Smith has pointed out how greatly it influenced the development of Scotland.[4] In reading the earlier ' Statistical Account for Scotland,' it is not easy to find a parish so remote that a cattle market was not held within walking distance of it, and the great fairs, where the animals were finally collected, were very large indeed. At Crieff twenty to thirty thousand head of cattle were sold at the October Tryst, and the total number of cattle sent to England from Scotland annually was estimated at 100,000.[5]

The stocks of cattle that were kept on a Highland farm must have been extraordinarily large. The bullocks were not ready for slaughtering till their fourth or fifth year, and a constant succession of young beasts had to be kept up. Even on a small farm it was usual to have four or five cows and their ' followers,' i.e. a calf, a one-year-old, a two-year-old, and a three-year-old for every cow.[6]

In the summer the cattle were driven up to the

---

[1] Stuart of Garth, *Sketch of the Manners and Character of the Highlanders of Scotland*, p. 172 ; Sir Eneas Mackintosh's *Historical Notes*, p. 37.
[2] See Sir John Sinclair's dietary of a farmer in his *General View of the Northern Counties*, p. 76.
[3] Mr. Walker, *On the Hebrides*, vol. ii. p. 47 ; see also p. 46. Sir Eneas Mackintosh in his *Memoirs*, written at the same time as the *Account Book*, says the same thing (p. 17.)
[4] Adam Smith, *Wealth of Nations*, p. 222.
[5] Alexander's *Northern Rural Life*, pp. 68 and 73.
[6] Mr. Walker, *On the Hebrides*, vol. i. p. 56.

shielings, to feed on the patches of hill pasture. They
were accompanied by herds and milkmaids, who lived
all the summer in huts. The summer pasture attached
to Dunachton was at the head-waters of the Dulnan,
about six miles off across the hills. The Account Book
has several lists of Balnespick's cattle ' in the Glen.'
The older people can remember their parents' stories
of the great migration up to the shielings. It was
quite general for the cattle to have to go a considerable
distance to find suitable pasturage, for before the introduction of sheep, and the increase of grass due to their
enrichment of the ground, fully two-thirds of the hill
grazings were unfit for cattle.[1] In the autumn the
cattle were driven down from the hills, and those that
the farmer wished to sell were sent to market. ' About
the latter end of August or the beginning of September
the cattle are brought into good order by their summer
feed, and the beef is extremely sweet and succulent,
which, I suppose, is owing in good part to their being
reduced to such poverty in the Spring, and made up
again with new flesh. Now the drovers collect their
herds and drive them to fairs and markets on the borders
of the Lowlands, sometimes to the North of England.'[2]
The rest of them, in Balnespick's own words, ' eat
promiscuously ' on the bare stubbles and open-field land.

The laborious system of ' tathing ' has already been
described. Owing to the lack of fences the cattle had
to be herded—' a disgraceful practise,' as Marshall
calls it (' General View of Central Highlands,' p. 59).
Many of the animals seemed to have remained out all
winter, although in very severe weather Balnespick's cows
were under shelter (see p. 180), and a certain number
of young beasts were wintered by sub-tenants, often
as part-payment of arrears of rent (see p. 201). All old
writers unite in describing the poorness of the feeding
of Highland cattle. As Mr. Marshall says : ' At the
end of winter every blade of grass is eaten up by the

[1] Mr. Walker, *On the Hebrides*, vol. ii. p. 66.
[2] *Northern Rural Life*, p. 73.

starving animals, so that they are finally forced to follow
the plough to eat the upturned roots.'[1] At the end
of a hard winter the cattle were so reduced by starvation that they had to be carried out of the cowshed
to the fresh pasture,[2] and the mortality among them
was said to be one in five every winter because of
starvation.[3] Balnespick was specially well provided
with hay, and he also seems to have grown a good
deal of 'rush,' or corn sown on exhausted land and
not worth threshing, for his live stock. The allowance of food, however, cannot have been a very large
one, for the cost of wintering a beast was estimated at
1s. 6d. for the whole winter, and 2s. for a heifer in calf.
With hay at 5d. a stone, the former figure would only
allow under four stone for the whole season. (The cost
of wintering a bullock would now be about 2s. 6d. a
week, and 5s. a week for a cow. Turnips and oil-cake
would, of course, be given ; but a farmer who fed his cows
on hay one winter, because of the failure of the turnip
crop, told me he allowed them 28 lb. a head a day.)

It is not surprising that the cattle were small and
unproductive. A five-year-old bullock was said to be
no bigger than a Guernsey, and the best cows only gave
a Scots pint of milk a day, and calved every second
year.[4] The price of a bullock was from £1, and
that of a cow from £3.[5]

Balnespick had not begun to improve his breed of
cattle, for he bought and sold freely with his sub-tenants,

---

[1] Mr. Marshall, *General View of the Agriculture in the Central
Highlands of Scotland*, p. 38 ; see also p. 37. *Lectures from the
Mountains*, Section II of Series I, also gives a full account.

[2] It was known as 'the lifting.' See Burt's *Letters from the Highlands*, vol. ii. p. 132.

[3] Sir John Sinclair, *General View of the Agriculture of the Northern
Counties*, p. 114. *The Investigation into the Cost of Milk Production*, by
the Scottish Board of Agriculture in 1921, states that the average mortality
on the farms investigated was—cows, 2 per cent. ; calves, 12 per cent.

[4] Mr. Walker, *On the Hebrides*, vol. ii. pp. 59–60.

[5] Figures in the Account Book are borne out by those in *Northern
Rural Life*, p. 62.

and the ordinary breed of cattle in Badenoch at that
time seems to have been very inferior and mongrel.[1]
He generally kept from 11 to 19 milch cows and a
bull, and a varying number of younger beasts. If
the three lists given both for 1771 and 1772 are compared, it will be seen that the numbers in each age-
group vary considerably, so that he must have bought
and sold a good many animals. In 1768 he had 73
head, including 29 cows. The next list is for 1771,
the numbers had fallen to 40, including only 13 cows :
no doubt he helped to pay for the very heavy expenditure on corn for himself and his tenants by selling some
of his stock. In 1772 he was gradually increasing his
stock to 52. In 1773 there is an unusually full account
of income and expenditure, and there is no mention of
the sale of cattle; but in 1774 he notes that 13 beasts
were sold. In 1775 he had 40 head, and evidently
sold at least 6. In 1777 the herd numbered 42, and
7 beasts at least were disposed of. In 1778 he had
54 cattle, including 17 cows, and does not seem to have
sold any. The next entry is in 1780, when there were
only 23 head ; but it is evident from the rest of the
Account Book that most of the farm work was slipping
from old Balnespick's hands to those of his son Lachie
by that time. Balnespick generally seems to have sold
his beasts as four-year-olds, or when they were about a
year old, and to have bought them as two- or three-year-
olds. He only had one half the number of calves that
he had of cows, showing that Mr. Walker's description
was no exaggeration. Beyond the casual mention of
a keg of butter, that his wife was sending as a present,
there is only one entry in the Account Book that refers

---

[1] *Lectures from the Mountains*, Series II, p. 7. The following is a
list of the cattle that were sold in 1786 after Lachlan's death : ' A din
stot and brandered stot, £4 11s. A rigged Stirk, £2 4s. A Humle
Black Heifer, £3 0s. A Brandered Stirk, £2 3s. A Black Humle
Cow and one Calf, £11 10s. A Rigged Cow, £4 7s.   A Black
Yell Cow, £3 16s. A Black Tagged Cow, £3 15s. A Brandered
Heifer, £2 3s. A Din Stot and a Heifer, £5 7s.'

to dairy produce. In 1773, in 'An Account of my Situation,' Balnespick notes among his credit entries £22 'ffor Bark, butter and cheese' (see p. 270). The proportion of money received for bark must have been very small that year, because there are no entries for 1773 relating to its stripping and carrying, such as Balnespick made so copiously in the year when he disposed of even a couple of pounds worth of it ; but it is very unfortunate that we do not know how many cows he had at that particular time, though it is probable that there were rather more than usual.

By the kindness of Mr. Alexander McEwan I quote from another old farming diary, written about the same time as Balnespick's, by a Colonel George Sutherland, tacksman of Rearchar and Evelix in Ross-shire, which gives a very full cattle account, dated 1783. He had at the time 20 cows.

	£	s	d
'25 stones butter at 10/- . . .	12	10	0
25 „ cheese at 3/4 . . .	4	3	4
To two fed veals at one 6/-, one 4/-.	0	10	0
To ten stirks at 10/- . . .	5	0	0
	£22	3	4
To wintering 24 head at 1/4 . .	2	0	0[?]
To grazing and herding all my yell[1] cattle	2	12	2
	£4	12	2

Benefit from my cows . . . £17 11 2
My cows cost upon an average £3 each, from which £60 I must take Double Interest for interest and accidentall loss etc. £6 0 0.

	£	s	d
To 3 stirks that die yearly one year with another	1	10	0
To rent	8	10	0

---

[1] Yell = barren, a Scotch expression.

To a peck of salt for each couple, 10
    pecks salt at 1/6 .   .   .   .   £0 15 0
To ankers, cheese clothes, etc. .   .   0 10 0
To loss by a couple of cows short of
    the 20 most years, 5 Double Stones
    at 13/4 .   .   .   .   .
To by do. a stirk short at 10/– a stirk '

These figures seem to agree with Mr. Walker's
account and Sir John Sinclair's more general estimate.[1]

An old Highland dairy and the methods of milking
are racily described by Mr. Osgood Mackenzie in ' A
Hundred Years in the Highlands.' He quotes from
his uncle's memoirs of the home farm at Flowerburn,
in a very out-of-the-way part, early in the nineteenth
century : ' There were at Flowerburn 60 cows with their
calves, and to attend them 20 herds and milkers.' The
milking only took place night and morning, but it
lasted three hours each time. The cows and calves
were kept separate, but at milking times they were
driven to each side of a wall. One by one the ' bawling
mob of cows ' were shackled, and then their individual
calves were picked out and let through a gate in the
wall : ' and after a moment's dashing at the wrong
cow by mistake, and being quickly horned away, there
was "Busdubh" [black muzzle, a common Highland
name for a cow or calf] opposite to its mother's milker,
and sucking away like mad for its supply, while the
milkmaid milked like mad also to get her share of it.'
The calf was then dragged back through the gates
and another let in. There are indications that this
was quite the usual method of milking in older times.
The dairy is described as follows : ' No finery of china
or glass or even coarse earthenware was ever seen in
those days ; instead of these were very many flat, shallow
wooden dishes, and a multitude of churns and casks

---

[1] Mr. Walker, *On the Hebrides*, vol. ii. p. 60; Sir John Sinclair,
General View of the Agriculture of the Northern Counties, p. 114.

and kegs, needing great cleansing, otherwise the milk
would have gone bad.'   At Flowerburn this cleansing
was done by scrubbing the dishes with heather brushes
and then filling them with cold water and dropping
in red-hot pebbles.[1]   But although wooden dishes
were certainly used elsewhere, and large supplies of
hot water must have been difficult to obtain, no other
reference that I have consulted mentions such a method
of cleansing them.

About forty head of cattle are now kept on Dunachton-
more.   All the animals are, of course, housed all through
the winter.   It is difficult to estimate the difference in
cost between old and new methods.   A utility cow
would cost about ten times as much to buy and about
fifty times as much to winter.   But she would calve
every year instead of every second year, and would
give about two gallons of milk : taking an average over
the whole period of lactation, that is at least sixteen
times as much, when the double calving is remembered.
The value of the calves and milk has increased in proportion.[2]   A bullock would now fetch from £24 to

[1] Sir John Sinclair's inventory of a typical farm in *General View of
the Agriculture of the Northern Counties*, p. 76.
[2] *The Investigation into the Cost of Milk Production*, published by
the Scottish Board of Agriculture in 1921, gives the following proportion
of costs per gallon of milk produced on selected dairy farms in the east
and north-east of Scotland :

—	Cost of Productive Labour.	Cost of Purchased Feeding Stuffs.	Value of Home Grown Feeding Stuffs.	Cost of Live Stock.	General Expenses, including Rents.	Interest.	Management.
Farms with breeding stocks	4·48	9·24	12·4	..	1·17	2·21	1·27
Farms where cows are purchased	3·20	7·23	10·11	5·02	1·05	0·97	0·88

The cost of providing steadings would, of course, fall on the landlord,
and on an average Highland farm he would not be able to obtain an
increase of rent that would pay him more than one or two per cent.
on the expenditure.

F

£30, and to winter him would cost fully thirty times as much, but he would sell ready for the butcher by the end of the second winter. The farmer stands to gain considerably from the manure of stall-fed animals. Adam Smith explains how largely the improvement of Scottish land was due to the introduction of winter housing. On the other hand, the capital outlay on the necessary buildings is a heavy burden on the owner of land and steadings.

In ancient times in the Highlands cattle rearing was the main resource of the farmer, and sheep farming only ' formed a secondary object.' [1] The native breed had fine, scanty wool,[2] but was ' of an inferior, naughty size.' [3] The sheep were treated rather like goats, for only a small number were kept,[4] and they were sometimes tethered out and ' always housed.' [5] As Sinclair says : ' Dung and wool are their objects, for by the ordinary tenantry there is not, perhaps, an ounce of meat consumed from one end of the year to the other.' [6] They were also regularly milked. The wool of their light fleeces did little more than suffice for the needs of the families who kept them : hardly any of it was sold. The great stocking industry of Aberdeenshire was almost entirely dependent on wool imported from the south during the earlier and middle parts of the eighteenth century,[7] and the export of wool from Inverness was only $1\frac{3}{20}$ tons [8]

[1] General David Stuart of Garth, *Sketch of the Manners and Character of the Highlanders of Scotland*, p. 172.

[2] Mr. Walker, *On the Hebrides*, vol. i. pp. 69–70.

[3] Sir John Sinclair, *General View of the Agriculture of the Northern Counties*, p. 14.

[4] Mr. Walker, *On the Hebrides*, vol. i. p. 67.

[5] Sir John Sinclair, *General View of the Agriculture of the Northern Counties*, p. 14 ; see also Miller's *Survey of Moray*, p. 331.

[6] Sir John Sinclair, *General View of the Agriculture of the Northern Counties*, p. 14.

[7] See an article by the writer in the *Scottish Historical Review*, July, 1921.

[8] Robertson, *General View of the Agriculture of the County of Inverness*, p. 307.

in 1784, when the introduction of large-scale sheep farming had already begun. By 1804 the export had increased to 136½ tons. The wool was much spoilt by being smeared with tar and butter (the ' tarry 'oo ' of the old Scotch song) as a prevention from ailments and parasites, but the mortality amongst the sheep was very high from starvation and disease.[1]

The introduction of the coarse-wooled, hardy black-faced sheep, with their south-country shepherds, marked the beginning of a new era in the Highlands. The rapidly expanding woollen industry increased the demand for wool, and thus opened a new source of revenue from the barren heather hills. The use of the high hills for summer pasture for the sheep necessitated the provision of more sheltered grazing in the straths ; but the tragedy of the evictions and ' clearings ' lay in the fact that the movement came at a time of feverish expansion in the south, and therefore was so rapid that little or no time for adjustment was allowed, and that the old clannish ties of the Highlands were already breaking and were rudely snapped instead of slowly adjusting themselves to modern social relationships. The Clearances have left an aftermath of bitterness and evil that far eclipses all the effects of the sufferings and persecutions of the older, wilder times. In General David Stuart of Garth's ' Sketches of the Manners and Character of the Highlanders,' and the evidence of the 1848 Crofter Commission, the sordid story can best be traced ; and Charles Fraser Mackintosh, in his ' Antiquarian Notes,' gives fuller local details for Badenoch, though one is glad to find that he had no cause to mention Dunachton and Kincraig in his list of evictions.

At the time of the Account Book, Balnespick was evidently beginning to develop his sheep farming. He had a flock of between 80 and 110 sheep, and in three separate years he bought about 20 sheep from the

[1] Sir John Sinclair, *General View of the Agriculture of the Northern Counties*, p. 14.

south—no doubt animals of the black-faced border breed. In other respects he still seems to have clung to old-fashioned methods. The 'Cotes' or 'Coats' for housing the sheep are mentioned several times in the Account Book (see p. 248), and 'sheep dung' was spread on some of the rigs (see p. 255). He kept a considerable number—generally about 24—of ' milk sheeps.'

The management of the flock does not seem to have been very efficient. In his lists of cattle he invariably writes : ' so many 2 year olds against May,' etc. ; in the case of the sheep the formula on one occasion at least is ' so many year olds against May, if they live ' (see p. 267), and the figures that he mentions show that there was justification for this diffidence. In 1772 he lost 2 out of 19 lambs, and another year 11 sheep out of a flock of 88 died. (In healthy sheep country, such as Badenoch and Strathdearn, one death in twenty would now be the usual rate of mortality.) The proportion of lambs seems to have been surprisingly small. Under modern methods a given number of ewes would normally produce a lamb apiece, losses and barren sheep being counterbalanced by twins. Balnespick's ewes only produced about half their number of lambs in a season. The usual practice in the district is to sell off the lambs at five months old, with the exception of 25 per cent. of them, which are picked out for breeding stock. The ewes are cast at five years. If the numbers in each age group in Balnespick's lists are compared, it will be seen that he sold his animals off haphazard at any age, and that a very small proportion of the ewes—only four or five—survived till they were five years old. There are now 300 sheep on Dunachton, but as their grazing has been greatly extended it is not possible to make any comparison. In the Badenoch district sheep farming is now the most important branch of agriculture. The main value of the animals is for their meat.

At the time of the Account Book the great wool trade with the south had only just begun, although there was a small local manufacture of coarse white plaiding

at 9*d.* an ell.[1] There is no mention in the Account
Book of the sale of wool, although, judging from the
many entries recording payments to women, and the
large bill from one of the weavers—which was double
that due to the smith—the home consumption in cloth,
blankets, and carpeting must have been considerable.
Curiously enough, the production of wool has again
come to be a by-product in the district, and generally
the sale of it about covers the cost of dipping, etc.

   The value of lambs in Balnespick's time was about
1*s.* 6*d.*, and sheep fetched 3*s.* 6*d.* a head for small ones
and 8*s.* for larger ones.   According to another old
account book, from which I have already quoted,
48 large sheep (probably the reference meant black-
faced sheep) produced 45 lb. of wool valued at £1 19*s.*,
and 40 small sheep (perhaps survivors of the old breed)
29 lb. of wool.   From other entries it is evident that
this finer, shorter wool sold at a slightly higher price.

   At one time a considerable number of ponies seem to
have been bred in Badenoch, but cattle raising gradually
took the place of horse rearing.   Oxen were generally
used for ploughing, but the horses were required to
carry panniers or to draw the little wicker carts and
sleds.   The Highlanders preferred quantity to quality,
and both Sinclair and Walker describe the eight or
ten miserable, underworked and underfed little horses
that even small farmers kept.[2]   It is evident that Burt
uses little exaggeration when he describes the carts
as being 'about the size of a wheel barrow,'[3] and
with solid wooden wheels.   Even when fully loaded
they were generally turned in a narrow place by being
lifted round by their driver.[4]   Sinclair estimates that
they were worth about 2*s.* 6*d.* each.[5]   The ponies

[1] *First Statistical Account for Alvie Parish*, vol. xiii. p. 375.
[2] In the list of labour dues quoted farther on, the day's work of a
horse was estimated as being of less value than that of a man.
[3] Burt's *Letters from the North of Scotland*, vol. i. p. 74.
[4] *Ibid.*
[5] Sir John Sinclair, *General View of the Agriculture of the Northern
Counties*, p. 14.

stood about nine hands high, and were rough and
shaggy, although the hair of their manes and tails was
often all pulled out to make ropes.[1]   Their harness was
home-made and so badly adjusted that they constantly
suffered from sores.[2]   Of their feeding Burt says [3] :

'In winter the horse is allowed no more provender
than will barely keep him alive, and sometimes not even
that ; for I have known about 200 of them near the
Town [*i.e.* Inverness] to die of Want within a small
compass of time. . . . Certainly nothing can be more
disagreeable than to see them pass the streets before
this Mortality, hanging down their Heads, reeling with
weakness and having spots on their skins of a Foul
distemper, appearing without Hair, the effect of their
exceeding Poverty.'

One is glad to think that Balnespick's horses were
already in much better condition, for they certainly
had a small allowance of corn when they were working (see p. 240).   Very much improved carts were used,
for Balnespick took a set of spokes, valued at 17s. 6d., in
payment of a debt owed him by the wright, though two
of his other carts were only worth 10s. for the two of
them.   The horses' loads, whether they were used in
a cart or as pack beasts, were 9 stone—even the small
carts used in hilly parts of the Highlands would now
take three times this weight of any compact commodity.
Balnespick kept six horses and six carts, but he also had
the use of about twelve more carts and horses at times
when he most required them, as the 'long loads' due to
him from his sub-tenants (see the account of oak bark for
1770, p. 172).   Two pairs of modern Clydesdales would
now probably suffice for all the work on a farm of the
size of Dunachton.

The changes in agriculture have had a profound
effect upon the amount of labour that is required, and
therefore upon the population of the countryside.
The 'Second Statistical Accounts' for most of the rural

[1] Burt's *Letters from the North of Scotland*, vol. i. pp. 76–78.
[2] *Ibid*.   [3] *Ibid*., vol. i. p. 81.

parishes of Scotland bring this out very clearly.   Thus,
in the parish of Tarves, in Aberdeenshire,[1] it was
noted that one man was able to accomplish the same
amount of work as two had formerly performed.   (In
this parish there was no clearing of the population,
for it remained almost stationary between 1755 and
1841, whilst the land under arable cultivation doubled
and its produce increased ten-fold between the 1792 and
the 1841 statistical accounts.)   The demand for labour
has also changed in its character; the proportion of
seasonal, light work, especially for weeding, harvesting,
etc., has enormously decreased with the introduction
of binders and other agricultural machinery.[2]   Balnespick had the assistance of his younger son Geordie, and
of four men farm-servants and three lads or women.
He also had the very considerable labour dues of his
thirty-six sub-tenants and their families.

Sir Eneas Mackintosh (Balnespick's landlord), in
his 'Historical Notes' (p. 38), gives the following list
of such services :

> 'Faces of peat to cut, wind and lead to the Mansion
>   House.
> Days to plough, harrow and lead dung.
> Long loads.
> Days to reap corn and carry corn and hay.
> Days to carry necessaries for the use of the family.'

Another contemporary lease, relating to a farm in
Ross-shire, enumerates the following services : 'deliver-
ing of a load of candle fir, winning and carting peats,
ploughing, sowing, mucking and manuring the laird's
land, harvesting the corn, repairing dykes, wintering
a cow, giving four errands yearly and sending four
horses to carry loads home.'   Mr. T. Jolly, in an essay

---

[1] *Second Statistical Account*, vol. xii. p. 670.
[2] The beginning of this tendency can be seen in many of the 1845
reports, *cf.* Udny in vol. xii.; but its full effect is described in the 1906
Report on the Decline of the Population of Great Britain (Cd. 3273, Division
VI, p. 49).

published in the 'Transactions of the Highland Society' for 1799, states that tenants 'were bound to plough part of the mains ; to carry the manure to and harrow the whole ; to bring home the corns in harvest ; to carry the corns and what bear was needed to and from the miln ; and to carry the whole produce of the farm, both meal and bear to port, or market.' They also supplied the proprietor with fuel. An additional labour, where the practice of tathing—*i.e.* manuring fields by folding cattle upon them—was usual, was the building of the sod walls within which the beasts were confined. These folds were moved every eight or ten days (James Robertson's 'General View of the Agriculture in the County of Inverness,' pp. 109-110).

Balnespick only mentions two services in the Account Book—the long load and the fetching home of the mill stone—but among some other old papers there is 'A Note of the Advantage of the last Tack of the Davoch of Dunaughton and Dunaughton-begg and Kincraig,' dated 1769, which gives a list of the services and customs to be performed, 'wanting meat'—*i.e.* the tenants providing their own food—'by 17 Eightland parts,' or the value of the services in sterling.

'I first take notice of One Eightland part Converted to money.

	£		
To 2 spades and 2 harrows for one day at 6*d.*		2	
To 4 horses for 2 days leading Said peats at 3⅓*d.* each		2	2⅔
To 2 men for 2 days driving said horses 6*d.* each and one man for 2 days bigging said peats		3	

Nota Bene—One peck of meal allowed for winning said peats.

To cutting and leading Earth for bigging one day 3*d.*		3	
To 4 horses 2 days leading said earth at 3⅓*d.* per Day		2	2⅔

To 2 men 2 Days Driving said horses at 3*d.* £
    per Day each   1

To 2 men with four horses for One Day
    leading Timber 3*d.* per horse and 6*d.*
    per man   2

To 4 hooks one Day in harvest at 3*d.* each   1

To 2 men and 2 horses one Day leading
    Corn 3*d.* each   1

To 4 horses for two Days plowing at $3\frac{1}{3}d$.
    each .   .   .   .   .   .   2 $2\frac{2}{3}$

To 2 men for 2 Days Labouring with said
    horses 6*d.* each   2

                                               18 11

'The services of One Eightland part for One year
Amounts to £- 18 11 and for 17 Eightlands part is
£16 1 7.

'Without making mention of carrying corn to and
from the Miln housing Corn Stacks all the year Round
and the money of Grasing Cattle upon the Tenants
hill pasture.'

The service dues, in addition to Balnespick's servants'
work, seems to have sufficed for the ordinary routine
work of the farm. He makes no extra payments for
work on the farm—except in one or two exceptionally
heavy hay harvests, although he gives careful lists of
the money paid to men for stripping the oak bark, constructing his ditch, etc. The carrying of his bark to
Elgin was probably counted as a ' long load,' for he
records no payments for this service.

Balnespick paid his servants £2 a year, and supplied
them with two pairs of shoes annually at 1*s.* 6*d.* to 2*s.*
per pair ; in addition they seem to have received ' farings,'
and were paid like the other workers when ditching
or peeling bark. In some cases they received meal—
bear and oats—at the rate of 6 bolls annually (p. 15
in the Account Book), but in others they seem to have
had a cottage and scrap of holding, worth about £1 10*s.*

Thus Balnespick had a servant, Donald Roy, from 1769 to 1772, and a man of that name is mentioned at Carit, but he paid no rent. The McGlashans are mentioned as servants, and the same names appear as holding half an oxengate on Auchnabochin at an unusually low rent at the same date. Lachlan McIntosh was there later, and at the same time Balnespick had a servant of that name, and David Stuart was at Craigandow and paid no rent during those years that Balnespick mentions a servant of that name.

In comparing the wages bill of the past and present it must be remembered that, though the other tenants' services were nominally given for nothing, something should be added to an estimate of the labour cost on account of the inconvenience of subdividing the land so closely, and for the heavy arrears of rent. The present rate of wages received by a married farm servant is £60 in cash, with milk, meal and housing. The present farm of Dunachton-more, which has a considerably larger extent than that of the holding actually cultivated by Balnespick, is rented by a working farmer, who employs three labourers.

Although exact comparisons are impossible, it is easy to see that the old farming produced lower returns for a lower outlay. It directly supplied the cultivators with the necessaries of life, and with the manure, etc., required for carrying on the farm, instead of, as at present, providing saleable products which the farmer can sell in order to buy what he requires. The standard of living of the people dependent upon the old methods will be described more fully. In Highland farming the point where diminishing returns to capital expenditure begin seems to be quickly reached, and, even with all our modern inventions, it is difficult to see how many of the deserted little homesteads on the hills could be repeopled except under the conditions of almost privation of the past. The cost of labour is generally given as the reason why the poorer land that was let to sub-tenants in Balnespick's time, and is now only used for grazing, cannot be brought under partial cultivation.

Comparing Balnespick's old-fashioned methods, the prognostications of the reformers, and present-day agriculture, it is rather striking to see how largely the results have fallen short of anticipations. Thus, both Sir John Sinclair ('General View of the Northern Counties,' p. 80) and the anonymous author of 'A Treatise concerning the Manner of Fallowing the Ground,' p. 8 (1724), in advising improved measures, promise returns of eight times, and even twelve times, the quantity of seed sown, whereas, with all our increased improvements, the average return in Badenoch at the present time is six, and Dunachton is quite exceptional, by reason of generous farming and good soil, in sometimes attaining to eight. Again Robertson, in his official report to the Board of Agriculture on Inverness-shire (see pp. 178–226), urges the draining of the low-lying hay-meadows by the river, saying that the ground could be put to more profitable uses. All along this part of the Spey one can still see the hollows where would-be improvers sank capital in digging trenches and ditches, but the ground has not been found worth reclaiming and, once more, rank grass, sedges, and rushes cover it, and only give a little pasture to cattle in the drier parts.

Balnespick's own small improvements are equally discredited. Some of his new ground was carefully 'lymed,' and the old 'Statistical Account for Alves' (vol. xiii. p. 375) states that 'the gentlemen of the parish have begun of late to lime their grounds, which has answered extremely well, producing luxuriant crops of corn and grass'; yet the present-day local farmers consider that there is fully sufficient lime in the soil naturally.

His crops of peas, the seed of which he procured from Nairn, and of which he sold so many small quantities—probably for sowing—were no doubt looked upon as one of the latest improvements; for the introduction of a pea crop was strongly recommended by earlier improvers as a method of fallowing the ground (p. 28 of 'A Treatise concerning the Manner of Fallowing the Ground' (1724)). Yet, by 1808, James Robertson, in his report on Inverness-shire, states that Badenoch is unsuitable for their culture, and discourages it there (p. 132). Colonel Fullerton's description of the losses that the adoption of the newer methods entailed on a good many gentlemen farmers was probably true of very many parts of Scotland besides his own country (Colonel Fullerton's 'Report on the Agriculture of Ayrshire').

For Scotland, with its uncertain climate and peculiarly variable soil, is a difficult land to theorise about, and one is irresistibly reminded of the elemental spirit of insubordination to human control in Byron's 'Ode to the Ocean' when one reads of all the schools of agrarian thought and theory that have arisen, worked their will upon the ancient hill-sides and straths, and passed away.

CHAPTER V

BALNESPICK was a practical, professional farmer, and his capital was almost all invested in loans to farming lairds. He was thus almost entirely dependent on arable land, as was then probably the custom in the north. It is significant of the difference from modern conditions that a man of Balnespick's enterprise and position, with capital that was considerable for the times in that district, should have chosen the career of gentleman farmer on Dunachton, and that it should have proved so successful a one. William Mackintosh had sold his own property of Balnespick in 1748 (though he continued to be called by its name), and his successors bought the properties of Clune and Corrybroughmore in 1778 and 1791. In the Valuation Roll of 1624 Balnespick is valued at £226 13s. 4d. Scots, and Clune and Corrybroughmore at £143 6s. 8d. and £337 6s. respectively, and it seems certain, from lack of any other family tradition, that much of this considerable improvement in worldly goods was earned by farming and investments in arable land.

Balnespick gives a summary of his investments in ' Ane account of my situation Ag^t. Marts 1773 ' (p. 270).

' Lord A. G. [Lord Adam Gordon]
    Debiter with Interest agt. Marts . £1025
Sir L. G. [Sir Ludovic Grant of Dalvey] 645
Corrie [Macqueen of Corrybrough] . 115
Lurie 86
Invereshie [Macpherson of Invereshie]. 102 '

The first three loans are mentioned several times. The interest on them was at the rate of 5 per cent. per annum, and Balnespick seems to have either allowed it to accumulate or to have reinvested it, and to have lived entirely on his farm.

The Davoch of Dunachton, which Balnespick rented from Mackintosh, consisted of the sub-holdings of Dunachton-more, Dunachton-beg, Lealt, Cuilintuie, Achnabeuchin, the Carit, Craigandhu, and the Cluanach. They seem to have been leased as a whole from early times, as can be seen in the Gordon Rent Rolls of 1691 (reprinted in vol. iv. of the Spalding Club's 'Miscellany.') The group of holdings was assessed as one unit in the valuations for the minister's stipend preserved in the Office of Teinds (information kindly supplied by Mr. Maclean, the present minister of Alvie). Sir Eneas Mackintosh, writing contemporarily with old Balnespick, mentions 'on a farm rented from me by Mc.Intosh of Balnespick for £84.13.4 sterling, 240 people are supported, of which 60 are able to carry arms' ('Memoirs by Sir Eneas Mackintosh,' p. 36).

By means of subletting some of his holding of Dunachton, Balnespick received back a considerable part of his outlay in rent. According to a list that he made in 1769 the nominal value of his subleases was £87 (see p. 221), but he never received as much as this. From 1770 his son Lachlan is known to have taken over the management of Kincraig and all the eastern end of the farm, including Luald, Prossnacalloch, and Dunachton-beg, and from that date the names of these particular holdings no longer appear on Balnespick's rent roll. They were rented at £36. Balnespick only mentions Lachlan's payment of his part of the rent in 1773, when he paid £35. As that year was a bad one for rents, coming as it did after two very poor harvests, and as the careful old gentleman nowhere notes that Lachlan owed him for rent, it is fairly evident that Lachlan was able to pay his full share. The smaller tenants, however, were far less regular. According to Burt[1] a Highland landlord never expected to get his

[1] Burt's *Letters from the North of Scotland*, vol. ii. p. 160.

full rental, and to lose the value of one year's rents
out of five was quite usual. But in the ten years during
which Balnespick kept accounts he seldom received
four-fifths of his rents. In the very good season of
1769 he only got £64, and after the bad season of 1770
and 1771 he received less than one-third of what was
due for the crofts on his part of the Davoch. On an
average he only received about half the amount of his
rents. Part of this deficit was caused by allowing a
' melioration ' of the first year's rent to an incoming
tenant in order to enable him to put his steadings, etc.,
in repair. Sir John Sinclair describes the custom,
which was not a universal one,[1] and of course entirely
took the place of the modern landlord's obligation to
give compensation for improvements, or the very heavy
expenditure on present-day farms—not small holdings—for the maintenance of deep-drainage, fencing,
steadings, farm buildings, etc., which nowadays must
probably amount to over a quarter of the value of the
rental of the arable land on an average Highland
property, exclusive of larger expenditure at intervals,
when rebuilding is required.

It is evident, from the incidental mention of new
tenants' names in the years preceding that in which they
figure in the rent accounts, that Balnespick gave such
a melioration, and as there were about forty changes
recorded in the ten years, this item meant a considerable loss to him.

Apart from the comparatively heavy expenditure on
rent, and the very low cost of labour, Balnespick's
expenses were extraordinarily small. The description
of the domestic economy of her old home at Rothiemurchus by ' the Highland Lady '[2] is that of a typical
Highland family: 'We were so remote from markets
that we had to depend very much on our own produce for
some of the necessaries of life. Our flocks and herds
supplied us not only with the chief part of our food, but

[1] Sir John Sinclair's *Northern Counties*, p. 50.
[2] Mrs. Smith, *Memoirs of a Highland Lady*, p. 179.

with fleeces to be woven into clothing, blanketing and carpets, horn for spoons, leather to be dressed at home for various purposes, hair for the masons, lint seed was sown to grow into sheeting, shirting, sacking, etc. My mother even succeeded in table linen. . . . We brewed our own beer, made our bread, made our candles ; nothing was brought from afar but wine, groceries, and flour, wheat not ripening so far from the sea. Yet we lived in luxury. Game was so plentiful, red deer, roe, hares, grouse, ptarmigan and partridge ; the river provided trout and salmon, the different lochs pike and char ; the garden abounded in common fruits and vegetables, cranberries and raspberries ran over the countryside and the poultry yard was ever well furnished.'

At Dunachton wheat flour does not seem to have been used,[1] but otherwise there are many entries in the book that show that the family lived in much the same style as that here described. Balnespick kept a gardener. Two smaller beasts or a bullock and six sheep were slaughtered at Martinmas to be salted down for use—for before the introduction of turnips winter killed meat was unheard of. Except in the autumn the Highland cattle seem to have seldom been slaughtered for food. The following letter from Mr. Clerk, the Inverness merchant who supplied Balnespick's daughter-in-law with flannel, bread, ' taxes[2] and sprigs,' raisins, coffee, bone buttons, brandy, a ham, and other articles, is dated May 1785 :

' I am sorry it is not possible to get any beeff to be sent, Baillie McIntosh went to the Butchers himself but they had none and he went to the principle public houses but there was not any to be got there was but little at our last weeks market and it was all disposed of.'

---

[1] Apparently old Balnespick's daughter-in-law used two loaves of white bread a month at Kincraig. They were specially sent from Inverness ; several old letters from the local schoolmaster survive, arranging for their transport.

[2] *I.e.* tin tacks.

About 1792 Pennant says that in Perth fresh butcher meat was being sold in the winter for the first time. There are entries regarding spinning and weaving, and as Balnespick's wife specially got the linen for his finer shirts from Strathspey, it is fairly obvious that coarser linen as well as wool was home produced. A list of the house linen is given on p. 274, which shows that the supplies were very ample, according to modern ideas, but from other old family inventories, etc., it is evident that the stock was, if anything, below the average. Even the critical Burt, ' speaking of sheeting and table linen,' was obliged to admit ' people are much better furnished in that particular than those of the same rank in England ' (Burt's ' Letters,' p. 18, vol. i).

Balnespick malted his barley and brewed beer and distilled whisky. The corn produced on the farm was not sufficient for the needs of the household in bad years, but the sales after good harvests, when there was a surplus, seem to have very nearly covered the expenditure incurred in buying meal after bad ones.

As well as actually providing what was needed by the household, the produce of the farm was exchanged directly for goods and services. The six bolls of meal that the farm servants received were the most valuable part of their wages. There are many entries showing that labourers were paid in meal for digging the ditch, and women for spinning. The shoemaker's bill was settled with a hide (p. 200), and the wright's account was paid in wood (p. 174). The weaver gave services in payment for rent for a strip of the farm, and there is an amusing entry : ' To the taylor and the hens 1 boll, 2 firlots, 2 pecks of bear' (p. 261). No doubt, like old Colonel Sutherland, from whom I have already quoted, Balnespick employed an itinerant tailor who, for a yearly payment in money and meal, did what repairing and making as was required. Colonel Sutherland paid his tailor 20s. sterling and a boll of meal yearly, and it is evident from his long list of elaborate clothes that he was a bit of a dandy.

G

There is even a complicated transaction with a
London firm, who had interests in the Spey timber
trade, in which a bill for ' wine and oyr articles ' is
more than balanced by the ' deals and backs,' hay and
oats, salmon—at 5s. apiece—and straw ropes supplied
to their local employees (see p. 185).

Corn, hay, bark, wood, cattle, dairy produce, and
sheep were sold from time to time. It is almost certain
that the Account Book does not give a complete list
except in the case of grain, and that towards the end of
the ten years the entries are less and less full. The
bark was an occasional source of income, and it was
used to make good some of the heavy expenditure incurred during two bad seasons. Dairy produce was
generally an important item in the household accounts
of Scotch farmers, as may be seen from the description
of the minister's second wife in ' Galt's Annals of the
Parish,' and Miss Grant's description of local ' bodies '
in ' Memoirs of a Highland Lady.' But it was under
the management of the lady of the house, which may
account for so little being said about it in the Account
Book. Colonel George Sutherland, whose dairy accounts
I quoted from on a previous page, was a bachelor.

Balnespick's purchases consisted of iron for shoeing
horses, making ' bands,' probably for agricultural implements, etc. ; he bought 24 stone in one year, with
a quantity of nails, and retailed a certain proportion
to his son and neighbours. Tea at 5s. per lb. for
' breakfast tea,' and 7s. 6d. per lb. Fish from Inverness—probably salt fish—salt, sugar, soap, port and
malaga, for which he paid 15s. a dozen, and whisky
brought from Ferintosh and Glenlivat at 1s. 10d. a pint.
There is no complete list of his yearly expenditure or
groceries, but if the list of tea that is noted on p. 268
covers the year's consumption, it would be at the rate
of 3½ lb. per annum for the whole family. Colonel
George Sutherland gives a very full list of the groceries
he bought and the prices he paid. It is as
follows :

'Sugar . . . . . 1/4 per lb.
Hyson green tea . . . 8/– ,,
Suchong . . . . 4/10 ,,
Coffee beans . . . . 3/– ,,
Black Pepper . . . . 2/– ,,
Flour of Mustard . . . 1/6 ,,
Barley . . . . . 2d. ,,
Rice . . . . . 3d. ,,
Raisins . . . . . 1/4 ,,
Split Peas . . . . 4d. ,,
Vinegar . . . . . 2/2 per bottle.
White Soap . . . . 9d. per lb.
Yellow ,, ... 8½d. ,,
Florence Oyl . . . . 2/3 per bottle.
400 herrings . . . . 3/– '

Balnespick incurred heavy expenditure in importing meal in bad harvests from Strathspey, the shores of the Moray Firth, and even from Perthshire, for retailing to his neighbours. In 1770 25 bolls were resold, in 1771 37 bolls, in 1772 159 bolls, in 1773 6 bolls, and in 1774 54½ bolls. It is not easy to follow exactly what Balnespick paid or received, for different lots of meal cost different sums, but by means of a discount he generally seems to have charged cost price, including the expenses of carriage, for payments made in ready money or not later than the end of the following harvest. After that an addition of 5 per cent. was charged. In 1771–72 the purchasers seem to have been given the full advantage of an early purchase of meal before prices rose, and in 1773 some of them were only charged 18s. a boll, when meal at £1 3s. 10d. and £1 4s. a boll, including cost of carriage, was being imported. Perhaps the inferior local corn was sold that year. There were also a number of bad debts, such as that owed by the smith, so Balnespick probably lost something over the transaction, although it is not clear how much.

Balnespick also contributed a certain amount to

public burdens as ' cess,' or land-tax, payment towards the minister's stipend and the schoolmaster's salary, and in poor relief. Cess, or land-tax, was levied on the land-rent of Scotland, and was the only tax on land at the time Balnespick wrote his diary. In the shires the tax was levied by the Commissioners of Supply, who had power to revalue lands that were overvalued. The amount of the tax was fixed permanently at £47,954 per annum, and the share contributed by Inverness-shire at £806 15s. 8d.[1] If Dunachton had not decreased in value since the preceding valuation in 1624, when it was assessed at £468 3s. 4d. Scots, and the total value of Inverness-shire was £161,167 Scots, Balnespick's contribution to the tax would probably be £14 0s. 8d. Scots, or about £1 3s. 8d. The contribution towards the minister's stipend was £14 12s. 2d. sterling, over 2 bolls of grain, and 24 ' long loads ' that could be commuted upon the payment of 1s. 6d. apiece.[2] The payment towards the schoolmaster's salary was £2 2s. 7d. quarterly. It is not clear what Balnespick paid towards the funds for the relief of the parish poor, which was at that time administered by the local presbyteries, but the sum cannot have been considerable. In 1791 there were only twenty-five persons in receipt of public relief in Alvie parish,[3] and the amount of help that was given individually was probably amazingly small according to modern standards. In many Scotch parishes the relief averaged 3s. per pauper per annum.[4] The sub-tenants contributed to the payments of cess, stipend, and salary, but it is not clear what proportion they paid. Balnespick

---

[1] I am indebted to the kindness of Mr. Angus, curator of the Historical Department of the Scottish Register House, for the foregoing information.

[2] *Records in the Office of Teinds.* Information kindly supplied by the minister of Alvie.

[3] *First Statistical Account,* vol. xiii. p. 376.

[4] Stuart of Garth (*Sketch of the Manners and Character of the Highlanders in Scotland,* pp. 107 and 233) and Sir F. Eden (*The State of the Poor,* Appendix x. p. ccxiv) both quote figures. The latter reference gives an account of two methods of local Scotch Poor Law Administration.

was responsible for the whole amount, and collected their contributions with the rent ; but they were often in arrears, so that the entire payment had to be made by him.

It is rather interesting to compare the public burdens in Balnespick's time and at present. A pamphlet published by the Scottish Land and Property Federation, dealing with 'the development of Scottish agriculture,' classifies them under two headings : '(1) Annual Charges, and (2) Intermittent Charges upon land at irregular or uncertain intervals.' They may be detailed as follows, the net income derived from them being for Scotland only, and for 1922 :

(1) Annual Charges—
    Income-tax, £15,897,924 (the tax levied under
        Schedule A).
    Super-tax.
    Land-tax, £32,531.
    County rates.
    Parish rates.
    Ministers' stipends and surplus teinds.
    Heritors' assessments, £45,000 in pre-war
        days.
    Crown duties and feu duties.
    Inhabited house duty (now abolished).
(2) Intermittent Charges—
    Death duties, £5,709,271.
    Casualties of superiority.

Of these income-tax and death duties are, of course, the heaviest burdens.

The rates actually paid in Alvie parish are as follows :

PARISH RATES.

Owners—
    Poor Rate, 8d. in the £
    Registration Rate, 8d. in the £   1s. 8·625d. in the £.
    Education Rate, 1s. 6½d. in the £

Occupier—
    Poor Rate, 9d. in the £
    Registration Rate, 8d. in the £   1s. 10·75d. in the £.
    Education, 1s. 1d. in the £

COUNTY RATES.

Owner—
    Police, 5·584*d*. in the £ . . . .
    County General Assessment, 1·118*d*. in the £
    Lunacy, 4·175*d*. in the £ . . .
    Diseases of Animals, 0·057*d*. in the £ . } 2s. 6·410*d*. in the £.
    General Purposes, 0·766*d*. in the £ .
    Roads and Bridges, 16·000*d*. in the £ .
    Public Health, 2·710*d*. in the £ . . .

Occupier—
    Police, 3·004*d*. in the £ . . . .
    County General Assessment, 0·359*d*. in the £
    Lunacy, 3·803*d*. in the £ . . .
    Diseases of Animals, 0·057*d*. in the £ . } 2s. 2·66*d*. in the £.
    General Purposes, 0·766*d*. in the £ .
    Roads and Bridges, 16·000*d*. in the £.
    Public Health, 2·710*d*. in the £ . . .

The rates on the farm are, of course, liable to the reductions made on arable land. As a result of the Agricultural Rates Act passed this year, the agricultural landowner will be relieved of rather less than a quarter of his county rates. As regards parish rates, the relief would vary from about one-sixth to almost nil, as the relief depends on the amount of non-agricultural subjects in the parish. (Information kindly supplied by Mr. Erskine Jackson.)

The reference already quoted from gives 'an example of the actual incidence of the more important of the annual burdens.' The figures are said to be quoted from the annual expenditure of 'a fairly large estate in the south of Scotland, where the local rates, and also the stipends, are comparatively low—certainly well below an average.' The figures are for 'the year ending Whit-Sunday 1917, and are calculated on the Valuation Rent Roll.' The amounts payable in income-tax and super-tax would, of course, be less at the present day.

'The total owners' public and parochial burdens, other than income-tax and super-tax, averaged over several parishes 4s. 0·03*d*. per £, of which about one-half was stipend. The owners' income-tax and super-tax, after all deductions allowed, amounted to 6s. 4·67*d*. per £, making a total of 10s. 4·7*d*. per £ for these annual burdens and taxes alone.'

' According to the Inland Revenue valuation of this estate at the last succession—and assuming an interval of twenty years between successions—the burden of death duties is equivalent to an annual charge of 3*s*. 10·8*d*. per £ of Valuation Roll Rental. Adding this sum to the amount of annual taxation above stated, gives a total average annual payment in taxation of 14*s*. 3·5*d*. per £, irrespective of mortgage interest and all costs of management, insurance, repairs and maintenance.'

It is not easy to make out a connected statement of Balnespick's yearly income and expenditure from the old Account Book. In the following table many of the figures are based on little more than guess-work, and in only a few columns is it possible to feel that they at all approach completeness. Yet, rough and ready as are the methods of calculation, perhaps the table does give some general idea of how a tacksman of the eighteenth century lived.

APPROXIMATE ACCOUNT.

INCOMINGS.

—	Sale of Home Grown Corn.	Sale of Hay.[1]	Cattle.[2]	Dairy.[3]	Sheep.[3]	Miscellaneous.[4]	Rents.
	bolls.	st.		£ s. d.		£ s. d.	£ s. d.
1769	89 at 10/- £44 10	515 at 5d. £10 12 0 / 163 at 3d. £2 0 3	Not stated	£24 0 9	Not stated	Malt . 1 0 0	64 0 0
1770	None	None	16 cows at £3 / 43 stirks £1 16 } £112 10s.	Cannot be worked out	Not stated	Malt . 1 2 0; Hides . 0 19 0; Whisky . 6 11 4; Bark . 28 3 6; Wood . 0 12 0	34 15 1
1771	None	£2 15 0	..	£10 15 7	..	Bark . 15 4 0; A mare (?)	7 19 7
1772	None	Not stated	Not stated	£9 2 5	..	Bark . 27⁵ 0 0	19 12 3
1773	None	..	None	£22 0 0 (with bark)	24,⁵ at 5/- £6	Wood . 4 8 0	17 0 0
1774	None bolls.	..	13, £19 10	£15 15 1	..	..	39 15 0
1775	10 at 10/- £7 10⁵	..	6,⁵ £9⁵	£10 15 1	9⁵ at 5/- £2 5	2 hides . 1 12 0	33 3 9
1776	None	..	7,⁵ £10 10	Uncertain	40,⁵ £10⁵		25 11 10
1777	15	..	7,⁵ £10 10	£8 5 4	8,⁵ £2⁵	Hides . 1 5 0	33 12 3
1778	11½	£1 0 10	None	£9 1 11	Not stated	Hide . 0 9 0	38 18 6

[1] Considerably more was evidently sold in small quantities.
[2] These figures are certainly inadequate. He bought and sold constantly. The calculations for most years are only based on the numbers of animals in the age groups compared with the preceding year.
[3] With the exception of 1773 these figures are calculated from the rates of production in Colonel Sutherland's account, pp. 63-64.
[4] It is almost certain that more hides were sold. ⁵ Approximate figures, deducted from general information.

EXPENDITURE.

—	Rent.	Wages.	Special Payments.	Minister's Stipend, Schoolmaster's Salary.[1]	Purchases of Corn.[3]	Cess.
					bolls.	
1769	£86 13 4	£8	..	£16 14 9	..	£1 3 9
1770	48 13 4	8	£3 0 0	16 14 9	25 at 18/-² £22 10 0	1 3 9
1771	48 13 4	8	0 10 2	16 14 9	40 ,, £1² 40 0 0	1 3 9
1772	48 13 4	8	3 2 0	16 14 9	46 ,, £1² 46 0 0	1 3 9
1773	48 13 4	8	..	16 14 9	14 ,, 18/-² 12 12 0	1 3 9

[1] The sub-tenants' payments are included in their rents and this is the lump sum Balnespick transmitted.
[2] Approximately. Payment varied. Balnespick also expended money in buying those stirks that he resold.
[3] Only counting the corn that was consumed at home and not resold.

CHAPTER VI

THE type of gentleman farmer, either tacksmen (*i.e.* holder of a lease) or small lairds, of which Balnespick was a prosperous specimen, is as much out of date in Badenoch as runrig fields or wooden ploughs, and as such men were an integral part of the eighteenth-century rural economy of the Highlands, the fragments in the Account Book that deal with Balnespick's personal life are well worth consideration.

Practically every one of the farms in the district, which usually run to 90 or 100 acres, and which are now leased by ordinary small working farmers, were owned or held on tacks in the eighteenth century by the cadets of the families of the Clan Chiefs Grants, Mackintoshes, Macphersons, and Shaws.[1]

The following are a few of the neighbouring families of this class whom Balnespick mentions, and who have all died out or left the district. Grant of Clury, from whom he bought meal, was head of an old sept of Clan Grant.[2] Balnespick's own wife was a member of this family. Crathie, another family with which he had dealings, was Macpherson ; Dalraddy was even older. Phoness, which is mentioned once, was also Macpherson, and the last member of the family, who gave up his land in 1788, ' was the seventeenth heritor who sat in Phoness.[3] Two other old Macpherson families mentioned are those of Lynvuilg and Neod. Gallavie was Macdonald. The Mackintoshes of Borlum have

---

[1] C. Fraser Mackintosh, in *Minor Septs of Clan Chattan*, and Alex. Macpherson, in *Church and Social Life in the Highlands*, describe most of them.

[2] *Lectures from the Mountains*, Series II., p. 252.

[3] C. Fraser Mackintosh, *Antiquarian Notes*, vol. ii. p. 375.

already been mentioned. They were a very ancient family. Invernahaven, now absorbed in Belleville, was held by a branch of the Shaws so old that they claimed to be the real heads of Clan Chattan. Dolphour was also rented by Shaws, and Shaw of Dalnavert, with whom Balnespick had constant dealings, buying and selling seed, corn, and meal from and to him, and acting like a trustee and executor during his illness and after his death (see p. 270), was the head of the family that owned Rothiemurchus before the Grants seized it about 1556. Of all the neighbours that Balnespick mentions, only two have left descendants who still own their land, Grant of Rothiemurchus and Macpherson of Invereshie, with whom Balnespick shared the *Edinburgh Journal*, and who is now represented by Sir George Macpherson Grant of Ballindalloch and Invereshie.

Some of these old Highland gentlefolk lived in extraordinary simplicity. Miss Grant of Rothie-murchus,[1] writing of the last of the Shaws at Dalnavert —the son of Balnespick's friend—says the house 'was a mere peat bothy, no better outside than the common huts of the same material, already falling into disuse. It was larger, for it contained three rooms, each of which had a window with four panes, not made to open, however ; . . . for the kitchen fire there was as usual a stone on the floor and a hole in the roof.' Later in her book she describes this old man's funeral, the two companies of volunteers turned out, and amid a great concourse of people he was carried in state to rest by the old lairds of Rothiemurchus. Sir Eneas Mackintosh, in his ' Historical Notes,' describes the house of the Macqueens of Corrybrough as also built of turf.[2]

Many of the lairds and tacksmen had, of course, far better houses,[3] and Balnespick certainly employed both a mason and a slater.

---

[1] *Memoirs of a Highland Lady*, p. 193.
[2] P. 3.
[3] Farmer Robertson, *General View of the Agriculture of Inverness*, p. vii.

A little silver and Sheffield plate has come down to his descendants from Balnespick, but one can only imagine his furniture.   Two old inventories which I have been fortunate enough to read, both of this period, are so very much alike that it is fairly certain that they describe what was typical of the times.   There were probably a mahogany table and leather-seated chairs, both in the dining-room and in the drawing-room, and the latter may have had some ' pire glasses,' and perhaps ' sewed work footstools.'   There would have been an imposing four-post bed with steps and curtains in the family bedroom, and smaller beds with ' damity ' curtains for the guests and grown-up children.   The servants had ' timber chairs ' and box beds.   The kitchen would be very generously supplied with ' sass pans,' spits, a ham kittle, a candle-making machine, and other utensils.   There were two or three small carpets for the floors, and prints and ' family picters ' on the walls.

Balnespick gives several lists of his shirts, of which he had about thirty-five (see p. 275).   He was no dandy, for he was content with Strathspey linen instead of sending for the finer material from Edinburgh or Holland, as did many men.   His shoes were made locally, as seems to have been the custom,[1] but he is disappointingly silent about the rest of his wardrobe. The Highlanders of all but the lowest classes were said to be extremely careful of their personal appearance,[2] and it was an age when men went finely dressed.   Even the typical very small farmer, whose balance-sheet was quoted by Sinclair,[3] although he lived on meal and could barely afford a little salt fish as a special luxury, had his Sunday suit of ' shop-cloth.'   The ex-officer gentlemen farmers generally adopted an elaborate, semi-military style of dress, worn with a peruke.

---

[1] Colonel Sutherland of Rearchar, from whose Account Book I have already quoted by kind permission of Mr. Alex McEwan, went very fine, but he also had his shoes made locally.

[2] General Stuart, *Manners and Character of the Highlanders*, p. 93.

[3] Sir John Sinclair, *View of the Northern Counties*, p. 76.

Balnespick does not say how many indoor servants he employed, but it is probable that he kept three or four. The meal used in the house was rather over fifty bolls before 1775, and rather under that figure for the remaining three years, which may have been accounted for by Lachie's taking over a larger part of the farm and employing more of the farm labour. In the earlier years he employed four farm servants, who received six bolls apiece, twenty-four bolls in all (see p. 166). The family, after 1771, when 'dear Geordie' went to America (see p. 273), consisted of Balnespick his wife, and one or two unmarried daughters. According to Sir John Sinclair, the amount of oatmeal eaten by the Highland peasantry was six bolls by a man and four bolls by a woman, but the country people's main diet consisted of oatmeal, whereas Balnespick's family had both meat and fish. Even if they ate as much as fourteen bolls, there would be the following surplus to be consumed by the maid-servants and for the many current payments that were made in meal :

Year.	Total of Meal.	Surplus (after allowing for the out-door servants and the family).
1769	65	27
1770	(not stated)	(not stated)
1771	53	15
1772	57	19
1773	66	28
1774	54	16

From various casual remarks by old writers, such as Mrs. Grant of Laggan, and Heron's 'General View of the Natural Circumstances of the Hebrides,' p. 77, it is evident that the servants of those days performed an extraordinary variety of duties. The following is a good account of the 'general' of the period[1] : 'A useful canny servant at all work about the cows, the dairy,

[1] *Moray and Nairn*, County Histories of Scotland Series, C. Rampini, LL.D., p. 361.

the sick nurse, the harvest—hay and corn—the services
of the parlour and bedchambers, and of late years the
cook.' This servant had been fifteen years in the
service of the minister of Lhanbride.

Balnespick's own gardener was a handy man. He
worked on the farm, delivered hay to customers, served
a notice on Borlum, etc.

The family food has been largely described in the
account of Balnespick's expenditure. Besides the farm
produce and the poultry on Dunachton, which are mentioned several times, they were probably largely fed on
the ' Kaim hens,' an item of rent in kind that was paid
in many parts of Scotland long after all other dues had
been commuted.[1] In another Inverness-shire rent roll,
contemporary to Balnespick's book, the total rental was
under £300, and 200 fowls and 46 dozen of eggs were
supplied by the tenants. Kaim hens had the merit of
being fresh-killed meat, and must have been welcomed
on that account when so much of the meat was eaten
salt.

It is evident that Mrs. Mackintosh exercised what
another old Scotch ancestress described as ' a prudent
and decent economy.' The proportion of meal to meat
is very high, and rye was sometimes mixed with the
better kinds of meal. Pron (*i.e.* meal mixed with husks,
which nowadays is only used as hen food) was regularly
used in the house, as was also skilling. Skilling means
the husks of corn in which a certain proportion of meal
remains. Eden, in his ' State of the Poor,' describes
how the prudent Scots and north country folk extracted
this meal by frequent steepings, and made a sort of
frumenty or blancmange. He urged the south country
labourers to adopt this economical dish instead of seek-
ing aid from the parish. Mixed meal, such as was
used in war bread, was also used. On p. 261 three
bolls one firlot one peck of bear meal was brought from
the miln ' servants' meal, in which there was five firlots

[1] Traditional. Kaim hens are mentioned in *Johnnie Gib of Geushet Neuk*, the classic of early nineteenth-century Aberdeenshire rural life.

rye, six firlots small oats '—leaving only three firlots one peck of the bear in the whole amount.

Balnespick, like his contemporaries, was essentially a practical farmer. Unlike the majority of present-day country gentlemen, whose home farms are managed by grieves, and who probably make their money else-where, either in business or professions or by invest-ment, and spend it on their land, Balnespick was mainly dependent on his holding for the necessaries of life, and farmed as his serious profession. The practical, daily supervision of the work was evidently carried on by him. He delivered his hay personally to a customer in Aviemore (see p. 184). He directed the men cutting the hay (see p. 186). He knew where every peck of his diverse crops were sown, and exactly where every sheaf in his strangely mixed stacks was placed. No detail in the working of the farm seems to have been too small for his careful, fussy note-taking. Lachie, his son, seems to have taken the sheep to market, and George went up to 'the glen' with the cattle (see p. 264). In Mrs. Grant of Laggan's letters, and in the reminis-cences of her mother by the Highland lady, the activi-ties that fell to the lot of the lady of the house are described. The servants' ' stents ' of spinning were reeled and measured, the dyeings supervised. All the kitchen activities of an almost self-supplying household had to be organised. The care of the milch cows, calves, and the dairy were within her province, and in the summer, when the herds and milkers were up in the remote glens, the arrangements for sending up food and fetching down butter and cheese were not easy. Sometimes the housewife went up to the sheilings herself to see that all was well, and in this way a member of the Balnespick family, old William Mackintosh's son or grandson, it is not known which, came to be born in a hut at the head of the Dulnan, and one of the lairds of Rothiemurchus was likewise born in a shieling.

There is no information in the Account Book of how Balnespick himself or his sons were educated.

General Stuart of Garth, in 'Manners and Customs of the Highlanders,' Appendix III, says that the gentry and tacksmen in the Highlands were 'certainly better classical scholars than men holding the same occupation and rank in society further South.' He adds that he personally knew many tacksmen and innkeepers (a very gentlemanly profession according to old Highland standards) who were good Latin scholars, and that in Skye the gentry commonly talked Latin together. The drafts of two letters in the Account Book show that Balnespick could write a well-expressed letter, but C. Fraser Mackintosh's 'Letters of Two Centuries' contains many better examples of the dignified, gentlemanly style of many of the old Highland lairds and tacksmen.   A University education seems to have been fairly common, but as Mrs. Grant of Laggan pointed out, it was their almost universal custom of serving in the army for a few years that most formed their manners and widened their minds.[1]   Miss Grant of Rothiemurchus, describing the local volunteers in 1813, writes that most of the elder officers 'had served in the regular army and had retired in middle life upon their half-pay to little Highland farms in Strathspey and Badenoch, by the names of which they were familiarly known. Very soldierly they looked in the drawing-room in their uniforms and very well the Regiment looked on the ground.'

How gloriously these 'Badenoch Bodies' did credit to their gentle blood and simple upbringing may easily be seen from the constant allusions in 'Memoirs of a Highland Lady' (see for instance pp. 82 and 372), and the admittedly very imperfect list in 'Lectures from the Mountains,' p. 237. Twenty-nine local men became colonels, or attained higher rank. There was a field-marshal, several generals, two or three governors of provinces, and eight or nine men were knighted for distinguished services to their country.

[1] *Memoirs of a Highland Lady*, by Mrs. Smith (*née* Miss Grant of Rothiemurchus), pp. 175, 176, 181, and especially p. 226.

In addition, the names of five younger soldiers are
associated with special deeds of outstanding gallantry,
among them being that of Eneas Mackintosh, grandson
of Balnespick, who was promoted a colonel, by the
recommendation of the Duke of Wellington, on account
of gallant service.

In 'Memoirs of a Highland Lady' there are many
charming glimpses of the less well-dowered collaterals
of the Rothiemurchus family, and of their simple,
unpretentious rooms, with flagged floors, home-spun rugs
and curtains, and a few good pieces of furniture and
china ; the men working hard on their little farms
and yet with courtly manners and cultivated minds ;
the ladies actively supervising byre and dairy and
kitchen and yet able to join naturally, and as a matter
of course, in the society of the folks up at the big house ;
of their pleasant hospitality, and of the dignity and seem-
liness of their bearing in times of trial and bereavement.[1]

---

[1] Captain Grant, a younger son of a farmer laird of Rothiemurchus,
lived at the farm of Inverdruie. He was old and frail and sat by the fire
in peruke and clothes of quasi-military cut. She was a shabby, bustling
little body, running the farm and the house, spinning for the simple
plenishing of her home, yet well able to talk and play and sing when
asked to dine with the Laird. The parlour is described with flagged floor,
home-made carpet and curtains, mahogany furniture, fine old glass, silver
and china for best use kept in a corner cupboard and old arms set criss-
crosswise above the mantelpiece. When the old captain died the body
lay in state in a room shrouded with white napkins, and gentle and simple
came to pay their respects.

Mrs. Grant ' sat on the Captain's three-cornered chair in the best
bedroom, dressed in a black gown and with a white handkerchief pinned
on her head . . . if addressed she either nodded or waved her hand.
. . . The room was full, crowded by comers and goers and yet a pin could
be heard to drop in it ; the short question asked gravely in the lowest
possible tone, the dignified sign in reply, alone broke the silence of the
scene—for scene it was. Early in the morning before company hours,
who had been so busy as the widow ? Streaking the corpse, dressing
the chamber, settling her own attire, giving out every bit and every drop
that was to be used upstairs and down . . . . there was nothing, from
the meanest trifle to the matter of the most importance she had not, her
own active self seen to.'

The rather flippant writer, for once thoroughly awed, goes on to

Mrs. Grant of Laggan drew a delightful picture of Highland society when she wrote : ' People hereabouts, when they have good ancestry and manners, are so supported by the consciousness of these advantages and the credit allowed for them that they seem not the least disconcerted at the deficiency of the goods of fortune.' How true it was that gentle birth was the real passport to society can best be seen by the study of old family trees.   Even the smaller gentlemen farmers' families not only mixed socially but intermarried with those of the greater landowners.   Thus Balnespick's son married a daughter of the Chief of Mackintosh, and his grandson a niece of The Chisholm, but he cannot be quoted as a typical example, for he was a man of considerably larger capital and had a more valuable holding than had a good many of his contemporaries.

describe the solemnity and formality of the proceedings, and the dignity and self-restraint of the widow, ' a plain woman in her ordinary rather shabby attire,' who looked ' an elderly gentlewoman ' in her mourning.   A collation was set out in the parlour and another in the kitchen, and then with the Laird of Rothiemurchus, the head of his house, as chief mourner, the solemn procession set forth.   ' Hundreds attended the funeral.   A young girl in her usual best attire walked first, then the coffin borne by four sets of stout shoulders, extra bearers grouping round, as the distance to the kirkyard was a couple of miles at least.   Next came the near of kin, then all friends fell in according to their rank without being marshalled.'

H

CHAPTER VII

THE SUB-TENANTS

AT the time the Account Book was written the Highlands of Scotland were very densely populated. Mr. Marshall says that in earlier times Scotland was essentially a place ' where a good soldier or a foolhardy desperado was of more value than a good husbandman. As a consequence of these extraordinary circumstances the farms were frittered down to the atoms in which they are now [*i.e.* in 1794] found : and the country is burdened with a load of tenantry which had hitherto been considered a bar, even under a change of circumstances, to the prosecution of any rational plan of management.' [1]

How entirely the clans were organised as fighting forces may best be realised by reading the memorandum of their military strength, by President Forbes of Culloden, that is published as an appendix to Stuart of Garth's ' Sketch of the Manners and Character of the Highlanders of Scotland.' President Forbes estimated that 31,930 fighting men could be put into the field by the Highland chiefs. In the wild old days the prosperity and power of chief and clan depended on the strength of the armed following the former was able to command. General Stuart of Garth quotes figures showing how extraordinarily large were the forces that the chiefs with comparatively low rentals were able to put into the field. At the time of the '45 Lochiel's revenues were £700, and he was able to call out 1400 men. Several other chiefs with a following of 5000 men and more had total incomes of between

[1] Mr. Marshall's *General View of the Agriculture of the Central Highlands*, p. 24.

£5000 and £6000. He quotes the proud retort of Keppoch, when questioned as to his income : ' I can call out and command 500 men.'[1] Burt tells of a Highland chief who said that he preferred his estate, which was worth £500, to an English one worth £30,000 a year, because of his following, as an illustration of this feeling.[2] In the case of Clan Mackintosh, C. Fraser Mackintosh has traced the determined efforts of one chief after another to get possession of considerable holdings in the corn lands bordering the Moray Firth, and ascribes their eagerness to do so to the necessity of providing additional grain for their numerous followers in Strathdearn and Strath Nairn.[3]

Sir Walter Scott, in his preface to ' Rob Roy,' emphasises the superabundance of the Highland population—due to lack of all outlet and this deliberate clan policy. He quotes Graham of Gartmore : ' The people are extremely prolific, and therefore so numerous that there is not business in that country, according to its present order and economy, for one half of them. Every place is full of idle people accustomed to arms, and lazy in everything but rapines and depredations.' There is hardly a writer on Highland agriculture in the eighteenth century who does not allude to the dense crowding. Sir John Sinclair [4] describes the subdivision in some detail. Mr. Jolly, whose sympathies are obviously democratic, says that the farms were so small and poor as to give ' scanty subsistence' in good years.[5] Lachlan Shaw, in his ' History of the Province of Moray,' written in 1760, says : ' The principal cause why they fell short in corn is that the inhabitants are too

---

[1] General David Stuart of Garth, *Sketch of the Manners and Character of the Highlanders*, p. 31 and onwards, deals specially with this subject, but the tone of the whole book shows the attitude of mind that even yet lingered.

[2] Burt's *Letters from the North of Scotland*, vol. ii. p. 164.

[3] C. Fraser Mackintosh, *Letters of Two Centuries*, p. 187.

[4] Sir John Sinclair, *General View of the Northern Counties*, pp. 194–5.

[5] An essay published in the *First Transactions of the Highland Society*.

many for the small extent of land, in so much that I
have often seen ten persons on a poor farm of twenty
pounds Scots.'[1]   The 'First Statistical Account for
Alvie Parish' itself states that 'the greatest bar to the
improvement of the country is the smallness of the
holdings.'[2]   The same fact is mentioned in local
accounts from all over the country,[3] and Mr. Walker
gives the most amazing figures in his description of
the Hebrides.   The average size of farms was, he says,
20 to 25 acres, and yet they maintained a tacksman
and his family with several men and women servants
and herds.[4]   But Mr. Marshall's description is the
most detailed one of all.[5]   He says that in Perthshire
the average joint tenant had about five acres of infield,
four acres of outfield, with muir, wood, and pasture.
(Stuart of Garth, writing of the same district about
thirty years later, puts the average amount of infield
at from 5 to 20 acres.)   'Yet even these subdivisions
are diminished by a still lower order of occupier,'
'under the name of acre-men or crofters,' who were
sub-tenants of the joint tenant, and in return for the
pasturage of a limited number of beasts, and a small
piece of infield land, helped with the harvest, etc., 'the
tenant fetching home the crofter's share.'   Below these
acre-men were a lower class of cotters, who had no
land, but received 'assistance' in return for work.

By the time Balnespick came to write his Account
Book the need for an armed following had ceased (or
almost so).   A commission could still be obtained by
a chief or landowner who brought a large following

[1] Vol. ii. p. 7.

[2] *First Statistical Account*, vol. xiii. No. 26, p. 375.

[3] Anderson's *Report on the Agriculture of Aberdeenshire* and the
Second Statistical Account for Wick (vol. xv. p. 145) are good examples
selected at random from a mass of material.

[4] Mr. Walker, *On the Hebrides*, vol. i. p. 52.

[5] Mr. Marshall, *General View of the Central Highlands*, pp. 32-3.
The extraordinary variety of small holdings may be gathered from the
letters relating to the Drummond Estate, quoted by Cosmo Innes in
Scotch Legal Antiquities, p. 226.

of recruits to the Colours.   C. Fraser Mackintosh, in
'Letters of Two Centuries' for the year dated 1794,
quotes a curious illustration of the survival of the practice.
Alexander Macdonald of Glengarry was made a colonel,
and was given the right of raising a regiment.   He
writes to his agent : ' Enclosed you have a list of small
tenants belonging to my Knoydart property.   Their
leases being expired by Whitsunday first.   And having
refused to serve me I have fully determined to warn
them out and turn them off my property without loss
of time.'   Glengarry thus initiated clearances in Knoydart in an attempt to revive the old ' feacher ' or military
service due to the chief.   Yet something of the old
spirit probably still lingered, as in the Chief of Mackintosh's description of Dunachton, when he specially
notes that there were sixty men on it ' able to bear arms.'
The labour of a large number of tenants was also still
essential to the working of the farm and the getting in
of the harvests.   The Account Book therefore throws
very valuable light upon the economic position of the
' inferior tenants ' on the eve of the very great changes
that for good and ill have so greatly affected the
population of the countryside of Scotland.

Cosmo Innes has worked out that the old Scotch
land measure on church lands was by ploughgates of
104 acres, the ploughgate being subdivided into four
husbandlands of two oxgates each.[1]   The oxgate therefore consisted of 13 acres.   The actual acreage was
probably variable.   On Dunachton the oxgates were
sown with 17 bolls of grain, and therefore probably
consisted of 17 acres of land.   The ploughgate was
supposed to represent the extent of the season's ploughing of the common plough, and each oxgate to support
one ox for the team that drew it.

In the list of rents of Dunachton, oxgates and half
oxgates are mentioned, but not ploughgates or husbandlands.   From allusion to ' Sandy's Ox,' etc., it is evident that the tenants kept single oxen, but no light is

[1] Cosmo Innes, *Scotch Legal Antiquities*, pp. 241, 254.

thrown upon how the numerous holders of half oxgates compounded for their share of the animal.

The farms were generally held jointly, either by a principal tenant with a number of sub-tenants, or by a group of joint tenants. The Gordon Rent Roll, quoted by Cosmo Innes in ‘ Scotch Legal Antiquities,’ and published in vol. iv. of the ‘ Spalding Club Miscellany,’ shows that all the farms in Lower Badenoch were held in this way, and that the usual size was generally two ploughgates and rather less often four ploughgates. The infield was divided into rigs or ridges, and held without fence or other divisions. The older practice was for the different tenants to draw lots annually for the possession of their rigs, but it is probable, from the wording of the rent accounts, that by Balnespick’s time they were held continuously by the same tenants. The pasturage was common. The system was known as runrig. From such entries as that mentioning ‘ my row next to the widow’s,’ etc., it is evident that Balnespick held some rigs in the joint farm of Dunachton-more.

It is possible to construct a fairly detailed account of how Balnespick’s farm was sublet. In a curious old volume of notes, written by Sir Eneas Mackintosh, Balnespick’s landlord, about 1774, and privately printed by the present Mackintosh, the dense population on Dunachton is alluded to. It maintained, he wrote, 240 people, of whom 60 were able to bear arms. Balnespick himself, his wife and unmarried daughter, his son Lachie, with his family, four farm servants and four maid-servants, would leave 223 persons and 52 men to be accounted for, and, as a matter of fact, the Account Book mentions the names of 40 tenants and of 11 more men who were obviously living upon the Davoch, and were probably cotters and servants to the larger sub-tenants, or were Lachie’s servants. The sub-holdings may be roughly classified as follows :

Group I.

    (*a*) *Craigan-dhu*, a holding of 40 to 50 acres held by a single sub-tenant. Now out of cultivation.

(*b*) *Cluanach*, a holding of about 40 acres held by two joint tenants. Now out of cultivation.

(*c*) *Carit*, a holding of about 40 acres held by three joint tenants. Now out of cultivation.

Group II.

Cuilintuie, a holding of about 50 acres, held jointly by two or three tenants. Now partially cultivated.

Group III.

Kincraig, a holding of about 65 acres, held singly. Probably a large part of this holding is now out of cultivation. It does not appear to have covered the present arable of Kincraig.

Tomackach, Prossnacaillach. Both of them were about 39 acres each, held singly. Still under cultivation.

There were also ' crofts at the gate,' very small patches of 3 or 4 acres of cultivation that evidently lay on the steep, bushy bank between the present house and the old road. All these holdings were on less fertile soil than that now under permanent cultivation on Dunachton itself. Group II is distinctly less fertile than Group III, and Group I is decidedly inferior to Group II, both as regards soil and accessibility.

In addition there were one holding of 3 oxgates = 39 acres, held by a single tenant; five holdings of 1 oxgate = 13 acres, each held by a single tenant; four holdings of 1 oxgate, each held jointly by two tenants; and fourteen holdings of half an oxgate each. Most of these holdings were on the exceptionally good land that now forms the arable of Dunachton-more and Kincraig. Some of them were on portions of the ground cultivated by the principal tenant himself and his son, others were held by a small group of tenants on Drumstank (now a field on Dunachton-more), and by a larger group of tenants on Achnabochin. The position and boundaries of this joint farm can easily be identified, the better parts of it being now covered by the 50-acre field of Auchnabeuchin, which is now included in the modern farm of Dunachton-more. At present the soil is equal in quality to the rest of the farm, but in those days it was far less good, and was probably much broken up by rushy, swampy patches, for this portion of the farm is naturally damper than the rest, and therefore owes considerably more to deep drainage.

The rentals charged for the holdings varied considerably with the productiveness of the soil. The land now forming part of the permanent arable of the two present farms, viz. Dunachton-more, Dunachton Beg, Auchnabeuchin, Drumstank, and Luald, let for over £3 per oxgate. Cuilintuie brought in about 19s. per oxgate, Carit let at the rate of 16s. for about an oxgate, and Craigan-dhu probably for 2s. less. The rent of Kincraig, which included portions of land that are now waste, varied from about 16s. 9d. to 11s. 1d. The entire holding of the Cluanach, the extent of which cannot be exactly estimated, but which was fairly extensive, let for £2 10s.

In some cases the smaller holdings on Achnabochin and Dunachton-more were let unusually cheaply, or for no money rent at all; but it is obvious that in these cases there was some special arrangement whereby the occupier was supplied with land, corn, implements, etc., and in return for his labour received a proportion of the crop. Thus Sanders Mackintosh rented a half oxengate on Auchnabeuchin. He paid only half the amount of rent that some of the other sub-tenants on that farm did, but apparently he received only a portion of the crop, for on p. 198 the entry occurs :

'The amount of Saunders McIntoshes corns as proof :

	B.	F.	P.
To bear	3	2	3½
To oats, allowing ten firlots and two pecks to the boll . . .	2	1	0 '

The entry is dated 1772, and in that year the yield of a half oxgate was probably about 15⅓ bolls.

On p. 255, in 1777, Balnespick writes : ' Cut on the ground given Coll and Donald More of brocked corn 63 thrave, of which they got 6 thraw and 7 shaves. The remaining 57 thrave and 34 thrave of the highth is put in furthest east small stack and 3 thraw of small oats from Drumvote.'

Coll Mackintosh also held a half oxgate on cheap terms on Achnabochin. He paid no rent at all for it between 1769 and 1774, so his services were probably very valuable. Donald More McAlbea, with his father and brother, lived on Dunachton Beg until 1774, but paid no rent. In that year the family moved to Dunachton-more, where they had three holdings. From 1777 onwards rent was only paid for two of them. That very varying conditions of tenure were usual can be seen from Cosmo Innes's 'Scotch Legal Antiquities' (p. 266), where six different kinds of lease for small-holders are noted on the Drummond estate.

The income and expenditure of a sub-tenant on Dunachton were probably somewhat as follows, but unfortunately they cannot be taken as typical of their class, owing to the unusual richness of the soil, which at the present day gives on an average as much as two-fold more than the neighbouring land, and a higher proportion compared to many other districts.

From a ' just calcule ' of the sowings on one of the oxengates on Dunachton it is evident that 17 bolls of grain to the oxgate were sown. The proportion of grains was probably two-thirds of oats and one-third of bear, with some addition of barley, rye, and pease (Sir John Sinclair, ' View of the Agriculture in the Northern Counties,' p. 80). If the tenants' harvests are calculated on the rough-and-ready returns of Balnespick's own crops, and if one return is allowed for the resowing of the ground, the following figures are reached :

Year.	Amount of Grain and Meal used by Balnespick for every Boll sown.		Crop on an Oxgate allowing for a Sowing of 17 Bolls.			Crop on a Half Oxgate allowing for a Sowing of 8½ Bolls.		
	Oats.	Bear.	Oats.	Bear.	Total.	Oats.	Bear.	Total.
1769	2·26	5·75	25·539	32·583	58·196	12·806	16·291	29·098
1770	Deficit of 0·5 for seed	Not stated	−5·6	..	..	−2·8	..	..
1771	0·12	2·68	1·359	15·185	16·544	0·679	7·592	8·272
1772	0·88	3·64	9·973	20·626	30·599	4·986	10·313	15·299
1773	2·16	4·17	24·479	23·629	48·118	12·239	11·814	24·054
1774	1·45	1·37	16·43	7·763	24·196	8·216	3·881	12·098
1775	2·86	3·8	32·413	21·466	53·935	16·206	10·766	26·817
1776	Total, 1·53		..	..	26·01	..	..	13·005
1777	1·13	2·14	12·806	12·126	24·932	6·403	6·063	12·466
1778	1·66	0·33	13·813	1·869	20·682	9·406	0·934	10·341

This harvest had to supply the direct needs of the family, to provide some feeding for the live stock, and to help to cover certain additional expenses.

Sir John Sinclair, in his 'View of the Northern Counties' (p. 76), estimates that the ordinary consumption of meal by a man would be at the rate of 6 bolls per annum, by a woman at the rate of 4 bolls, and by a child at 1 boll. If the families were of average size the consumption of meal would therefore be about 13 bolls at least, but Highland families appear to have been famous for their large size, and according to Adam Smith[1] 'a half-starved Highland woman frequently bears more than twenty children.'

The dietary, according to Sinclair, consisted of :

'Breakfast.—Water gruel and bread, or pottage and milk, or flummery and milk.

'Dinner.—Potatoes and milk, bread and milk, sowans and milk.

'Supper.—Potatoes, gruel or kail, except in the months of May, June, July and August, when gruel pottage and milk, with some bread constitute their food invariably and without a change, in the distribution of

[1] *Wealth of Nations*, p. 81 in Methuen's edition, edited by Professor Cannan. See also Sir Walter Scott's preface to *Rob Roy*.

which it may be imagined that the milk must be sparingly divided. There is not 5 lb. of meat consumed within the family throughout the year ; an egg is a luxury that is seldom or never indulged in, far less a fowl; we have seen in the summer season a haddock occasion-ally, as a wonderful regalement. By this mode of living, two men, two women, three children and a grown girl or perhaps lad may subsist in all upon £15 4s. per annum, but hardly in a manner adequate to give spirit or strength for labour.' [1]

The 'Second Statistical Account for Kingussie '—the neighbouring parish to Alvie—says that : ' Potatoes and milk may be said to constitute the principal food of the peasantry. For the meal which the small tenants can raise on their farms, in their mode of cultivating them, would not support their families during one-third of the year. . . . In regard to animal food, such as beef, mutton and poultry, that is a luxury in which the small tenants never indulge, except at marriage feasts, bap-tisms, Christmas and the New Year ' (p. 90 in Black-wood's edition).

At the time of the Account Book it is hardly likely that the country people on Dunachton grew potatoes to any large extent, and it is obvious, from the calculation already worked out, that in many years their harvests were insufficient for supporting the needs of their families. From casual mention in the Account Book it is evident that eight or nine deaths occurred among the actual sub-tenants—women and children are not mentioned—

[1] Adam Smith in *The Wealth of Nations*, p. 161 in the edition published by Messrs. Methuen and edited by Professor Cannan, gives the following very unflattering account of the national dietary : ' The Common People of Scotland, who are fed with oatmeal, are in general neither so strong nor so handsome as the same rank of people in England who are fed with wheaten bread. They neither work so well nor look so well, and as there is not the same difference between the people of fashion in the two countries experience would seem to show that the food of the common people is not so suitable to the human constitution as that of their neighbours in the same rank in England.' Perhaps the shortage of food rather than its nature was to blame.

soon after the bad harvests of 1770 and 1771. Perhaps
there was an epidemic of some kind, or the season was
unusually unhealthy, but it is only too probable that
starvation was a contributory cause. The fate of the
people on poorer land, and in the far worse harvests
of 1782–83 (which came after Balnespick ceased to
keep his Account Book), must have been terrible.

But in addition to supplying the needs of the families
of the lesser sub-tenants themselves, some small proportion of food had to be given to the live stock. It is
not easy to see how any sub-tenant could have maintained fewer than the following list of animals :

1. The share of the maintenance of an ox to work
in the common plough.

2. Two or three garrons or ponies for carts or
panniers. Walker ('On the Hebrides') alludes to the large
number of miserable horses that were never properly
fed or worked (p. 49), and on Sinclair's typical small
farm no fewer than five were kept. Balnespick was
able to send twenty-one carts and pack-horses to Elgin
with oak bark, all apparently off Dunachton.

3. Milk and dairy products were an important item
in the family dietary, and the rearing of young stock
was the usual method of paying the rent ; a milch cow
was therefore essential to the holder of the smallest
pendicle of land. As Balnespick's own cattle only
calved every second year, and the yield of milk of the
native breed was very small, it is probable that two
cows very barely met the needs of the ordinary
family.

4. Sir Eneas Mackintosh pointed out that the rents
in the Highlands were generally paid out of the money
made by the sale of bullocks, and attributes to this reason
the fact that the rents were usually paid in money.[1]
This was evidently the case in Badenoch, for both
Balnespick himself and his sub-tenants paid in money,
whereas in Sir John Sinclair's specimen farm account,
which is dated nearly twenty years later, and in two

[1] Sir Eneas Mackintosh, *Historical Notes*, p. 38.

other old manuscript farm account books relating to the same period, which deal with districts that were more definitely arable, and where agriculture was in some ways further advanced than in Badenoch, the rents are principally paid in kind. The rent of half an oxgate of land on Dunachton averaged about £1 10s., and that of an oxgate about £3. The price of bullocks was about 30s. for a four- or five-year-old beast. Allowing for the high mortality then usual, it would therefore be necessary to have at least four or five calves and stirks of different ages coming on upon every half oxgate, and double that number on an oxgate.

5. From entries in the Account Book it is evident that the sub-tenants also kept sheep. As Sir John Sinclair says[1] : ' Most of the tenants, however, have a very few sheep. . . . The dung and wool are their objects, for by the ordinary tenantry there is not, perhaps, an ounce of meat consumed from one end of the year to the other.' They were also useful for their milk.

The hill feeding for these animals during the summer appears to have been included in the rent of the sublets, and it also covered ' promiscuous eating ' on the stubbles in the autumn, but an additional charge was made for extra grazing, or for a share of the ' hay midow.' If the unfortunate stirks, sheep, and ponies had to depend on what they could pick up all through the severe winters Balnespick describes, one may well wonder that any at all survived. It is unthinkable that the cows that were actually in milk and the oxen that were to be used for the early ploughing—most of the ploughing was evidently done in the spring—did not receive some extra feeding, either hay purchased from Balnespick or grown on meadow rented from him—as was certainly the case in some instances—or else by feeding with ' rush corn ' from the holding itself, or by leaving some portion of it under pasturage. The current cost of wintering a stirk was 1s. 6d., according to the Account

[1] *General View of the Agriculture of the Northern Counties*, p. 14.

Book, and the wintering of a cow would amount to at least 2*s*. To allow two bolls of grain or their equivalent in money or grazing for the animals would probably be a very conservative estimate.

It is certain from entries in the Account Book that all the sub-tenants were often obliged to buy meal for their own maintenance, and, unfortunately for themselves, the local price of grain was very variable, and tended to rise in those bad years when their own supplies were insufficient. Balnespick does not give the price he received or paid for corn every year, but from figures taken from the Account Book and from other sources I have worked out the following rough table :

Year.	Price of Meal.	Surplus and Deficit on the Crop of a Half Oxgate in Bolls.	Profit and Loss on a Half Oxgate.
			£ s. d.
1769	14/–	+ 14	+ 9 16 0
1770	20/–	− 15 at least	− 15 0 0
1771	19/–	− 6·7	− 6 6 11¾
1772	18/–	+ 0·3	+ 0 5 4½
1773	15/–	+ 9	+ 6 15 0
1774	16/–	− 3	− 2 8 0
1775	14/–	+ 11·9	+ 8 16 7½
1776	..	− 2·0	..
1777	16/–	− 2·5	− 2 0 0
1778	18/-	− 4·7	− 4 6 4¾

Additional expenditure was probably incurred under the following headings:

	£	s.	d.	
Fox killer	0	1	0	per annum.
Cess	0	0	4 (?)	,,
Minister's stipend . .	0	0	2½ (?)	
Schoolmaster's salary . .			(?)	
School dues paid by the parents . . .	0	4	0	for reading, 8/– for Latin or arithmetic.
Multures to the miller for grinding . . .			(?)	

Whisky	.	.	.	.	(in several cases this item was a very heavy one).	
Salt for the cattle		.	.	0	1	6 at least.
Shoes, or leather for making them	.	.	.	0	3	0 for the man at least.
Flax (unless this was home grown, when it would take up ground)	.	.	.			
Weaving	.	.	.	.		
Tailoring	.	.	.	.		
Replacement of implements		2	0	0[1]		

To meet such incidental expenditure there were various supplementary sources of income. Sir John Sinclair estimates that the yearly 'earnings of lint, wool, eggs, spinning, etc.,' on a small farm employing a maid and herd, were £5. From the 'First Statistical Account' for the parish one learns that the 'inferior tenants' were said 'to procure their small necessaries from the nearest market town by the sale of small parcels of wood they bring there.' It also mentions that a considerable amount of coarse, white plaiding, worth 10d. an ell, was manufactured. Burt, in his 'Letters from the North of Scotland,' vol. i. p. 83, describes the Inverness market : 'Here are four or five Fairs in the year, when the Highlanders bring their commodities to market ; but, Good God ! you could not conceive there was such misery in this island. One has under his arm a Small Roll of Linen, another a piece of coarse plaiding ; these are considerable dealers. But the merchandise of the greatest Part of them is of a most contemptible value, such as these, viz.—two or three cheeses, of about three or four pounds weight a-piece ; a Kid sold for sixpence or eightpence at the most ; a small quantity of Butter, in something that

---

[1] See Sinclair's *Northern Counties*, p. 76, and *Northern Rural Life*, chap. vi.

looks like a bladder and is sometimes set down upon
the Dirt in the street ; three or four Goat Skins, a piece
of wood for an axle tree to one of the little carts.   With
the produce of what each of them sells, they generally
buy something, viz.—a Horn or Wooden Spoon or
two, a Knife, a Wooden Platter, and suchlike Necessary
for their Huts and carry them home with them little
or no money. . . .' He continues on p. 86 : ' If
you would conceive rightly of it, you must imagine
to see two or three Hundred half-naked, half-starved
creatures of both sexes, without so much as a smile or
any cheerfulness among them, stalking about with goods
such as I have described, up to their Axles in Dirt,
and at night Numbers of them lying together in Stables
or other Outhouse Hovels that are hardly any Defence
against the weather.'

It is probable that the system of runrig had a good
deal to recommend it when the land was so minutely
subdivided and under primitive methods of agriculture.

The grouping of the little patches of oats, bear, etc.,
would obviously facilitate ploughing and reaping ; and
co-operation in the constant herding required on unfenced land for the grazing of the animals, and in the
work of ploughing, harvesting, etc., with implements
' fabricated by themselves in all their pristine rude-
ness,' [1] would be almost essential to the carrying on of
farming under such conditions.

It is obvious that such methods of joint cultivation
would be liable to lead to disputes, and it is a tribute
to the people's forbearance [2] and orderliness that they
should have proved so universally workable.   In all
the miscellaneous entries in the Account Book there is
only one mention of a quarrel, and even in that case
it was between some of the joint tenants on Dunachton
and a man called Forbes, who was a tenant on Raits,
and whose sheep strayed.   It was usual, in old leases,

[1] Miller's *Survey of Moray*, published 1790, p. 325.
[2] *Northern Rural Life in the Eighteenth Century*, p. 17 and onwards,
gives an amusing account of such quarrels.

for the tenants to agree ' to keep good neighbourhood,'
and ' birley-men ' or ' proof men ' [1] were appointed by
the people themselves and by the tacksman or laird,
to whom all questions regarding assessment of improvements, the amount to be performed as the ' stent ' of
a labour due, the value of unthreshed corn, etc., were
referred.[2] To dispute the decision of these arbitrators
was considered to be in the highest degree disgraceful.
Judging from the petty squabbles among the small
holders that the Land Court is often called upon to
adjust, and the very small advance that co-operative enterprise has made in the very districts where it would seem
most advantageous, one cannot help wondering if the
modern Highlander has not very largely lost the sense
of communal life, and the powers of working in with
other people, that his predecessors undoubtedly possessed.

In the ' Sutherland Account Book,' from which I
have already quoted, it is noted that the proof man

[1] Cosmo Innes, *Scotch Legal Antiquities*, p. 524. *Aberdeen Journal*,
' Notes and Queries,' vol. vii. p. 82, derives ' birleyman ' from
' byrlawman ' = ' chosen by common consent.'

[2] The birley-men were called upon to make important assessments,
as can be seen from the heading of an old paper, dated 1764 : ' The
comprising of the biggings of the Barrony of Dunaughton as the same
were estimate and valued upon the twenty-second day of May one
thousand, seven hundred and sixty-four years in terms of the Tack granted,
by Æneas McIntosh of McIntosh heritable proprietor of the Lands of
Dunaughton more, Dunaughton beg and Kincraig, dated at Moynall the
second day of February, one thousand and seven hundred and sixty-four
years, To William McIntosh of Balnespick, by the persons afternamed,
viz., Alexander McLean in Contalavit, John McPherson in Sylbrie
both tenants to Invereshie; Alexander McDonald Smith and Patrick
McDonald mason both tenants in Dunaughton. Birlie men mutually
chosen by the aforesaid Laird of McIntosh and the foresaid William
McIntosh Tacksman of said lands who gave their oath *de fideli
administratione.*' Unfortunately, the document is incomplete, but the
total value of the biggings mentioned in the very incomplete piece that
remains amount to over £500. One of the birley-men could only
sign rough initials, and it is an interesting sidelight on the manners and
customs of the times that birley-men, in the station of life these men
occupied, should have been called upon to assess in a transaction between
Mackintosh of Mackintosh and the father-in-law of his niece.

I

received a small allowance of corn for his services—Balnespick's book contains two loose folded slips : ' a just calcule ' of the rental and sowings on a holding in Dunachton-more (see p. 276), and ' a note of the comprising of Paul McPhails Biggings' (p. 236), as drawn up by the birley-men. They are both rather complicated documents, written in a neat clerkly hand —perhaps by the local schoolmaster. The note on Paul McPhail's biggings is signed by Alexander Macdonald, who was the smith, and Alexander Mackintosh, who is mentioned several times as belonging to Dunachton, but paid no rent, and was therefore probably only a cotter. Both the signatures are written in firm, well-formed hands.

The arrangement of the land into ploughgates and oxgates seems distinctly superior to the present lack of organisation of most small holdings. For although the need is not so great now that two horses have replaced six or eight oxen as a plough team, yet even now, when it is remembered that it is usual for a crofter to keep his own ploughing team, although a pair or a pair and a half of horses can work 60 acres of arable farm even in hilly districts, and that the average size of small holdings in the Highlands would appear to be under 20 acres, it is obvious that there must be a considerable amount of waste. In the words of the ' Report on the Economies of Small Farms and Small Holdings in Scotland,' issued by the Scottish Board of Agriculture in 1919,[1] ' there is a tendency for the number of horses to be in excess of requirements, and still more the quantity of food consumed by horses of a low degree of efficiency.'

The changed system of agriculture was, of course, quite unsuitable for the old open-field method of farming, or for very minute holdings. With the improved breeding of cattle, communal herding became undesirable. There was little reward for carrying out liming, draining, and other improvements on runrig fields, and the introduction of a five-shift course made fencing

[1] P. 36.

almost a necessity. Some capital was also required to introduce and carry on such methods. Gradually all but the smallest crofters enclosed their land and followed the new system.

In addition the improved processes led to a great reduction in the amount of labour that was required (see Chap. IV.). The labour dues of the lesser tenants were no longer needed, and in many parts of the country the introduction of sheep-farming on the bare hill-tops made the provision of sheltered grazing for the winter essential. All the writers on the new system without exception deplore the dense crowding of the small holders. Marshall's allusion to a 'load of Tenantry' sums up the attitude of his contemporaries.

The following description of the sub-tenants' methods, written as late as 1845 in the 'Second Statistical Account of Alvie Parish,'[1] would no doubt apply with equal force to those living at the time of the Account Book, and describes the old system as observed by a modern agriculturist: 'The absurd and unproductive system of farming pursued by their rude ancestors from time immemorial is still continued by the tenants who have small holdings, to the prejudice of their own interests as well as the deterioration of the small pendicles of land which they occupy. The little manure they collect, they lay on the patches of ground nearest to their dwelling houses, which they keep in perpetual rotation of potatoes, barley, and oats, without ever resting them, till the ground is very greatly reduced. The distant parts of the farm, which they call outfields, never receive a single load of manure, but are allowed to lay waste for three years, and are then cropped again for three years alternately, the last crop scarcely returning the seed. They seldom or never think of removing a stone out of their way, or of draining away the abundant moisture that chills the ground and renders it unfit for bearing. The tenants occupying small pendicles have neither skill nor capital for carrying on

[1] P. 92 in Blackwood's edition.

an improved system of farming ; but if they had both it cannot be denied that very little encouragement has hitherto been given by the proprietors of land to improving tenants. On a lease of from seven to eleven years, the longest given till of late in the parish, without any security to an improving tenant for payment of his outlays, in case of being removed from his farm at the expiration of a short lease, no extensive improvement will ever be attempted. Another insurmountable obstacle in the way of agricultural improvements is the absurd division of the land among the small tenants. It is not uncommon to see a piece of land, not half an acre in extent, divided into five or six lots, called runrigs ; which makes it impossible for any one of the six to improve his small lot, unless the other five concur with him.'

Fortunately, at this time, among the small tenants themselves, there was considerable inducement to leave the runrig farms and very minute holdings. The rising standard of living demanded more lucrative occupations, and there was ample opportunity for obtaining better positions in the growing industrial life of the Lowlands and by emigration. The Account Book does not mention emigration, but among the papers relating to Captain Lachlan's affairs—he died in 1785—three sub-tenants are mentioned as having emigrated, and Donald McDonald, ' being low in circumstances left this country for England where he remains.' Colonel Thornton, who revisited Raits in 1785, wrote from there : ' Went to Church, where I found a much thinner audience than I had ever remembered, and, conversing upon this subject with the Rothiemurcos and other gentlemen of the neighbourhood, they informed me that the spirit of emigration had seized the people of these parts, and that many handicraftsmen and others, whose services I much wanted, had actually left the country. My shoemaker and carpenter were both gone, and with them many more : this fully accounted for the thin congregation ' (' Sporting Tour,' p. 83).

At that time there had been no clearing anywhere in that part of the country.   On Dunachton-more and Achnabochin the people were not turned off their holdings.   The descendant of one of the families who lived for generations on Dunachton described to me how a little later on, within the memory of her grand-mother and mother, the younger folk gradually drifted away to better openings, and the men who remained tended more and more to supplement the produce of their holdings by seasonal work in the south ; till at last the old folk died out, and the wide fields, or mossy pasturage, swallowed up their patchwork strips of cultivation.

In many cases their descendants can still be traced. A great-grandson of some of the Davidsons is a much-respected craftsman in Strathdearn, and is a tenant on the land of old Balnespick's great-great-grandson there. Some families have representatives still living in Badenoch, and the great-grandson of some of the Macbeans in Dunachton was at one time tenant farmer of Kincraig.   Other families, among them some of the Mackintoshes and Robertsons, emigrated, and are now in a good position in Australia.   Several of their soldier sons, when they came home to fight for their old mother-land in the Great War, found their way up north to seek out the old people who still remembered their for-bears, and to visit the little heaps of grey, weathered stones that lie on the sheltered slopes of the birch woods, and are all that is left of the old homes of their people.

Unfortunately, in many parts of the Highlands there were evictions, and the bitterness that they have left has surely coloured with some prejudice what was, after all, to a large extent a healthy movement.   It is only fair to remember that Highland lairds supported the beneficial and public-spirited Highland Society. In the district round Dunachton C. Fraser Mackintosh describes evictions both on the Belleville property and at Kinrara, yet both the Highland lady and Mrs. Grant of Luggan, who were themselves devoted to the country people and on very good terms with them, speak highly of the Macphersons of Belleville, and of the Duchess of Gordon, and describe much useful service that they did for the local people.

From the Account Book itself, and from contemporary writings, one may gather a good deal about the daily life of the people.

Their work was spasmodic. At harvest time and during the spring ploughing they were very busy, but in the winter there was little work to do, and in the summer many of them went up to the summer pastures with the cattle. This migration was known as the glaning. Mrs. Grant of Laggan describes seeing them pass on their way to the hills driving their cattle before them : 'The people looked so glad and contented, for they rejoice at going up, but by the time the cattle have eaten all the grass, and the time arrives when they dare no longer fish and shoot,[1] they find their old home a better place, and return with nearly as much alacrity as they went.'[2] The cattle were driven up early in May and returned in August in time for the people to take part in the harvest. The old folk can still remember hearing accounts of the stir and bustle in their parents' young days, when the start was made for the 'glen.' Blankets, food-stuffs, churns, and dishes were loaded on to carts, with caillachs (*i.e.* old women) and spinning-wheels set on the top of them, and with lowing of cattle and barking of dogs, more than half the community would set off up the rough track that wound over the shoulder of the hill to picnic in the rude little huts of the shielings.

Nor did they perform their tasks in a gloomy spirit. Of their old working songs I have already spoken, and Mrs. Grant of Laggan speaks of the labourers dancing on the stacks to a reel tune as they piled and arranged the sheaves (p. 206). I have been told that the minister or tacksman would sometimes hire a piper or fiddler

[1] Apparently on account of the weather and short days.
[2] Mrs. Grant, *Letters from the Mountains*, p. 136.

to encourage the people at their work at harvest time, and that the women, in 'wauking' the cloth—a very toilsome process—sang all the time, and commonly said the cloth would take so many more songs to do, instead of so much more work to finish.

About the whole relationship of the people there seems to have been an extraordinarily close bond of clannishness and good-fellowship. They were all more or less intermarried, and the families seem to have clung together very closely : thus there were three generations of McAlbea, all sharing a holding, and the Davidsons, the Macbeans, the Macphadrucks, and the Macphails were all groups of relatives living together, although the exact relationship between the different men is not quite clear. Not only was the land held runrig, but meal was constantly bought jointly by two or three men, and money was sometimes raised by whole family groups.

The housing of the people must have been deplorable. ' The greater number by far of the farm houses and offices of the tenants and cottagers are mere wretched hovels, made up (not built) of stone and feal (sod or turf), without any regard to either proper construction, convenience, or situation. The family live in one end of the house, and the cows and young store in the other, even without a partition, all enter and come out at the same door. The out offices of the tenant are in a similar style.' It is quite evident, from the Note of the comprising of Paul McPhail Biggings already mentioned, that the Dunachton tenants were little better off, for although separate byres, stables, and sheepcotes are mentioned, the total value of the house and steadings was £1 10s. 3d. sterling. According to the 'First Statistical Account for Alvie,' the 'inferior tenants' habitations were wretched.'

It is not to be expected that these hovels would contain much furniture. Louis Simond, a French traveller,[1] describes a typical cottage : ' You find in it

[1] Louis Simond, *Journal of a Tour and Residence in Great Britain*, p. 398.

not a chimney, but a fireplace on the ground with a few
stones round it, immediately under a hole in the roof ;
a hook and chain fastened to a stick to hang an iron
kettle on ; a deal table ; a piece of board on which
oatcakes are prepared ; a dresser and some little earthenware ; an old press ; a pickling tub for mutton ; some
pieces of mutton hung in the smoke which winds round
them on its way to the roof ; a shelf with many cheeses,
and among the cheeses a few books . . . the beds
were a filthy mattress and a filthy blanket—no sheets,
no floor, only the ground trodden hard ; a window of
four small panes, not one entire.' The lighting was
mainly by resinous splinters of fir wood (Sir Eneas
Mackintosh), which were often taken from wood buried
in the peat moss. In the neighbouring valley of the
Findhorn the older folk can remember hearing that
every year the country people used to make an expedition to Strathspey, where the pine grows more luxuri-
antly, to collect especially resinous pieces for making
into fir candles. Probably the Dunachton folk did
likewise, for birch and oak seem to flourish more than
pine trees in their district.

Sinclair gives an inventory of the furniture of a
small farmer in the Black Isle, but he was evidently
a man in considerably better position than were most
of Balnespick's sub-tenants [1] :

	£	s.	d.
'Bedstead	0	4	0
Press	1	10	0
Meal chest	0	4	0
Clothes chest.	0	4	0
Three chairs and three stools .	0	5	0
Two spinning-wheels . .	0	8	0
A reel	0	3	0
Four wooden dishes and four cogs .	0	5	0
Three pots	0	10	0
A pan	0	2	0

[1] Sir John Sinclair, *Survey of the Northern Counties*, p. 76.

	£	s.	d.
Ten horn spoons	0	2	0
Tongs	0	1	0
Crook or chain for fireplace	0	4	0
Table	0	2	0
Eight blankets	3	0	0
Three rugs or coverings	0	12	0 '

The description of a family's belongings, on p. 268 of the Account Book, gives some idea of the plenishings and clothing of one of Balnespick's sub-tenants. Sinclair gives the following list of clothing [1] :

'For the man :	£	s.	d.
One bonnet at	0	1	0
One coat, waistcoat, and breeches of home-made cloth	0	15	0
Three pairs coarse worsted hose at 1s. 6d.	0	4	6
One pair brogues 1s. 6d., one pair shoes 5s.	0	6	6
Linens	0	18	0
Greatcoat and long coat of shop-cloth and one pair corduroy breeches for Sunday	1	4	0
	£3	9	6

'For the wife :	£	s.	d.
Gown and coat of blue dyed woollen stuff	0	9	0
Aprons and stockings	0	3	0
One pair shoes	0	2	6
Linens	0	12	0
One printed cotton gown	0	10	0
A cloak of shop-cloth or tartan plaid	0	18	0
The three children 2s. 6d. each.	0	7	6
	£3	1	0 '

[1] Sir John Sinclair, *Survey of the Northern Counties*, p. 76.

From entries in the Account Book relating to money advanced to servants to buy black cloth, it is evident that in Badenoch also ' shop-cloth ' was used for best, and such was certainly the custom as far back as any one now living can remember. It would be interesting to know how far the Act forbidding the wearing of Highland dress that was passed after Culloden led to the abandonment of the kilt, and how far it had died out already in this district. The Act was repealed in 1782.[1] Stuart of Garth, in his ' Sketch of the Manners and Character of the Highlands,'[2] says that the country people were particular about their appearance, and that they willingly submitted to ' personal privations in regard to food and accommodation ' in order ' to procure arms and habiliments which may set off to advantage a person unbent and unsubdued by conscious inferiority. . . . The point of personal decoration once secured, it mattered not to the Highlander that his dwelling was mean, his domestic utensils scanty and of the simplest construction, and his household furniture merely such as could be prepared by his own hands.' A tailor was always employed to make the men's clothing, and, according to the ' First Statistical Account for the Parish of Alvie,' there were no less than four tailors in the total population of 1011.[3]

The outward surroundings of the people were squalid, and that they were exceedingly poor is admitted by every traveller who visited the North of Scotland. Pages of quotations might be made from Tennant, Johnstone, Burt, and others. The very appearance of the people was affected by the poorness of their living, for as the latter says : ' The stature of the better sort, so far as I can make the comparison, is much the same with the English or Low country Scots, but the common people are generally small ; nor is it likely

[1] General David Stuart of Garth, *Sketches of the Manners and Character of the Highlanders of Scotland*, pp. 140–4.
[2] *Ibid.*
[3] Vol. xiii. p. 375.

that being half starved in the wombs and never after-
ward well fed, they should by that means be rendered
larger than other people.'[1]   The 'Second Statistical
Account for Alvie' also notices that the people are below
middle size owing to poverty and privation, and that
most of the diseases of the parish were due to the low
diet of the people (p. 90 in Blackwood's edition of the
'Second Statistical Account for Inverness-shire'), and
Sir Eneas Mackintosh [2] notices that 'the size of men
in general over the Highlands is from 5 feet 4 to 5 feet
6 inches, but they make excellent soldiers, being able
to bear much fatigue and live upon little.'

There can be no doubt that the greater part of the
population of the Highlands were living under conditions that would now be considered incompatible with
a civilised existence, and that they were often on the
very verge of absolute starvation.   Yet it is amazing
to find how utterly unaffected by such miserable material
conditions were the character and mental outlook of
the people.   General David Stuart of Garth has pointed
out how indifferent were the Highlanders to worldly
wealth and the gratifications it could procure (see
p. 315) : 'In a word they are equally void of the two
chief curses of mankind, luxury and ambition.'   Simond
writes of their 'proud indolence' and 'superiority to
want,' and of their courage, carelessness, and hospitality.
'It is very remarkable that the inns of these mountains
have hardly any fastening and that the heavier baggage
of travellers remains on the carriage out of doors all
night—for there are, of course, no coach houses ; yet
all the treasures contained in a trunk of clothes do not
tempt people who have scarce a shirt to steal it !   Surely
poverty of this sort need not be pitied, much less
despised.'[3]   The critical Burt said that he could carry
£400 to £500 about with him in the wildest parts of

1 Vol. ii. p. 85.
2 Sir Eneas Mackintosh's *Historical Notes*, p. 37.
3 Louis Simond, *Journal of a Tour and Residence in Great Britain*,
p. 398.

the Highlands with far more confidence than in London
(p. 234, vol. ii., ' Letters from the North of Scotland ').
And Stuart of Garth says that keys and locks on dwelling-
houses were unknown in the Highlands,[1] and that among
themselves even the cattle lifters maintained the ' strictest
honesty.'

The ' Second Statistical Account ' describes the
country people as follows : ' Considering their limited
means of information they are surprisingly intelligent and
well informed, naturally inquisitive and shrewd in their
remarks, and always ready to communicate what they
know in exchange for the information they receive.'[2]
In the list of debts owed to Lachie by country people
and remitted, out of twenty-four debtors sixteen could
not sign their names, but those who could do so wrote
very firm, good hands.

Their courteous, self-respecting manners are described by many writers. The ' Second Statistical
Account' for the neighbouring parish of Kingussie says :
' The bravery of many of them has been well proved
and they maintain a high reputation for politeness.'
Mrs. Grant of Laggan has much to say of the ' gentle
cottagers ' near her home, and Miss Grant of Rothiemurchus tells how the meanest of them would mix
simply and easily with the laird's party at the various
harvest home dances.[3] ' The servants and labourers
and neighbours of that class came by turns into the
parlour. We were accustomed to dance with all the
company, as if they had been our equals ; it was always
done . . . a vein of good breeding ran through all
ranks, influencing their manners and rendering the inter-
course of all most particularly agreeable.' She gives
many examples of the gracious hospitality offered in
the smallest and poorest huts, and of the charming

---

[1] General David Stuart of Garth, *Sketches of the Manners and
Character of the Highlanders of Scotland*, p. 42.

[2] *Second Statistical Account for Inverness-shire*, p. 91, in the edition
published by Blackwood.

[3] *Memoirs of a Highland Lady*, p. 196.

manners of even the roughest men in the river gangs.
Most of all does one gain a picture of the bearing of
the old race from the pages of Stuart of Garth. He
quotes from Dalrymple's 'Memoirs' : 'The Highlanders, whom more savage nations called savage,
carried in the outward expression of their manners
the politeness of courts without their vices, and in their
bosoms the high point of honour without its follies,'[1]
and he goes on to describe the self-respecting respect
of the country people who treated their chiefs with perfect deference, and yet argued, jested, and chatted with
them with ease.[2] He gives one charming glimpse of
a typical Highlander of the old school—a man who
had fought for his clan in his youth, and whose brother
had died to save his chief's life : 'By trade he was a
smith ; and although of the lowest order of the people,
he walked about with the air and manner of a field
marshal.'

Although the chiefs held absolute powers over
their people, both by the consent of the clan and by
law of the land, through the 'Hereditable Jurisdictions,'
and the much-prized 'right of Pit and Gallows,' yet
class distinctions, such as were so strongly marked in
eighteenth-century England, must have been almost
non-existent in the Highlands, where the very word
for landlord was 'ceann-cinnidh,' or 'Head of Kin,'[3]
and where every member of a clan claimed, with or
without foundation, to be related to the Chief. In
'Memoirs of a Cavalier,' dated 1640, there is a far
from flattering description of the poverty and dirt of
the Highlanders who fought under General Leslie,
but it goes on to say : 'They are all gentlemen and
proud enough to be kings. The meanest fellow
among them is as tenacious of his honour as the best
nobleman in the country' (quoted by General Stuart of

[1] General David Stuart of Garth, *Sketches of the Manners and
Character of the Highlanders of Scotland*, p. 60.
[2] *Ibid.*, p. 117.
[3] M. W. Mackenzie, *Home Life of the Highlanders*, p. 5.

Garth, p. 331). The rather underbred Burt allows himself cheap sneers over the simple pride of the poor piper, and of his own washerwoman, in their gentle blood : ' Here is Gentility in Disguise, and I am sorry to say that this kind of Vanity of People of no fortune makes them ridiculous to strangers ' ; but he is obliged to admit that : ' You will never see among the meanest of them the clumsy stooping gait of the French Paysons or of our own Country Fellows, but on the contrary a kind of stateliness in the midst of their poverty. . . . They have a pride in their family, as almost every one is a genealogist.'[1] General Stuart of Garth quotes figures showing how carefully were the records of their actual descent preserved by the country people : thus James Stewart, the Wolf of Badenoch, settled at Garth in 1390, and in 1882 there were 1937 people living in that neighbourhood who claimed to be directly descended from him (p. 27 ; for other examples see p. 344). It was a well-known and universal custom that the meanest clansman had the right of shaking his Chief by the hand, and the Chief was never addressed by any title, but directly by the appellation by which he was known to all ranks—either that of his estate, the name of his ancestor, or by a nickname—Lochiel, Macalum More, etc.[2] Sir Eneas Mackintosh—Balnespick's Chief and his landlord—in his ' Notes,'[3] gives some indications of how closely a very powerful Chief mingled with his people. The Laird of Mackintosh was such an important person that General Wade was obliged to ask his permission and favour and to consult him before constructing the famous military road on his land. Three times, during the eighteenth century, the Chiefs of Mackintosh called out over 500 men, twice to oppose the King and once to support him (to be more correct, the Chiefs called out their tenants

---

[1] Burt's *Letters from the North of Scotland*, vol. i. p. 72 ; vol. ii. p. 26.

[2] General David Stuart of Garth, *Sketches of the Manners and Character of the Highlanders of Scotland*, p. 117.

[3] See pp. 12 and 33.

only twice. In the '45 it was the Chief's wife who raised the clan). Yet Sir Eneas as direct heir to the Chiefship and to the wide Mackintosh estates attended the village school, and when he was Chief he often used to go to the wedding feasts and funerals of his smaller tenants. One is not at all surprised to find that Mrs. Grant of Laggan and her husband the minister were guests at the wedding banquet of their shepherd and housemaid quite as a matter of course. In eighteenth-century England such ' condescension ' on the part of a beneficed clergyman, let alone in the case of one of the largest landowners in the country, would surely have been unusual.

One could not expect to find any information with regard to the people's manners in an account book, but of their independence and energy there is ample evidence. ' Donald Davidson alias McIntyre ' is mentioned several times as a purchaser of very small quantities of grain. He was a cotter on Croft, apparently working for two men of the same name—perhaps his brothers—who rented a portion of the holding, and his name is given in the list of ' men proper for proving the marches twixt McIntosh and Borlum,' yet ' when the late Borlum called for this man to examine him about the marches he was displeased as he pointed out the marches as he pleased ' (see p. 273). Buchanan, in his ' Travels in the Hebrides,' gives a terrible picture of the oppression and masterfulness of the tacksmen, but the rather obscure note on p. 201, ' To Donald, Sanders More's son of the birlie from the South, 2 pecks which stands me 20 pence each, as it made at his own sight but $3\frac{1}{2}$,' and several other entries certainly suggest that Balnespick's sub-tenants were quite able to carry their own point in a difference of opinion (for instance that on p. 258, ' To Sanders Bains wife or he entered my service only a firlot of meat that she acknowledges '). Of the enterprise of the people there are many examples. It seemed to have been quite usual for them to go to Inverness and Forres or Elgin. The smith set off to buy corn in Ross, and in one year (p. 191) Sanders more Mackintosh borrowed £3 to go to Glasgow, and Mrs. MacPhadruck set out for Aberdeen, but cannot have stayed there for long, for the sequence of her purchases of malt, borrowings of bottles and sales of whisky is hardly interrupted. On another occasion (p. 264) two of the farm servants bought a hide from Balnespick with part of their wages, apparently to make and sell harness or shoes in their spare time. Another tenant borrowed money to fetch a load of whisky from Ferintosh. He paid this debt by the sale to Balnespick of part of this whisky, the rest he probably retailed to his neighbours. The most interesting example of all occurs on p. 265, in which two men borrow money from Balnespick to apprentice a young relative to Johnathan Ross, merchant in Ruthven, and then to pay for shoes, linnens, etc., when the boy was sent to London, and for 'a whole suit of clothes bought at said time and for making.' In all £12 19s. was spent.

A less estimable trait of the old Highlanders was their partiality for whisky. The 'First Statistical Account for Alvie' states there were thirteen houses in the parish where drams were sold, and that the people were 'much addicted to drinking whiskey' (vol. xiii. p. 375). Miss Grant of Rothiemurchus tells of how neat whisky was taken by men, women, and children, and how it was supplied to the men and maid-servants at the house and to all who came there on errands as a matter of course.[1]   There is surely a tinge of admiration in Louis Simond's attitude when he says that the Highlanders were able to drink a quart of whisky a day, and adds: 'Men able to bear that quantity of ardent spirits must have practised much and often' (p. 406). Whisky seems to have been distilled by several of the Dunachton sub-tenants and by Balnespick himself, and there is ample evidence, by many of the entries, of a fairly extensive 'practising' of the kind Simond describes.

[1] *Memoirs of a Highland Lady*, p. 38.

The ' Second Statistical Account ' of the parish says
that the principal amusements of the people were
' camack matches, raffles and dancing ' (p. 90).   No
other authority mentions the raffles, but Sir Eneas
Mackintosh describes the camack or shinty matches
as follows:

' Playing at Shiney is thus performed—an equal
number of men draw up on opposite sides, having clubs
in their hands, each party has a Goal, and which party
drives a Wooden Ball to their adversary's goal, wins
the game, which is rewarded by a share of a cask of
Whiskey, on which both partys get drunk.   This
game is often played upon the Ice, by one Parish against
another, when they come to blows if intoxicated.   The
players legs being frequently broke, may give it the
name of shiney.'[1]

Many people can remember their fathers' stories of
this rather ferocious game.   In Strathdearn, at the time
of the New Year, the ball was hit off on the high road,
at the old boundary between Moy and Dalarossie.   It
was then played over walls, fields, and ditches until it
grew too dark to see, or till it ended in a free fight, almost
the entire male population joining in the fray.   The
celebrations that took place after the game were far
from ' pussyfoot.'

The old Highlanders treated their dancing as an
art.   Miss Grant of Rothiemurchus (' Memoirs of a
Highland Lady,' p. 34) says that in her childhood ' a
dancing master taught us every variety of wonderful
highland step. . . . The servants . . . all took lessons
too, in common with the rest of the population.   The
Highlanders considering this art an essential in the
education of all classes and never losing an opportunity
of acquiring a few more flings and shuffles.'   My own
mother and aunt can remember when it was usual to
find a local dancing-master in country districts, of whom
the children took lessons as a matter of course.   Such

[1] *Notes Descriptive and Historical, principally relating to the Parish
of Moy in Strathdearn*, p. 31.

K

masters could play the fiddle and demonstrate the steps
at the same time, poking awkward pupils' toes into the
way they should go with the bow in the intervals.
They generally took their profession very seriously.
Allied to the love of dancing is that of music, to which
I have already alluded.

According to an old story, ' putting the stone '
was played, and Sir Eneas Mackintosh mentions other
pastimes and sports that were usual among his tenantry.
' Wrestling,' he says, ' is a great amusement among
schoolboys, which generally ends in earnest fighting.'
It also was ' a pastime to play with a football made of
a bladder covered with leather, and when a couple are
married they must pay a groat to the School Boys to
keep the Ball in order and is named Ball Money.'

Sir Eneas also describes the practice of ' burning
the water,' which was forbidden by law. It took place
in the late autumn, and at night. One man carried
a lighted torch to attract the salmon, and another speared
them with a trident when they came near it. The
salmon in October and November were in very poor
condition, and we should not now consider that they
were fit for food at that time. He also describes how
the lads caught trout in nets of basket-work and with
coarse flies.

The killing of foxes is mentioned several times in
the Account Book, but Sir Eneas [1] gives full details of
the sport, which would scarcely be one that would
commend itself to a keen English rider to hounds.

' During the Christmas Holy Days, the Country
people convene armed with Guns, poles, hooks and
spades, having a number of Hounds and Tarriers, and
go in pursuit of the Foxes which are numerous in the
Country. If the animal earths, some dig to him and
when they come to the mouth of his Den, they send in
the Tarriers who strive to get behind the fox, who,
seeing himself thus attacked, makes a stout defence,

[1] *Notes Descriptive and Historical, principally relating to the Parish
of Moy in Strathdearn*, p. 35.

barking like a dog.   Should it happen that the Animal
is too strong for the Dogs, the pole is put in and the
hook being fixed in his body, he is thus dragged out
and the tail carried in tryumph to the Chief's House,
where plenty of good cheer is ready.'

In spite of their poverty, Mrs. Grant of Laggan
describes how the people gloried in being ' splendidly
hospitable ' upon the great occasion of a wedding or a
funeral. ('Letters from the Mountains,' p. 115, describes
how four sheep were killed for the celebrations attending
the shepherd's wedding.   See also 'Second Statistical
Account for Kingussie,' p. 90.)   No wedding feasts are
mentioned in the Account Book, but Sir Eneas Mackintosh describes the whole ceremony very fully, and his
account closely resembles the personal reminiscences
told me by an old woman in one of the decaying fisher
villages on the east coast—a place where the memory
of more old customs and traditions seems to survive
than in almost any other part of Scotland.

' As soon as the partys have agreed upon the Day
of Marriage, the Clerk of the parish (sometimes the
Parson) is sent for, and in the presence of their mutual
Relations, a Writting called the contract is signed,
whereby the Parties bind themselves to marry, and in
case of non-performance (without just cause) to pay
such a sum as is thought proper.'

' The night before Marriage, the ceremony of Feet
Washing is performed at the Bride and Bride Grooms
own Lodgings : among the men it is an excuse for
drinking. Next morning, being dressed, the Bridegroom first (preceded by a Bag pipe,) having a young man
on each side of him, next comes the Bride with her two
maids, proceed for Church ; when the ceremony is
over, and the partys come out, pistols and guns are
fired over their heads by their acquaintances who then
join, and a cake broke over the bride's head, where a
great struggle is made for a piece of it.   Upon their
return a dinner is ready, several Cows and Sheep being
frequently killed for that purpose. When it is over

the Bride Groom goes round the guests with a plate, when everyone gives according to his Inclination, and if the Bride and Bride groom are liked, they get as much as will enable them to stock their farm. The Lord of the Manor frequently attends in order to encourage Matrimony. . . . I have been frequently well entertained at them when a company of young people have scampered to them from Moyhall. The country people sometimes dance to a pipe, but oftener to the fiddle. At the commencement and finishing of each reel or dance, the Swain kiss their Numphs. The fiddler receives one penny for each Dance. . . . The company continue dancing and drinking till the hour for the young peoples going to bed, when the whole accompany them to the Barn (for they are not allowed to sleep in the house the first night). All the men remain on the outside till the Bride is undressed, then, (the Bridegroom being undressed) they kiss the Bride. . . . It was and still is a custom to make the husband drunk the second night, that the wife might know how to treat him on similar occasions. The wedding continues several Days. If the young couple were very poor, they frequently went round the country to Thigg, which is a gentle name for begging, when the farmers gave corn and Shepherds sheep to stock the farm. The first work the married woman undertook was making her winding sheet, which put her in mind of Mortality ' (p. 33). Mrs. Grant of Laggan describes the formality and decorum of the banquet and the dancing.

Funerals were as important social functions as weddings, or even more so. In ' Memoirs of a Highland Lady,' p. 192, there is the following account of the lyke-wake of the hen-wife's husband : '. . . he was waked after the old fashion, shaved and partly dressed, and set up in his bed, all the country side collecting round him. After abundance of refreshment the company set to dancing, when, from the jolting of the floor out tumbled the corpse into the midst of the reel.' Sir Eneas Mackintosh (' Notes,' p. 34) gives a rather different account : ' During the night all the deceased's Relatives and Acquaintances convene to watch the Body and this ceremony is called Latewake ; a good fire is put on (if in winter), plenty of whiskey and snuff goes round, the young folks play at several country games while the graver sort tell tales of Ghosts and hobgoblins, every word of which they believe. As late as the year 1740 music was introduced and the nearest relative began the dance.' He goes on to say that this custom has entirely died out. Balnespick's Account Book has many items relating to the funeral feasts of the sub-tenants, which seem to have cost from £1 to £2, even in the case of very poor families in debt for the necessaries of life. Balnespick advanced money for half a boll of meal = 4½ stone, ½ lb. of sugar, and for whisky for the funeral of Macdonald the smith (p. 139), and in the case of Alexander McIntosh 7s. of whisky was provided at 1s. 6d. a Scotch pint (p. 238).

The sociable instinct of the people also found expression in the ceillidhs, or informal evening gatherings round the cottage firesides. Miss Macbean, one of the last representatives of the Macbeans and Macalbeas in Dunachton-more, has told me of the extraordinarily vivid and happy memories of the old ceillidhs that her mother and aunts carried from their childhood, and of the haunting song-tunes and strange old stories that they heard there. Together we traced the half-obliterated rigs and furrows in an empty glade in the birch wood that had once been the infield of Craigandhu, and wandered over the deserted clearing, fringed by the alders at the burn-side, that was still called the Carit, and in a corner of a field saw the moss-grown heaps of stones where once stood the little clachan of Dunachton-more ; and as she talked the silent places became once more the homes of the long-dead folk she had known in her childhood. She spoke of the every-day conditions of a life that seemed almost incredibly hard and narrow according to modern standards, yet the memories that these old people had handed down to her were nearly all happy ones, fragrant with a joy of life and a poetic feeling that seems so utterly lost to the modern world that it could only be adopted as a conscious pose. The very vividness of the picture of the past that she called up, like those strangely clear-cut memories of childish days that we all cherish, showed how wide was the gulf that divided it from the present. It was because our old Scots forbears were what they were that they made of their struggle for bare existence a thing so wonderful that the very thought of our common ancestry rallies and unites the Scotch the whole world over ; and it was just as much because of some essential element in the race, that when the opportunity offered, the Highlanders abandoned the hard, old life on the tiny patches of sterile soil, putting aside from them the misty dreams and fancies in which they had been nurtured, as the growing youth inevitably puts away childish things, and went out into the wider world of men to hold their own and conquer by the sheer force of their indomitable character.

CHAPTER VIII

THE old Account Book throws some considerable light upon the relations between William Mackintosh of Balnespick, tacksman of Dunachton, and his sub-tenants there. It is a valuable contribution to our information regarding an important feature of eighteenth-century Scots rural life about which little has been collected or written. In making an investigation of the affairs of this individual tacksman, it is worth remembering that, although there is a tradition that old Balnespick was a popular and well-liked man in the district, nothing has been specially remembered as to his relations with his sub-tenants, and that there is no reason for thinking that he was more than a favourable specimen of his type and time.

In Carlisle's 'Topographical Description of Scotland' (1813) the Highland tacksmen are described in the following words : ' One who holds a lease from another, a tenant of a higher class : this term is usually used in contradistinction of tenants in general, who are such as rent only a portion of a farm.' What James Anderson says of the Hebridean tacksmen was no doubt true equally of those in other parts of the Highlands : ' The class of tacksmen occupy nearly the same rank in the Hebrides as belongs to that of men of landed property in other parts of Britain. They are called gentlemen and appear as such ; and obtain a title from the farm which they hold, nearly in the same manner as gentlemen in other parts of the country obtain from their estates ' ('Account of the Present State of the Hebrides ').

Originally the tacksmen were the younger sons and relations of the Chief—as may be seen from the pedigrees of many old families—and, as M. I. Adams says, in an article on Highland emigration in *The Scottish Historical Review*, vol. xvi. p. 286, they tended to consider their leases as ' a sort of property, subjected to a moderate quitrent to their superior, rather as a fair and full rent for land in Scotland. . . . In the military organisation of the clan, the tacksmen formed an essential element, since by blood, instincts, and training they were its natural lieutenants. As such they were indispensable to the Chief, and they paid for their lands in full by their services.'

It is probably widely realised that the tacksmen had this semi-military, semi-dynastic *raison d'être*. The study of an individual farm, such as Dunachton, tends to show how important they also were to the carrying on of the old methods of tillage and the due organisation of the rural social life of the times. In the seventeenth century Dunachton, and a large part of the rest of Badenoch, formed part of the Huntly estates. The great Aberdeenshire family of Gordon, of which the Marquis of Huntly was the head, was not a clan in the true sense of the word, and its connection with such a distant and distinctively Highland district can have had but little of that patriarchal character that was the essence of clan organisation. Yet, in the Gordon Rent Roll, published in vol. iv. of the ' Spalding Miscellany,' almost every one of the Badenoch farms is described as having a ' principal ' tenant, and these principal tenants belonged to many different clans. Again, tacksmen abounded and flourished long after the most troublous times in the Highlands had passed (see ' Home Life of the Highlanders,' and the article by McMaster Campbell, p. 32). The explanation is surely that some kind of organiser was almost indispensable under the old system of complicated and very minute joint holdings. The advantages of dealing with one man, instead of with forty or fifty, is obvious, and in an uncertain climate, like

that of the Highlands, there must have been a distinct
inducement to encourage a man who was in a position
to accumulate a little reserve fund, and therefore to pay
his rent in bad years as well as in good. In those days
of slow and infrequent communication it would have
been extremely difficult for the factor of a large estate
to collect the enormous number of very small rents
and to be responsible for the even yet more minute
payments towards cess, stipend, and salary of the inferior tenants. It would have been even more impossible for the factor to organise the armies of small joint
cultivators, so that 'good neighbourhood' was kept
and the fields were properly tilled. As long as the old
system of tillage continued, it is easy to see that it was
well worth the landlord's while to give the tacksman
an advantageous lease, and that his presence was a
useful part of the organisation of a big Highland
estate. His functions were to a large extent the
counterparts of those of the bailiffs of English manorial
farms.

On Dunachton, according to the Account Book,
there does not seem to have been any particular tie of
common clanship between Balnespick and his sub-
tenants, for amongst the latter were Campbells, Mac-
donalds, Macbeans, Macalbeas, Frasers, Camerons, etc.,
as well as Mackintoshes, and members of other septs
of Clan Chattan, such as Gillespies, Davidsons, Shaws,
and others. There does not seem to be a single entry
in the old Account Book that even remotely suggests
that Balnespick especially favoured his fellow-clansmen:
the smith, to whom so much money was advanced with
little possibility of repayment, was a Macdonald, and
among the birley-men the name Mackintosh is not
disproportionately numerous. On the other hand,
although Balnespick sold some of his imported meal
and gave credit to neighbours who were not sub-tenants
on exactly the same terms as to the people on Dunachton,
and although he employed them frequently, it is quite
evident that on the whole he did considerably more for

the people who sub-rented his farm and for those who were evidently old tenants of his on Balnespick.

The connection between a laird or tacksman and his 'inferior tenants' was indeed an extraordinarily close interweaving of interests. They were not only both landlord and tenants, and employer and farm labourers. Their animals grazed in common, and they were mutually responsible for the tillage of the runrig fields. They also bought and sold largely from and to each other. Balnespick's purchases of young stock, grain, meal, yarn, etc., from his own sub-tenants must have been considerable, although it is not possible to calculate exactly how much his purchases actually totalled. Of his own sales of grain and meal, out of the 396 transactions that the Account Book records, about 239 were to sub-tenants. By making a sort of ledger account for those people whose names appear most often, I have tried to untangle the record of some of these mutual buyings and sellings. The following is the completest record, for several versions of it are scattered through the Account Book ; but in the case of the Macphadrucks and of Alexander Mackintosh, Balnespick bought a good deal more and lent much less, although, owing to the use of Christian names and nicknames that belonged to several tenants, it is impossible to make out a complete list.

ALEXANDER McDONALD, Smith, Tenant, 1 oxengate Auchnabochin, 2 oxengates Drumstank.

Paid Balnespick.	£	s.	d.	Due to Balnespick.	£	s.	d.
1768. To part of rent .	o	16	10	1768. Owed for rent .	2	6	7
1770. To credit for 7 fir-lots oats supplied to Balnespick .	1	15	o	1769. ,, ,, .	2	6	o
				,, To 4 st. hay . (?)	o	1	o
1770. To rent . .	2	6	o	,, Due by Smith .	6	13	7
1771. Sold Balnespick 1 boll meal . . (?)	o	18	o	Undated. 1 f. oat seed . (?)	o	5	o
1772. Credit for bill fall-				1770. To rent . .	2	10	9
ing due. Her own share, £10 Scots. Payd by McGlashan, £2 Scots. Brother-in-law, £2 Scots				,, To loan . .	o	10	o
				Undated. Per Duncan Bain advanced .	o	5	o
				1771. Advanced to Mc-Donald upon Mrs. Stuart's account	o	6	o
	2	1	8	,, To loan for meal .	1	4	o[1]

[1] This entry is quoted three times for different amounts.

Paid Balnespick.	£	s.	d.
1772. Paid towards 3 bolls meal	1	0	0
,, Credit for work done by the Smith in 1769-70-71	0	19	6
1772. Price of three queys sold to Lieut. McPherson	6	6	0
,, Recovered from widow	0	1	8[1]
	£16	4	8

Due to Balnespick.	£	s.	d.
1772. To rent of Drumstank	2	10	0
,, To payment of bill given to F. Davidson for a cow	3	12	0
,, Due for 3 bolls meal bought in 1771, 1772 and one undated (£1 0 0 of above pd.)	2	10	0
Undated. To loan of 10/6 and interest	0	12	0
1772. Lent Mrs. McDonald	0	1	0
,, Advanced to D. Davidson for bear for above	0	1	6[2]
,, Advanced to F. Davidson for meal for funeral of above	0	10	0
,, To whisky and sugar supplied for McDonald's funeral	0	1	8
,, To 1 f. meal supplied when the widow's manure was put out	0	5	0
,, To 2 bolls meal supplied to above	2	0	0
,, Advanced to Sanders McQueen for cloth for the boy	0	3	0
Undated. Advanced to a widow in Pitourie for ½ a hide	0	6	0
1772. To the woman who took the children to their uncle	0	1	0
,, Sent to children's uncle	2	0	0
,, For a cow and calf	2	0	0
,, Paid to John Bain for whisky supplied	0	15	0[3]
	£33	16	1

[1] This entry was £1 0 0, and it was not quite clear if it was Scots or sterling. Several of the entries are repeated once or twice in varying form.

[2] Once noted as 1/-.

[3] The original debt was for £1 4 0, but John Bain owed 10/- to the smith for meal.

The following accounts happen to be fairly full. They give some idea of the mutual relationship.

John McIntosh, Shoemaker.   Tenant in Dunachton-more.   Between 1768–1776 he paid an annual rent of £17 15s. 6d. Scots, *i.e.* £1 9s. 7d. sterling.   After 1776 his rent was increased to £37 13s. 4d. Scots, and it is probable that he took over part of Paul Macphail's holding which Balnespick cultivated in the interval after the latter's death.   There is a most interesting memorandum upon this man's holding drawn up by the birley-men, on the last page of the Account Book. It is undated, but probably refers to the taking on of this extra piece of land.   In 1769 he did not the 'Long Carriage,' but promises double next year.

(P. 178.)   In 1771 he bought half a hide from Balnespick at 5s. 6d., and paid for it (a later entry).

(P. 200.)   In 1773 Balnespick notes that he had made 26 pairs of shoes for the Dunachton family, 2 pairs of which were pumps at 4s. 5d. a pair, and that he still owes 1s. 1d. of the price of a half hide bought in the preceding spring.

(P. 200.)   In 1774 (?) Balnespick notes that he has paid John McIntosh for all the shoes made for him.

[The pumps rather suggest articles made for Balnespick's own wear, but no doubt most of the shoes were for the servants as part wages, for on p. 268 an extensive purchase of shoes for Mrs. Mackintosh and her daughter from Newton (*i.e.* Newton-more) is recorded.]

(On a slip.)   Undated.   An entry states that Balnespick lent him ' his own pound and one from me.'   The shoe-maker later on returned them both.   Either he had had to give security or had used Balnespick as his banker.

(P. 191.)   Undated.   An entry states that he owes Balnespick £2.   It probably refers to the first part of the earlier entry, the second part of which was evidently added later.

Balnespick sold the shoemaker:

> In 1776. 1 firlot barley.
> In 1778. 2 stone hay at 10s. Scots, *i.e.* 10d. or
> 5d. a stone.
> In 1778. 1 firlot barley.

Paul McPhail, also known as Buie (yellow), his relict and sons. He was tenant at Dunachton-more and paid an annual rent of £32 11s. Scots, *i.e.* £2 14s. 3d. sterling. His steadings were worth £19 15s. Scots.

In 1769 he did not the Long Carriage, and in 1770 he died. Apparently there was some delay in finding a tenant, for Balnespick cultivated part of the holding himself till 1774. In 1771 he sowed 5 bolls 1 firlot of small oats and reaped 17 thrave of oat rush and 10 thrave of rye there, and he also sowed and reaped there the two succeeding years. The widow seems to have remained on and held part of the croft, for in 1772 she paid £21 Scots (£1 15s. sterling) rent, which probably represented a part of the rent for 1770. In 1773 she paid £17 8s. Scots (£1 9s. sterling) for rent and meal. In 1774 she moved to a smaller holding on Cuilintuie, for which she paid a rent of £13 6s. 8d. (£1 2s. 2d.), and where she and her sons remained.

Whilst the family were at Dunachton they required a certain amount of additional grain or meal. Three bolls were paid to the sons for services at one time, and one of them, William, bought a firlot of oats. The widow also, as already noted, paid for corn as well as rent that year, and bought three bolls of meal in 1773 jointly with James Robertson in Cuilintuie. The price was to be 18s. a boll if paid for by Martinmas that year. An added note states that £2 17s. was paid for it, *i.e.* at the rate of 19s. per boll, so the discount for prompt payment was evidently not earned.

In 1774, the year they moved, the family owed Balnespick money, for he notes that 'after counting with the McPhails,' a composition of their debt was made for £1 10s. This sum was made up in the following

way : Balnespick himself owed them 6 s. 6 d. and they
agreed to winter seven head of his cattle, 'which will
amount to one pound, one shilling if they winter them
rightly and a shilling more if the brandered quey is
with calf,' i.e. £1 2s. One shilling and sixpence was
paid in cash.

In 1774 Balnespick sold them one boll meal, and
an undated entry states that they cut 'allers' for him
for five days (i.e. alders. The wood was much used for
implements, etc.). In 1776 he gave them a boll of
meal for services. In 1777 Mrs. McPhail bought and
paid for a boll of meal.

The usefulness of the sub-tenants to Balnespick is
obvious. The rental from those portions of the farm
which he sublet covered the amount of rent that he
himself had to pay for the whole Davoch, thus providing him with a considerable farm free of all charge,
and in addition he received very valuable labour dues.
As has already been pointed out, Balnespick never
received his full rents, and in the worst years, when
money was most scarce, he had to provide the larger
part himself, yet all the same, under the older methods
of farming, when an abundant supply of labour was
required and the extent of the acreage that a man could
personally manage was very limited, Balnespick's sub-
tenants were undoubtedly exceedingly useful to him.

The Account Book brings out not less strongly the
less obvious fact that a good and efficient tacksman was
also extremely useful to his sub-tenants. In the 'Second
Statistical Account for the Parish of Moy and Dalarossie' (p. 106), the minister wrote : 'Non-resident
proprietors are a bane to any country. Till of late the
number of gentlemen farmers made up the loss, but
of these there is not one now to whom the country
people can refer.' Eighty years earlier, when most
of the country people could not write, and when they
were considerably more rustic in their ideas, the need
of some one to whom they could refer must have been
much greater. In the Account Book there are entries

that show that Balnespick acted as a sort of bank for some of his tenants, and that he seems to have been a kind of executor in other cases. Some curious jottings relating to the affairs of his son Lachlan, who died in 1785, just a year after old William Mackintosh himself, give some details of the activities of the elder Balnespick. Thus on one occasion he received and administered the pay of a man who was with the army. The man happened to be in debt to Balnespick, but the whole of the money transmitted in this way was spent on his family and the debt was not claimed until after his return. On another occasion Balnespick seems to have arranged a sort of marriage settlement for the daughter of the ' weaver by the Gate,' mentioned in the Account Book, and there are numerous examples of cases when he administered the affairs of widows and orphans. One entry refers to the claim of James Macdonald at Cuilin-tuie, often mentioned in the Account Book, for the repayment of money that was owed him by a tenant on Raits, when the effects of the latter were being rouped, ' and that Borlum ' (the owner of Raits) ' had taken a concern in Cameron's affairs, and would see his Effects properly distributed among his Creditors—That Captain Mackintosh ' (*i.e.* old Balnespick, the writer of the Account Book) ' had taken a note of the debts due by Cameron in his Bounds of the Barony of Dunachton and upon knowing James Macdonald's share of the debt due him, told him that though he had his bill, yet he would collect the debt and retain it in lieu of what he (Macdonald) was due him (the Captain) which was accordingly done.'

The tacksman also, no doubt, brought a certain amount of employment, especially to the local crafts-men, but it is in two other respects that he was most useful, *i.e.* as an organiser and as a provider of credit, for he thus performed two functions of which the present-day smallholder is often considerably in need.

The services of a powerful organiser must have been extremely necessary under the system of runrig, just as it would be under any system of joint agriculture, such as the farm colonies that the Government tried and failed to found after the war. We do not know how far the authority of the birley-men was independent of the support of the tacksman, but it is at least probable that the backing of the latter was very valuable. 'Northern Rural Life in the Eighteenth Century' is written mainly about Aberdeenshire, where the tacksman system does not seem to have been established, and constant disputes are mentioned. On p. 273 of the Account Book a grazing dispute is referred to Balnespick and Borlum, and the proper regulation and control of the pasturage in the days of common grazing must have been most important, for it is evident, from Professor Gonner's book on enclosure, that overcrowding was a serious disadvantage of the open-field system, just as it has proved itself on the common pasturage of the Skye crofter townships (see the Reports of the Crofter Commissions). Under the system of runrig it must have been most important that all the portions of the farm should be kept equally under cultivation, and when, owing to the death, illness, or departure of a tenant, his share of a joint farm was without a cultivator, it evidently fell to Balnespick's lot to see that it was properly sowed and tilled. Thus when Paul Buie McPhail died Balnespick undertook the cultivation for two years, charging the widow for the seed and manure that he used and buying some of the crops from her. After the smith died he seems to have taken the management of Drumstank into his own hands for a time, and there are records of occasional sowings in Croft, Carit, and Craigan Dhu, probably for the same sort of reason.

In the course of his main business, that of a stock-raising farmer, Balnespick was probably quite useful to his tenants when he bought their yearlings and two-year-olds, for, as Miss Grant of Rothiemurchus, in 'Memoirs of a Highland Lady,' pointed out, the crofters were often unable to keep their cattle until as four- or five-year-olds they should be ready for selling to the drovers from the south, and their main source of income was the sale of the younger beasts to Rothiemurchus, Balnespick, and Belleville. In some of the purchases that Balnespick made and retailed to his neighbours he seems to have been the prototype of the modern agricultural co-operative society. The vital importance of the supplies of meal that he imported have already been alluded to. He also bought and resold pease and pease meal, seed corn—which it is still necessary to bring from the seaboard at least every two or three years in the Badenoch district—iron, nails, whisky from Ferintosh, malt, and corks. It seems probable that his bulls were the only ones in the common herd. As an elder of the parish church he was responsible for the administration of what relief was given to the poor, and although the service was compulsory, he contributed to the communal life of the district in collecting the sums due for the minister's stipend and the schoolmaster's salary. He also collected payments from his tenants, and administered a voluntary fund towards the payment of the fox-killers. The following is a copy of such an arrangement between Lachie, his son, and the fox-killer :

'Kincraig, 12 ffebry 1777. We Lachlan McIntosh Esqr at Kincraig and Duncan Macpharlin, foxkiller, having met here this day and after comuning concerning the killing of ffoxes within the bounds of the parish of Alvie benorth the water of Spey I the said Lachlan McIntosh doe hereby contract and bind me to pay to the said Duncan Mcpharlin nine shillings sterling money for every ffox young and old that he shall kill upon the real ground of the said parish betwixt Ardvordan and Lagnacaillich upon his makeing fforth or otherwise Testifying to me that he does kill the ffoxes upon the Ground and Lands of the Bounds above mentioned Instantly on proof as aforesaid And on other side I the said Duncan Mcpharlin

L

hereby bind and Oblidge me that I shall occupy and Labour in my Business of the ffox Killing in the said bounds and district in my severall rounds and Traversing upon the adjacent grounds undertaken for by me constantly and that I shall answer any call given to me by any of the people within the said Bounds where the ffox shall be hefted and is Destructive And in case these informers of ffoxhunting shall atempt to Kill or actually Kill young ffoxes Unknown to me the said Duncan Mcpharlin they shall not get any reward The premises we undertake and bind ourselves to fulfill and perform to one another Under the Penalty of ffive pounds sterlin to be payed to the party implementing to the party performing We are

(signed) Lach: McIntosh

D M P (The letters formed with difficulty.)

This man was the ' Duncan the Foxkiller ' mentioned in the Account Book.

The provision of easily obtained credit was probably quite as useful a service as the organisation of the farming, for the people were almost entirely without ready money and had hardly anything to pledge, had that even been possible. Balnespick, being on the spot and knowing the people intimately, was in a position to know when he could safely advance money as no one else could do. The Account Book abounds with entries recording the advance of money. Sometimes only the sum is given, but very often the purpose for which it was borrowed is mentioned—such as the purchase of a horse (see p. 171), a cow (see p. 271), some harness (see p. 191), the fittings of a plough (see p. 190), grain, meal, hay, etc. Once it was for the wintering of a horse, once or twice for the expenses of a journey (see p. 191), to discharge a bill that had suddenly fallen due (see p. 274), for funeral expenses (see p. 190), for whisky (see p. 190), for clothes for the children (see p. 271), for cloth, etc. Many of the entries that appear in the Account Book were not loans but gifts, for even among the later ones, very few appear in the list of debts due to the family that was drawn up in 1785 after Lachie's death. Thus it is quite evident that the moneys given to old McPhadruck and one or two others were never even formally loans. In other cases, as in those of Mrs. Macphail, Mrs. Macdonald, and one or two others, the loan can only have been a formality, and it is evident that no payment was expected. In the words of Lachie's widow, it would have been 'improper' and 'to the disgrace of the family' if such poor people had ever been expected to pay. Sometimes Balnespick seems to have charged interest at the rate of 5 per cent., in other cases the loans were given free. On the whole, the free loans seem to have been given more often to his sub-tenants, but not invariably so. The Account Book and the other old papers from which I have quoted show that the use of credit and bills instead of currency was universal in the district, in fact without it, owing to their shortage of currency, the people would probably have found it difficult to carry on at all. For the working of the system among such very poor people, the presence of a certain number of local men able to give bills upon little more security than their personal knowledge of the debtor's character must have been almost a necessity.

Unfortunately, among the writers of the eighteenth century, the tacksmen did not bear at all a good character. The article by M. I. Adam, from which I have already quoted, gives a good general summary of the charges against them. A reference dated 1785 is quoted as saying : ' The Chieftain lets out his land in large lots to the inferior branches of the family, all of whom must support the dignity of lairds. The renters let the land out in small parcels from year to year to the lower class of people, and to support their dignity squeeze everything out of them they can possibly get, leaving them only a bare subsistence. Until this evil is obviated, Scotland can never improve.' The tacksmen were also said to be obstinately set in the old ways, and to demand exorbitant labour dues.

Such strictures were probably largely due to the fact that by the end of the eighteenth century the tacksman system had survived its usefulness. They were made as a rule by the same writers who condemned the run-rig tenants. The tacksmen had long ceased to be necessary to the well-being of the clansmen as an integral part of the military organisation of the clan. With the opening up of the country, the improvement of agricultural processes, and the enclosing of the fields, the need for tacksmen as organisers and intermediaries tended to die away. Like the 'load of tenantry' on the patchwork open fields that they had ruled over, they were tending to become out of date and to give place to the present-day working tenant farmer, with his two or three hired labourers. With 'enlightened self-interest' the proprietors introduced the more productive system up the east coast and right across the Highlands of Scotland, raising the rents as the old tacks fell in. As M. I. Adams says : 'Under the new system leases are granted, but granted on rents which represent, or are intended to represent, the economic value of the land. These leases are granted to a much wider class and so far diminish the profit and prestige of those who had formerly held tacks. Again, the practice of sub-letting was abolished or the services which might be exacted from the sub-tenants limited. Some of the sub-tenants were promoted at once to the dignity of leaseholders. Finally the whole relation of landlord and tacksman was put on a simple business footing, thereby extinguishing the tacksman's partial sense of ownership, and the half traditional tie of kinship. The tacksmen, in fact, ceased to form a special and privileged class. Their status was lowered as that of the under tenants was raised.'

In the Hebrides the tacksmen were said even to treat their sub-tenants with gross personal cruelty, although Buchanan, one of their bitterest critics, admits that : 'There is a great difference between that mild treatment which is shown to sub-tenants and even scallags by the old lessees, descended of ancient and honourable families, and the outrageous rapacity shown by those necessitous strangers who have obtained leases from absent proprietors, who treat the natives as if they were a conquered and inferior race of mortals' ('Travels in the Hebrides,' p. 50).   It is unthinkable that the high-spirited and self-respecting people of Badenoch should ever have submitted tamely to personal maltreatment, nor is there a particle of evidence that anyone ever dared to offer it to them.

Perhaps one small fact will best indicate something of the tie that united an old Highland tacksman and his sub-tenants.

It is now more than one hundred years since the Balnespick family left Dunachton, but in trying to find out what became of the descendants of their old sub-tenants, I was much struck by the number of men, in those families which I was able to trace, who were called William.   It is not a particularly common name in the Highlands or in that especial district, and I finally came to the conclusion that even although the original derivation was forgotten, it must have been handed down through three generations from forbears who had been named after that William Mackintosh of Balnespick who wrote the old Account Book, and the grandson who afterwards succeeded him.

APPENDIX I

The Local Craftsmen and Workers

According to the ' First Statistical Account for Alvie Parish ' (vol. xiii. p. 375), the local craftsmen were ' fit only for the coarsest work.' They consisted of :

2 smiths.
6 weavers.
4 taylors.
2 brog makers (shoe or brogue makers).

The following local workers are mentioned in the Account Book. They seem to have paid their way by a mixture of farming, work at their handicrafts, and general labouring :

Tailors (1).—Alexander McPherson, cottager in Dunachton Beg. Balnespick sold him 1¼ bolls of meal.

Millers (3).—Alexander McIntosh, Birley man, tenant in Dunachton Beg. He died in 1774. There are about fifteen entries relating to this man, the general position being :

Paid to the miller in multure meal (about) 11 bolls, 1 firlot, ½ peck.
Sold to the miller, whiskey, to the value of £1–9–4.
malt.
iron.
grain, 4 bolls, 3 firlots, 1 peck.
Bought of the miller, grain, 5 bolls.

Angus Dow McDonald, tenant in Dunachton Beg. He was not employed by Balnespick as a miller, but peeled bark two days. He borrowed £2 5s. at different times and bought 2 bolls and 2 pecks of grain.

Alexander or John Meldrum. Balnespick paid him 5s. upon Duncan McBean's account. He sold him 2 bolls of grain.

Weavers (5).—John Campbell, tenant at the gate. He bought one boll of meal from Balnespick. Among Lachlan's papers there is a good deal about this man. He was ' in a condition to pay any little debt that he was due' (in his widow's own words). Old Balnespick arranged a marriage for him. The lady and her friends 'not desiring the connection,' he agreed to pay her eight pounds 'in slump' and two pounds a year and to leave her 'his effects,' and the marriage duly took place.

John Fraser, tenant at the gate. He bought hay and corn from Balnespick.

'Faryr the Weaver.' Is mentioned as cutting hay at two harvests.

William Dow. He bought grain from Balnespick.

Sanders More Cameron, cotter in Auchnabeuchin. He was employed as a weaver and earned 16s.; he also worked at the hay harvest. He bought small quantities of malt and meal, worth in all about 12s.

Carpenter (1).—Unnamed. He bought meal in the shortage of 1771 and borrowed money.

Fox killers (3).

Wrights (4).—Lachlan Roy. He bought wood from Balnespick.

John McIntosh. He borrowed £3 and bought one boll of meal.

ffraser. He received spars in payment of wages.

James Lee, cotter in Carit and afterwards in Raits. He bought 1 boll, 1 firlot, 1 peck of meal at different times, and borrowed £1 1s., of which he repaid 3s. 6d., and was to make a set of spokes in view of repaying the rest. He was also paid 16s. upon Donald Grant's account, and 1s. 'for news.'

Shoemakers (2).—McErish, cotter in Auchnabeuchin. He bought a boll of meal.

John McIntosh, tenant in Dunachton more. In 1773 Balnespick paid him for 26 pairs of shoes by giving him a hide. This more than balanced accounts and left him owing 1s. 1d. Later on he borrowed £2, and purchased hay and corn on five different occasions to the value of about £1 10s. 5d.

Mason (1).—Peter Macdonald, tenant of half an oxgate on Dunachton. He peeled bark and bought small quantities of malt and pease. After his death Balnespick lent the widow £5 16s. to pay for his funeral and that of his son, and later on gave her £2.

Smiths (2).—James Gow, who repaid a debt in 1771.

Alexander Macdonald, whose accounts have already been referred to.

Fiddlers (2).—John McPherson, who cut hay for 7½ days one summer and bought 1 boll, 1 firlot of meal.

William Mackintosh of Balnespick's Account Book

The spelling and figures are exactly reproduced from the original. In some pages Balnespick's addition seems to be faulty, but it is probable that in many cases the inaccuracy occurred in making one of the entries and that the totals are correct.

[Page one. 1769.]

An account of my sowing in the year 1769.   By the blessing of God I began sowing March 17th New Style.
Said Day sawn of Kininveys[1] oats by the ash tree

on Do ground 28th	02 – 00 – 0
It below Prosnapoil[2] of said oats . . .	01 – 02 – 2
It on said ground	00 – 00 – 1½
It upon the ley ground to the east of the bear	00 – 02 – 2
All the whole oats to the east of the Cross Dyke	05 – 00 – 0
It sawn of Kininveys oats on the two large divisions east and west	01 – 00 – 1
It of the said oats on the other divisions east and west of the Dyke	01 – 01 – 0
	07 – 01 – 0
It sawn of Kininveys oats clean to west the Dyke	00 – 03 – 0
It of Falconers[3] white oats for rush[4] .	01 – 00 – 0
It of Kiniveys and Falconers for rush . .	01 – 00 – 3
It of Rye of white seven firlots clean on above haugh	03 – 00 – 0
	13 – 01 – 0
Impr of small oats[5] 30th March on ley ground to the east side of the Cross Dyke . .	07 – 03 – 0
It on ditto ley ground	00 – 01 – 0
It on Do leys	00 – 03 – 2
In leys sown	09 – 01 – 0

[The measures on this page are bolls, firlots, and pecks. 4 pecks = 1 firlot, 4 firlots = 1 boll.]

[1] A place-name.

[2] The name of a part of Dunachton. It cannot now be identified.

[3] A variety of oat seed (?). It is never sown now.

[4] Oats sown on such exhausted ground that the crop is only fit to feed unthreshed to the live-stock.

[5] Oats so deteriorated that they are little better than the old black oats.

		B. f. p.
It of small oats on in rush above Priline[1] 31st April	03 – 02 – 0
It of brocked[2] corn in top of the Priline .	00 – 01 – 2
It of small oats by the Dyke on Dito ground .	02 – 02 – 0
It to the east of above Dyke this side of which a firlot bad white oats	02 – 01 – 2
It on the Cleckersnach[3] at and preceding 24th April	09 – 02 – 0
It above the Hill of the Stacke a firlot of what was in the stackes given the horses .	02 – 01 – 0
It of bear of the stackes to be sawn . .	02 – 2 – 0
It of birley in the yard and on the short rigs the remaining part on this side the garden to make brocken oats[4]	00 – 1 – 2
	29 – 2 – 2

[Page two.]

B. f. p.

Carried from the oyr side of small oats that was sown only in that number yr (was) a firlote refuse of white oats and six pecks birlie . . . . . . 29 – 2 – 2

At which time being the 27th April yrs of the oats of the last stacke sown 10 bolls 3 firlots over and above the small proof[5] only that yrs ten firlots yet of said oats in sacks to be sawn, so that all to be sawn is of the stack hereafter

It sawn the 28th April . . . . 00 – 3 – 0
It measured to be sown the 29th April . . 2 – 2 – 0

[The measures on this page are bolls, firlots, and pecks.
The arithmetic on this page is Balnespick's ; it is as likely that one of the items is wrong as the total.]

[1] A heathery knoll above Dunachton. The soil is very poor on it.
[2] Spoilt or spotted. See Wright's *Dialect Dictionary*.
[3] Now forms part of Belleville, the neighbouring property. It is now only grazing.
[4] Bruised oats (?) = crushed corn. This meaning was suggested by an old farmer.
[5] A sample taken from the sheaves and threshed to estimate the value of unthreshed corn. An obsolete term.

	B.	f.	p.
At and preceeding 29th April theres measured twixt what is sawn sold and for the horses of the oats of the stack last housed . . . 16 – 1 – 2			
It sown Monday 1st May	1 –	1 –	0
It Tuesday 2nd sown	2 –	0 –	0
It Wednesday sown	2 –	0 –	0
It Thursday 4th sown	1 –	0 –	0
It Friday 5th May by the blessing of God I finished my oat seed having sown today .	1 –	1 –	0
	39 –	1 –	2
It of white oats[1] and rye[2] carried from the other side	13 –	1 –	0
	52 –	2 –	2
Saturday the 6th May I began sowing my bear[3] sown then after muck and tathing[4] to the east the cross dyke the last of it by 9th of May	01 –	2 –	$2\frac{1}{2}$
It behind the Brew House and oyr parts to the west of cross Dyke[5] in muck . .	01 –	0 –	0
It below the Town[6] in tathing . . .	00 –	2 –	2
It in muck preceeding the 17th . . .	00 –	3 –	2
It more in muck 18 and 19 being of barley and Macphadrucks[7] bear . . .	00 –	3 –	3
	04 –	2 –	$1\frac{1}{2}$
It the 20th of my own bear in muck . .	1 –	0 –	0.
It from Dalnavert[8] a firlote in muck . .		1 –	0
It of my own bear all in muck . . .		1	
	06 –	0 –	1

[1] The variety of oats now usually sown.

[2] This grain is now never sown in Badenoch.

[3] An inferior variety of barley long given up in Scotland.

[4] Manuring outfield land by folding the animals grazing on it at night and moving the enclosure every ten days or so. The fold was built of turf sods.

[5] A turf dyke that divided the land of a farm in half.

[6] Old Scotch word for farm homestead and steading.

[7] A sub-tenant.

[8] A neighbouring farm. In Balnespick's time it was rented by the descendant of the old Shaws of Rothiemurchus. In 1860 its arable is said to have been doubled by judicious improvements. See *Lectures from the Mountains*, vol. ii. p. 26.

[Page three.   1769.]

Ane account of what whole oats, malt etc I disposed of in the year 1769 of Cropt 1768.

Imps to Invernahaven [1]	. . . .	20 – 00 – 0
It to Mr McLean of seed oats at ten merks	.	4 – 00 – 0
It to Mr Blair of seed oats	. . .	2 – 00 – 0
It Baillie Clerk [2] in Ruthven [3]	. .	00 – 03 – 0
It to McKinich tenant in Inverburnie (?)	.	00 – 03 – 0
It to Kinrara [4]	. . . . .	03 – 00 – 0
It to James Roy in Park [5]	. . .	0 – 01 – 0
It to Borllum [6] for bear	. . .	03 – 00 – 0
It to Mr Gordon [7] Minister of Alvie	.	01 – 00 – 0
It to James Stuart in Inverburnie	.	00 – 03 – 0
It to James Kennoch yr of Falconers oats	.	00 – 02 – 0
It of said oats to Peter McDonalds son on said place	. . . . .	00 – 02 – 0
It to ane oyr man yr also	. . .	00 – 02 – 0
It to Peter McDonol in (?)	. .	00 – 02 – 0
It of Kinveys oats to Mr Blair April	.	01 – 02 – 0
It to Dalnavert said day of seed oats	.	00 – 02 – 0
It to Mr Gordon Aberlour [8]	. . .	01 – 02 – 0
It to John McIntosh in Dun : more [9]	.	00 – 01 – 0

[The measures on this page are bolls, firlots, and pecks. The total is copied from the Account Book ; probably one of the entries is wrong.]

[1] Invernahaven : the scene of a clan battle in the fifteenth century and the seat at one time of a very ancient branch of the Macphersons. Invernahaven was bought by the poet Macpherson and his son cleared it. Its very name now seems to be forgotten by the country people. See C. Fraser Mackintosh, *Antiquarian Notes*, Second Series, p. 60.

[2] Clerk was a common name in Badenoch.

[3] At that time an important market town where five annual trysts were held and a garrison of soldiers was quartered. The modern town of Kingussie just across the Spey has entirely taken its place. It is about six miles from Dunachton. The trysts are described in Robertson's *Report on the Agriculture of Inverness-shire*, p. 30.

[4] The name of a place about seven miles off.

[5] A sub-tenant on the Davoch of Dunachton.

[6] The last descendant of the old Mackintosh family that owned Raits, the property adjoining Dunachton. He was the son of the well-known Jacobite general, the Brigadier Mackintosh. After his death the property was bought by the poet Macpherson and renamed Belleville.

[7] The brave minister of Alvie, whose exploit is described in chapter ii. of the Introduction.

[8] In lower Strathspey.

[9] A sub-tenant.   Dun : more is a contraction of Dunachtonmore.

It to Lachlan Toshach ½ boll small and two
    pecks white . . . . . 00 – 02 – 2
It to Donald Bain[1] 1 boll small oats and 1½
    boll white . . . . . . 00 – 02 – 0
It to Sanders McIntosh in Prossnakalach[2] of
    small oats a boll to ½ white oats . . 00 – 02 – 0
James McDonoll in Killintuie[3] of Falconers . 00 – 01 – 0
It of small oats to William Dow[4] a firlote (?) 00 – 00 – 2
It of small oats to Duncan Gordon in Croft
    Beg 2 firlotes (?) . . . . 00 – 01 – 00
It to Hugh my servant 2 pecks . . . 00 – 00 – 1
It to John Don[5] a firlote (?) . . . 00 – 00 – 02

                                        41 – 03 – 3

[Page four. 1769 (?). Date not stated.]
Ane account of white oats some of my tenants had from
Aberlour which I payed ten shillings ready cash.

	B.	f.	p.
Impr the Smith[6]	0 –	1 –	0
William Mc Donol[6] in Auchnabochin[7] .	0 –	1 –	0
Donald Mc-Glashan yr[6]	0 –	1 –	0
Alexr McIntosh yr[6]	0 –	1 –	0

                                          1 – 0 – 0
Carried from the oyr side of my own oats sold . 41 – 3 – 3
It of white oats given the miller[6] of falconers 0 – 0 – 1½
It of small oats to the Tulloch man a firlote . 0 – 0 – 2
It more to Sanders McIntosh[6] in Prosnacalich
    ½ bole . . . . . . 0 – 1 – 0
It to William Mcdonoll in Achnabochin[6] ½
    bole . . . . 0 – 1 – 0
It to Donald Mcglashan yr[6] ½ bole . . 0 – 1 – 0

[The entries on this page are evidently incorrect.]

[1] A subtenant. White Donald, a nickname.
[2] A smallholding on Kincraig.
[3] Cuillintuie, a smallholding on Dunachton.
[4] A sub-tenant. 'Dow' is a corruption of 'dhu,' i.e. 'black.'
[5] A sub-tenant, 'don,' i.e. 'brown.'
[6] Sub-tenants or cottagers of Balnespick on the Davoch of Dunachton
(including Kincraig).
[7] One of the holdings that Balnespick let to a group of sub-tenants.

B. f. p.

The above six firlots small oats being partly
    brocked and of my best small oats.
It May the 4th given Dollnavert of said oats .   0 – 2 – 0

                                          $42 – 3 – 2\frac{1}{2}$

It Sanders McIntosh in Achnabochin[1] of
    meale two stone
It to James Letter use of four stone meal
It to Donald McIntosh[1] a stone meall
It to Lach : Tosach of bear $\frac{1}{2}$ boll.
It to Sanders[1] more the weaver[2]
It to James Polson[3] in Pitourie[4]   .   . $\frac{1}{2}$

[Page five. 1769 (?)].

    I have by the blessing of God finished my labouring upon
Wednesday the 25th May New Style which day the Amount
of my white oats rye and peas is   .   .   .   13 – 01 – 03
Of small oats   .   .   .   .   .   .   29 – 01 – 01

It of bear in after muck and after tathing to the
    east of the dyke .   .   .   .   .   01 – 02 – 02
It in after muck on the west side of the head
    rig by the side of the dyke only a few
    loads of the muck on the uper side and
    on the side next the carse east and west   00 – 01 – 00
It by the brew house in third muck and a small
    allowance of muck given above to the
    whole of it   .   .   .   .   00 – 03 – 00
It below the town in tathing on a small divi-
    sion on the east side of the miding with
    some muck   .   .   .   .   00 – 02 – 02
It more in the miding and sheep muck and
    horse muck below the town   .   .   02 – 03 – 01

                                      $06 – 00 – 01\frac{1}{2}$

of the above there was three bolls and a half bear bought from
Borlum and old Mcphadruck[1] and a firlote from Dollnavert.

---

[1] Sub-tenants or cottagers of Balnespick on the Davoch of Dunachton
(including Kincraig).   [2] Big Alexander.
    [3] The name of this family occurs constantly. Their signatures on some
old papers left by Lachie is Wilson. Some members of the family were farm
servants or cottagers on Dunachton.
    [4] A small farm to the east of Dunachton now known as Balourie.

[Page six. 1771 (?).]
  Dunachton the 3rd Sepbr. Sent to Elgin of Oak Bark.[1]
Impr Seven Carts full weight and thirteen horses with back
  loads weight [2]
  given Lachlan Shaw of money . . .   2sh
  given Wm Davidson 1sh
  given John Roy in Dun: beg . . .   1
  It to Wm John Davidson . . .   1 – 6
  It to James McPhadruck . . .   2 – 0
  pd John McIntosh shoemaker a firlote of small
    oats for comprised corn [3] . . .
  It given to Wm Callum to pay the ballance of
    the meall to Donald Grant . . . 00 – 7 – 0
  It to him to buy (? ?) . . . . . 00 – 10 – 0
  It to bear his and servants expence . . 00 – 05 – 0
  It he is to recover from Mr Duff 6 sh:

[1773.]
  Ane account of oats, I mean small oats sold to different people.[4]
  To the Captain of Kinloch . . . . 08 –
  To Evan Roy in Dollrady and Stuart the
    Chelsaman [5] of my own oats. . . 02 – 02
  To James McIntosh in Keepoch moor [6] of the
    morry oats [7] . . . . . 00 – 01
  It to James McDonoll in Kylintuie [8] . . 00 – 01
  It to James Robertson yr 1
  It to Donald Sanders mor's son [9] . . . 2
  It to Faryr [10] in Dunachton more . . 1

 [1] The peeling of oak bark for tanning has long died out in the district.
 [2] This entry not only shows that pack horses were still used, it probably
refers to the ' long load,' one of the labour dues that the tenants had to perform.
It also shows what a very large number of horses were required to work the
holding under the old system.
 [3] The meaning of this word is not clear. It may mean corn estimated
from proof taken and threshed from a stack, and allotted to John Mackintosh
for cultivating a piece of land.
 [4] This is practically a duplicate list of that on p. 66 of the Account Book.
With the exception of four names, all the men mentioned are sub-tenants.
The figures refer to bolls, firlots, and pecks.
 [5] An old soldier in receipt of a pension from Chelsea Hospital.
 [6] One of Balnespick's subfarms. It cannot now be traced.
 [7] Oats grown in the county of Morayshire.
 [8] Cuillintuie, a subfarm still under cultivation as part of Dunachtonmore.
 [9] Big Alexander the weaver.
 [10] Father.

It to Faryr in Leult [1] .   .   .   .   .

To Donald Stuart he wroucht six days here   .   1 — 1

It to James Rob in Croft Carnoch [2]   .   .   1 — 0

It to Wm Campboll the above is marked on

    ane oyr page   .   .   .   .   .   1 — 0

[Page seven. 1769.]

By the blessing of God I began cutting down my bear friday the 22nd Sepbr New Style 1769. The season was so rainy that little was cutt only part of the days fair

	Thrv.	St.	Sh.
Cut of muck and Tathing bear below the Town			
It of affter muck and affter tathing bear to the east of the Cross Dyke . . .	070		
It behind the brew house of muck bear .	032	10	06
It closs by the Kerth [3] above the Allon [3] affter	008		
It of muck bear closs by the Cross Dyke on this side	006		
It below the town of muck and tathing bear .	159		
It one of the two divisions to the west of the stryp the division next the stryp being under bear of Donald McSorl's relict so my two was so all being muck bear. This being the last cut Saturday the 30th Sepbr which was the first day wee got shearing for the whole day [4] . .	019		
	294	01	06
Saturday the 30th Sepbr. affter finishing the bear			
Cut of bad Rye on the Haugh . . .	032	01	00
My servants got up Monday the 2nd Octbr and they had by eight in the morning the rest of the rye cutt	028	01	00
It of small oats to the east of the mid Dyke preceeding the 8th Octbr to west the Faishcallach [5] that was fully ripe . .	174	01	

[1] A subfarm on Kincraig.

[2] An adjoining farm at that time apparently part of Raits.

[3] Neither of these local place-names can now be identified.

[4] This entry shows that Dunachton was runrig among Balnespick and his sub-tenants. McSorl's widow's name does not appear among the list of sub-tenants, so she must have been a cotter of some kind.

[5] This local name cannot be identified. It was outfield, and probably an outlying piece like the Priline.

	Thrv.	St.	Sh.
It of small and rush and brocked oats put in the stack next the bear stack at this side	083		
It in said stack of small oats this side above dyke	063	00	
It of rye in said stack	024		
It put in said stack of the small oats to east side of the Dyke it is counted above 16 thrave	004	01	

[Page eight.]

Carried from the oyr side	381	01	
It on the Cleckersnach of small oats . .	147	00	0
It on this side of faishcalloch of green oats small	019	0	0
It to the east of small oats not ripe being the whole above the brae . . .	232	00	0
	779	1	0
Octbr 8th of white oats to the east of the aple tree that side of Kiniveys oats . .	127		
It below prosnapoil [1] and a small piece of Lagnalinhe [2] of said oats	039		
It of white oats to the west of the dyke put in the large stack next the one of the oat barn	141	1	
It of white oat rush	74		
It of birlie in the yard of Prosnacalloch and the little by Faishcalloch . . .	010		
	1170	00	
	300		
	1470	1	0

By the blessing of God I had done cutting friday 21st Octbr 1769.

The season was so rainy that I had 290 Thrave of my small oats in the field till Monday the 20th Novbr. and only then laid about flacks.[3]

[The measure on this page is the thrave or threave, used for unthreshed corn. It consisted of two stooks of twelve shaves (sheaves) each. The sheaves were rather smaller than modern ones. See Murray's *Dictionary*, and also local traditions.]

[1] Cannot be identified.
[2] One of the little clearings in the birch wood below the house.   [3] Flails.

[Page nine.   1768.]

Ane Acct of the number of cattle that I have Martinmas 1768.

Impr of cows that had calves 29

It of five year olds agt May 02
It of four year olds agt May 05
It of three year olds agt May 09
It of two year olds agt May 07
_____

That is she 23
It a large bull seven years agt May and a two year old agt
   May 2
It four he three year olds agt May 4
It of he two year olds agt May 7
_____

13
It of calves four he and six she 10
_____

75

Of the above 29 cows two are to be slaughtered.[1] One of
the calves died and therse but one the above cows slaughtered and
therse one bought in place of her and yrs still ten stirks yr being
eleven.

[Page ten.   1769.]

Octbr 5th 1769 then housed of bear that was below the Town
on muck and tathing in the bear barn.

Of which yrs six thrave of packman (? ? ?) on the top of
   the mow next the bear barn 124
It sent to Dunachton of the shortest of the said bear   049
therse reserved of the said bear to be put in the stack
   not being dry 005
It was not put in the stack.

[Page eleven.   1770.]

Ane Account of what white oats I disposed of the cropt being
1769

Sold in March 1770   B.   f.   p.
Impr to Invernahaven at 10 sh per boll payable
   agt martinmas first . . . . 25 – 0 – 0

_____
[1] The latter part of this entry was evidently added to the rest of it.

	B.	f.	p.

It payed him of what I was due since last year
three firlots being after above 25 bolls . 02 – 3 – 0
There was put in the Barn of Capt Shaw's meale
ten firlots which was taken out as follows
Impr to Donald Bain's wife [1] 1
To John Roy [2] and John Dow [3] in Kincraig . 2
To the slater 6th Sepbr 2
Received from Alexander McDonoll in Balla-
chroan [4] Decbr 11th 1773 to be joint with
James McPhadruck's [5] money to pay
Alexr McPherson in Dolbrady [6] . . £1 – 16 – 0

[Page twelve. 1769 (?).]
Ane account of what I malted of my own bear.
Impr put in steep of the bear that was in the barns
preceeding the 23rd March . . . 08 – 2 – 0
It of the stack put in steep 23rd March . 04 – 2 – 0
It of said stack put in steep. . . . 04 – 2 – 0
17 – 2 – 0
It sold of said malt to different people
to Cathelus McPherson in Islanddow [7] . 01 – 0 – 0
It to Mrs Stuart Inverslany she got non [8] . 00 – 0 – 1
It to Peter Robertson in Dunachton beg [9] . 00 – 0 – 1
It to the miller [9] 1
It to my Lord's wife on Luald [9] . . . 1
It to William Gow's wife in Pitourie . . 1
It to ffinley's relict in Dun : beg [9] . . 1
It to Cameron the weaver on Achnabochin [9] . 1
It to my son William of Malt 6th April . 1 – 0 – 0

[The measures on this page were apparently bolls, firlots, and pecks.]

[1] White Donald, a farm servant.
[2] Red John, a sub-tenant.
[3] Black John, a sub-tenant on the Davoch of Dunachton.
[4] Ballachroan. A farm at that time belonging to a very ancient Macpherson family. It was occupied by the famous 'Black Officer.' Alexander
Macdonald was no doubt a sub-tenant. This entry was evidently inserted later.
[5] A sub-tenant on the Davoch.
[6] A local farm.
[7] There is still a labourer's cottage here.
[8] The three last words in this entry were apparently added later.
[9] Sub-tenants of Balnespick on the Davoch.

[Page thirteen.   1769.]

Ane account of what multer[1] meal came from the milln for the crop 1769.

	B.	f.	p.
Impr upon the Monday 13th Novr 1769 of bear meall	01	1	1
It of oat meal 20th Decbr	00	2	0
It Janry 20th of bear meal	00	3	$3\frac{1}{2}$
It 24th said month of oat meall	01	3	$0\frac{1}{2}$

Payed all the above multers of skilling[2] of my own cropt

Ane account of what bear meal was made of my own bear of Cropt 1769

Thursday 21st Novbr	4	2	0
Wednesday 27th Decbr of bear meall	1	2	$0\frac{3}{4}$
It first of Febry. of bear meall	2	1	0
It to Dunach:[3] said day of bear meall	1	0	1
It to pay the multers 13th Febry of bear skilling	2	1	$0\frac{1}{2}$
It of bear meall March 14th	2	3	0
	14	1	2
It 13th April of bear meall	1	3	3
	16	1	3
It of bear meall that was dryed put in the large girnell[4] at Kin:[5]	7	1	0
	23	2	1

[Page fourteen.   1770.]

	B.	f.	p.
Novr. 21st of white oat meall and on the 26th Janry.	05	2	0

[1] Meal paid to the miller for the grinding of the crop at the mill to which the farms were 'thirlled.' The entries on this page are rather confusing, but it seems clear that Balnespick had to pay the miller.

[2] Corn from which the husks have been removed preparatory to grinding. See Eden's *State of the Poor*, p. 500.

[3] A contraction of Dunachton.

[4] A chest or barrel.

[5] A contraction of Kincraig.

		B.	f.	p.
Decr 22nd of small oat meall	. . .	01	1	3
Janry 3rd of small oat meall .	. . .	3	2	2
Janry 8th of said meall	. . . .	03	0	3
It to Donald McEvans wife of skilling fee	.	00	1	1
It Febry. 1st of oat meall	. . . .	2	1	1
It to Dunachton said day of oat meall	. .	01	0	2
It put in the multer chest of skilling to pay all that was brought out preceeding the 13th Febry.[1]	. . . . .	02	1	$0\frac{1}{2}$
It 13th Febry of white oat rush meall put in the chest in the stable	. . .	06 –	1 –	$1\frac{1}{2}$
It given of Dito meall to Sanders more weaver		06 –	1 –	0
It of small oat meall said day put in said chist		02 –	1 –	0
It of pron[2] put in said chist that had $\frac{1}{2}$ meall six firlots				
It of small oat meall March 14th	. .	07 –	0 –	0
		33 –	2 –	3
It of small oat meal April 13th	. . .	03 –	0 –	0
It of white oat meall	. . . .	2 –	0 –	3
It of oat meall April 19th	. . .	03 –	3	
		42 –	1 –	2
		23 –	2 –	1 [3]
		65 –	3 –	3
It of bear malted	. . . .	17 –	2 –	0 [4]
It of white oats to Dollwhinie[5] of sd cropt	.	27 –	0 –	0
It sold twixt small oats and white oats that was made victual	. . . . .	12 –	0 –	0 [6]
		122 –	1 –	3 [7]

[1] A duplicate entry with that on p. 13 of the Account Book.
[2] Meal mixed with husks, now only given to the fowls.
[3] The total of bear meal, see p. 13 of the Account Book.
[4] The total of malt sold, see p. 12 of the Account Book.
[5] Not the Dalwhinnie on the Highland line, but land now merged in Belleville. The very name is forgotten.
[6] This total is evidently included in the figures given on p. 16 of the Account Book.
[7] The complete total.

[Page fifteen. 1770.]

Ane account of what meal was given the servants at Kincraig 1770.

Tuesday the 30th Janry of oat meal . .	8 stones
Said day of bear meal	10
Tuesday 28th Febry. to Dito of oat meal .	10
Said day of bear meal	06
Wednesday 14th March of oat meal . .	06
Sd. day of bear meal	06
It Thursday 29th march given the servants of oat meal	06
It of pron then and formerly ½ boll for a firlot	02 – 2
It of bear meal said day	04
It Thurdsay 19th April of oat meal . .	10
It of bear meal	06
It of pron five good pecks	1 – 8
It Monday 7th May of oat meal 8 stone and of bear meal 6th	10
It Saturday for the two men and the other three of bear and oat meal . . .	07 –
It Friday the 1st June of oat meal and a third bear meal	03
To Alexr. Kennedy two pecks meal from Sanders more's wife	00 – 0 – 2
To him of bear and oat meal . . .	02
To Kennedy to begin Sunday 22nd April of bear meal	01 – 8
To oat meal said day	01
To Kennedy oat and bear meal 21st May .	01
To Kennedy of oat meal	00 – 8

[This account appears to cover five months. It amounts to 100 stones, and is therefore at the rate of 240 stones per annum, which would allow each of the men 6 bolls apiece, and leave 12 bolls for 'the other three.' Six bolls is the customary allowance for farm servants, who receive victuals as part of their wages at the present day.]

[Page sixteen. 1770.]

Ane acct. of what white oats I sold of Cropt 1769 payable martinmas.

	B.	f.	p.
Impr to Invernahaven per bill [1] . . .	25		
It to three tenants in Inverbromie three firlots each	2	3	0

[1] Entry duplicated on p. 11 of the Account Book.

		B.	f.	p.
It	to John Shaw in Inchkanch of Kinrara .	00 –	1 –	0
It	to my son William	00 –	3	
It	to ffaryr McAlbea [1] in Leald [4] . . .	00 –	2 –	0
It	to William Gow in Pitourie . . .	00 –	1 –	0
It	to the Sherriff officer in Pitchurn [2] . .	00 –	1 –	0
It	to Alex. Meldrum in the Isle of Dollnavert [3]	00 –	2 –	0
It	to Wm Mcpherson son to Thomas Roy in Dolbrady of rye	00 –	1 –	0
It	to Peter Grant McGregor in Kinrara of Rye	00 –	3 –	0
It	of white oats to Sanders McIntosh [4] in Prossnacallich	00 –	2 –	0
It	Sanders Duncan Davidson Dolphour [5] .	00 –	2 –	0
It	Wm McDonald Achnabochin [4] . .	00 –	2 –	0
It	to James Grant in Kinrara . . .	00 –	2 –	0
It	to the Boatman Gordon	00 –	1 –	0
It	to John Roy in Kincraig [4] . . .	00 –	1 –	0
It	to McGlashan [4] upon acctt. of James Grant in Kinrara	00 –	1 –	0
It	of small oats from Dunachton to Lach: Toshach	1 –	1 –	0
It	of the small oats at Kincraig to Peter Dow in Achnabochin [4]	2 –	2 –	0
It	to Alexr McKenzie Gardiner from Kincraig	1 –	0 –	0
It	to McQuibon in Torness . . .	1 –	0 –	0
It	to James more Grant in Kinrara . .	3 –	2 –	0
It	to the widow in Pitourie . . .	0 –	2 –	0
It	to Lachlan [6] for his horses . . .	0 –	1 –	0
It	to Wm. Grant ffactor to Rothie [7] out of Dun:	4 –	0 –	0
It	to Wm. McDonoll [4] in Achnabochin out of Do.	0 –	2 –	0
It	to McQuibon of Lachie's oats . . .	0 –	2 –	0
It	to Lachie of the best white oats for seed .	5 –	2 –	2
It	of hinderen [8] white oats to Do.. . .	5 –	0 –	0

[1] This name has entirely died out or become incorporated with that of Macbean. It was at one time a common local name in Badenoch. See *Northern Chronicle*, July 12, 1905.

[2] Now known as Ballourn. A small farm immediately to the east of Kincraig.   [3] There are two or three cottages here still.

[4] Sub-tenant to Balnespick.   [5] A neighbouring farm.

[6] Balnespick's eldest son, who lived at Kincraig and shared the farm.

[7] Contraction of Rothiemurchus, a property five miles down the river owned by a cadet branch of Clan Grant.

[8] Probably a variety of oat seed.

[Page seventeen.   1771.]

Ane account of what meal I disposed of Cropt 1770.

	B.	f.	p.
Impr to Donald McEvan April 13th of Bear meal nine pecks of good round meal for half boll oat meal payable against Jully or Marts [1]	0 —	2 —	0
It to him said day of miller oat meal . .	0 —	2 —	0
It to James Lee [2] of the millers four pecks and a lippie for which he is to give me a boll meal	1 —	0 —	0

The whole of the multers of Cropt 1769 amount to 9–0–0 of oat meal the above being included

| It of bear meal taken to Dun: 14th May . | 1 — | 1 — | 2 |

[1770.]

| It of bear multer to Dunachton 5th June . | 1 — | 0 — | 2 |

It to Donald McEvan Decbr. 14 ower and above payt, of the thraves fifteen pence.

There was seven bolls and two pecks put in above chist of the multers of oat meal yr was taken out of said meal the 7th Janry

	Stones		
To Dunachton	10		
It to Margrot Rob and Elspet said day being Thursday with a peck of bear . .	0 —	8 —	0
It to the Carpinter friday 15th June of said meal	2 —	0 —	0
It to Mr Shand's man Wednesday 20th .	8 —	0 —	0
It to the Carpinter of meal	1 —	8	

It to him of cash at two times two shillings

| It to the carpinter am not sure how much meal he got last . . . . . . | 1 — | 8 | |

More of cash given him a 20sh note and a sh:

It at annoyer time to the carpinter of cash five sh:

---

[1] This is a duplicate entry with p. 40 of the Account Book.

[2] Lee was part of the time a sub-tenant. He was the wright. The name is an unusual one in the Highlands, and it is possible that he was one of the ploughwrights from the Lothians who were encouraged to come north to introduce better methods.

[Page eighteen.   1770.]

Ane Account of my sowing in Dunachton 1770. By the blessing of God I began sowing friday the 13th of April. The ground being mostly covered with snow and frost for seven weeks preceeding from said date. There was only one rig sown with Rye friday.

	B.	f.	p.
Saturday the 14th sown in the Gardeners Croft of Rye	00 —	2 —	0
Said day a firlote grass [1] seed with Rye one rig clean	0 —	1 —	0
It in two furthest east rigs of white oats .	00 —	0 —	$3\frac{1}{4}$
It in the Croft of Lagnamer [2] of white oats .	00 —	2 —	3
It on the Croft on this side at the Gate .	00 —	1 —	2
It on the inside of the Park at the west on Monday the 16th April . . .	00 —	2 —	3
	[3] 02 —	3 —	$3\frac{1}{4}$
It said day of small oats in the Park . .	2 —	0 —	0
It April the 26th sown of small oats . .	2 —	2 —	0
It the 30th		3 —	0
It Saturday 5th May	2 —	0 —	0
It in a sack to be sown	1 —	1 —	0
It sown of small oats friday	1 —	2 —	2
	10 —	0 —	2
It of bear Monday 28th May . . .	00 —	2 —	2

[Page 19.   1771.]

By the blessing of God I began sowing on Thursday 4th April 1771.

	B.	f.	p.
Impr said day sown in Laginamer and on the side next the road of Gartannagowr [4] all to ane old stacke at the east end above of cropt .	01 —	0 —	0

[1] The only example of the sowing of grass seed in the Account Book. It was a most exceptionally early date, for there is an old letter showing that fully twenty years later grass seed was most difficult to buy in Inverness.

[2] A meadow of about three acres in the birch woods near the house. It is now used as grazing, as it is too small and inaccessible to be worth cultivating.

[3] This total covers white oats only.

[4] Patches of clearing in the birch-covered slopes below the farm.

		B.	f.	p.
It	on the side next the wood of my own white oats	00 –	0 –	2
It	of my own oats on the west end of Croftnacore [1] within the dyke . . .	00 –	0 –	2
It	of white oats within Dunachton on Achnabochin [2]	01 –	0 –	0
It	on the east end of Croftnacore . . .	00 –	2 –	0
It	of Rye sown on Dun: and Achnabochin clean	00 –	2 –	0
It	of Rye in Rush with six pecks lauder white oats	01 –	0 –	0
It	of peas sown on the gardeners Croft of the best peas	01 –	0 –	0
It	on the two small rigs next the kitchen of bad peas	00 –	0 –	2½
		05 –	1 –	2½
	Sown on the east end of Croftnacore of small oats being Saturday 13th April of which the leys six firlots . . .	02 –	2 –	0
	Then came on snow and drift the most disagreeable weather that would be Tuesday 16th None could go out of doors and no cattle got water. It pleased God Thursday 18th that the thaw came on.			
	There was sown Monday the 22nd of the oats I bought from the smith and from Kylintuie part Tuesday . . .	4 –	0 –	0
	To the west of the ground the bear was in of the Kincraig oats	3 –	1 –	0
It	more of the said oats twixt the bear ground and the bank above the water . .	1 –	1 –	0
It	of said oats	0 –	2 –	0
It	of the oats of the Park . . .	1 –	0 –	2
		12 –	2 –	2

[Page twenty.   1770.]

Ane acctt. of what bottles is twixt here and Kincraig 21 Janr 1770.

	doz.	botts.
Impr under Ale at Kincraig	10	5
It in the rack of bottles	3	10

[1] Patches of clearing in the birch-covered slopes below the farm.
[2] An example of Balnespick's sowing on part of one of the runrig subfarms.

	doz.	botts.
It with Mr Edward in Borrowing . .	4	00
It with McPhadruck's wife . . .	1	00
It under Port wine here	1	04
It under white wine and vinegar . . .	0	05
It under Rum and Whyskie . . .	0	04
It under Ale	0	4
It under Porter at Kincraig . . .		2
It in Mrs Roses		2
	22	00

There came from Garmouth in June under wine

It four dozen more under wine . . . 04 · 00

Ane acct of money given in borrowing to different poor people.[1]

Impr to James McPhadruck in Kylintuie to buy a horse £1		Pd
It to John Meldrum at the White Milln .	5sh	Pd
It to Alexr. the Smith's wife . . .	5sh	
It to Lachlan Toshach to buy hay . .	4sh	
It to Donald Roy in Caritnakyle Jully 2nd and at anoyer time	2sh	Pd
It to Sanders more the Weaver for which am to have days service	2sh	Pd
August 21 given Donald Dow McQueen to buy salt[2]	12 – 6	Pd
Janry 21 given little ffaryr in Borrowing .	4 – 0	
It given Sanders McDonol at Aban . .	1 – 0 – 0	
It to young John Dow in Dun : payable the 15th Janr at St Coms[3] Market . .	1 – 0 – 0	
It to Donald Gordon in ffarletter[4] of ten sh: May 22	0 – 10 – 0	
It to James Le ½ guinea	0 – 10 – 6	
It to the Smith	0 – 06 – 0	
It to Donald Roy Campboll . . .	0 – 01 – 0	
It to Donald Dow McQueen when going to Ins.[5]	0 – 02 – 0	

[1] This part of the page was apparently written at another time from the first part. Its probable date is 1770 or 1772. The word ' paid ' was evidently added some time after the entries. All the names, with the exception of Donald Gordon, and possibly Toshach, were those of sub-tenants.

[2] No doubt for his cattle.

[3] A market held on St. Colum's Day, probably one of the five fairs at Ruthven.   [4] A farm just across the Spey.

[5] Probably a contraction of Inverness. About forty miles off by road.

[Page twenty-one. 1770.]

Ane account of the days that my servants entered my service and Lachie's July 1770

Monday 4th Jully both the McGlashans [1] entered

They had meat in the house till after breakfast Thursday which day they got of oat and bear meall 8 stones.

Sanders Faryr's [2] son entered the same day

Hugh entered some days sooner.

The number of hands employed in peeling the oak Bark in the year 1770 178

Sent to Inverness 25th Jully of said bark 33 hirps [3] amounting to 21 bolls of which discounted for damaged bark etc 2 bolls so that I only got bill for . . . . . £8 – 11 – 0

August the 7th delivered at Elgin to Mr Alexander Duff shoemaker [4] 22 bolls 3 firlots at . . . . . £11 – 06 – 06

There was 18 carts [5] for the bark sent to Elgin.

It for three carts more sent to Mr. Duff by Lachie . . . . . . 01 – 19 – 0

It to Mr Shaw 14 bolls and 2 of the old bark 06 – 08 – 0

[Page twenty-two. 1770.]

Dunachton 14th Jully 1770 counted with Duncan McBain mercht at Inch. [6] I recovered in part payt of his bill and for Whyskie ten shillings payed by him upon my account to the Smith's wife and John Meldrum five to each . . . . £00 – 10

It payed to him for two salmon. . . [7] 07 – 10½

It of cash given me . . . . . 07 – 0

———————————

01 – 04 – 10½

[1] These were evidently the two McGlashans who were sub-tenants in Kylintuie.

[2] Probably Sanders more, Faryr McAlbea's son. The family was on Luald as cottagers, and then became sub-tenants on Dunachtonmore.

[3] Probably a measure of some kind.   [4] To be used for tanning.

[5] They must have each contained 1 boll 1 firlot of bark. As bark is not a very heavy substance, this shows that they cannot have been the primitive skellachs used in 1795 in Ross and Caithness. See Sir J. Sinclair's *Survey of the Northern Counties*, p. 96.

[6] A small hamlet on the other side of the Spey.

[7] This was rather a high price according to eighteenth-century standards.

It given the fox killer Duncan Cameron all he
     was due [1] . . . . . . £ 17 - 0
Impr given said Duncan eight pints and a chapon
     whyskie at . . . . . 00 17 -
It to Cathelus McPherson in Island dow for
     20 pints . . . . . . 1 - 13 - 4
It to my son the Captain 20 pints at . . 1 - 13 - 4
It to Borlum 10 pints for his feyrs burialls . 00 - 18 - 4
It to Alexr. McIntosh the miller 16 pints at . 01 - 09 - 4
It to my son the Captain a boll malt . . 00 - 16 - 00
It to Cathelus a boll at .. . . . 00 - 16 - 00

Given by Peter McDonoll upon my acct. to Sanders more
the weaver a peck meal for which he charges 13 pence.

And to Sanders Shaw the cupar to the value of twenty two
pence half penny Scots

[1771.]
Dunachton 27 May then recieved from John McIntosh in
Keepoch payment of the mare he bought from me last spring in
1771.

[Page twenty-three.]
Monday the 8th Jully 1771.
Said day there's in vault 2 dozen and one bottle of port one
bottle rum and 2 ankers also five bottles Malaga and in the press
there was a bottle of the port taken out when Aberlour was here.
Ane account of borrowed money by different people

Impr to Sanders McDonoll at Aban [2] . . 01 - 00 - 00
It to John Dow McAlbea payable St Coms
     Day last 01
It to James Lee Cartwright . . . 10 - 06
It to Donald Gordon . . . . . 00 - 10 - 00
It to John McIntosh in Keepock . . 00 - 10 - 00
It to Donald Robertson in Dunachton more . 2 - 16

[All the items on this page, except the Smiths, have ' paid ' written on them.
With the exception of Gordon and James more Grant, the borrowers were all
sub-tenants to Balnespick in Dunachton.]

[1] Before game was preserved, foxes were ' extreamly destructive of sheep
and poultry.'
[2] This is also mentioned as ' the new ground.' It seems to have been
near Cluanach ; it cannot long have remained in cultivation.

It to little Faryr in Dun: more march last . 00 – 04
It to the Smith upon Mrs Stuarts acct. . . 00 – 06

                                                6 – 16 – 6

It given James Lee Jully 24 a guinea note of
    which he gave me 3 sh and sixpence The
    ballance 17 sh 6 he is due me a gang of
    spokes which is 18 – 6 Am due him
    upon Donol Grants account 16 and a sh
    for newes
It to James more Grant in Kinrara [1] . . 1 – 0 – 0

[Page twenty-four. 1770.]

August the 5th I began cutting my hay   I had six men three
days at a sh: each, the season was very favourable the first four
days.   But friday came rain and very heavy showers most even-
ings till the 14th.

                                                         Carts.
I put into the Barns Friday 12 carts Load and thereafter
    sixteen making a whole 28
It in a stack made by George [2] 19th August . . . 46
It in the stack made by John more McAlbea and in the
    oyr stack brought up Saturday 24
It in the stack made on the midow that was cut to the
    west of the dyke 20
                                                       ——
                                                       118

Wednesday 19th Sepbr. I began by the blessing of God to
cut my (other ?) kind of cropt at Dunachton.

                                            Th. st. sh.
Said day cut of Rye on the Croft not good . 10
It of peas with rye and clean . . . 16
It Thursday the rain came on so did not cut
    any till 24th then cut my ten thrave
    white oats 10
It within the Park cut of small oats preceeding
    the 1st Octr. 105
It of white oats on Lagnamore 8th . . 23

---

[1] This man is mentioned in Lachlan's papers. He went to America.
[2] Balnespick's third son.

	Th.	st.	sh.
It on Gartangowr	17 –	0 –	0
It on the west end of the Park . . .	16 –	0 –	0
It of small oats on the east end of the Park .	35 –	0 –	0
	232 –	0 –	0

I had cut of bear at Dunachton at and pro-
    ceeding the 30th Sepbr. . . . 40
It at Kincraig of bear not very good . . 60

                      332

    Since the 19th Sepr. yr was hardly four days dry till the snow came on the corns the 12th Novr. my little cropt was only housed the last of it friday 31st Novr.

[Page twenty-five. Undated.]
    Bought of McIntosh Shaw and Company 11 barrs Iron weighing 24 stons.
    Sold of said iron to Lachie my son and to James Lessle in Kinrara
    Affter which remained 28 pieces of which to Lachie for shoing his mare and for swivles to his horse tethers
It to Lachie Monday 7th Octbr. a large piece
It to Sanders McIntosh Miller in Dun: the 9th Octbr. a large piece
It for my own use to make bands etc
It Iron to Mrs Shaw of Keepock
It to Lachlan in August of Iron
It to Sanders McIntosh miller of double double nails 30 of double nails 40
It to those brought home by Duncan Bain of double doubles 120 and the same number of doubles Ocbr. 9th
It brought out for my own use of those nails that Duncan Bain brought home of double doubles 62 of doubles 60 for the door of the barn etc:

[Page twenty-six.]
    Dunachton in October of date in the left of the stable 24 pieces of iron that weighed about   20 – 0 – 0
Taken out for making bands etc for my own use 19th Octbr. . . . .   10 – 0

Given Donald McDonald[1] in Dunachton Beg the use of the
four pound sterling but I am due him one anker whyskie
of the account received from Donald 30 sh: and one
anker whyskie at 21 sh: with three chopins at 2 sh:
and six pence.

To Peter McIntyre in Glenfeshie the use of one half-crown
March 27th, 1771 Pd at his return

It to Donald Gordon[2] the use of four Pd sterling 22nd May

Recovered from the above Donald by cash, whiskie and his
shoes the above four Pd Str all but six shillings and ten
pence May 13th 1771

Dun: 12 Nov then recovered from Sanders McIntosh[1] in
Prossnacallich twenty one pound and six pence[3] as payment of what he was due for oats since last year ½ boll
oats given him last year and ½ guinea borrowed money
I have eighteen pence more for want of change that
am due him

Said day given Rob the Mason five and six pence with six
firlots lime to make seven sh: given him formerly and 12
stone meal as also eight sh: when he paid for his watch.[4]

[Page twenty-seven. 1770.]

Ane Account of what money I received from Lachie since
August last 1770.

Impr I had a twenty sh: note sent me when the
sheeps were sent for to the South and
three and ten from McDonald in whole
as also 20sh: as balance of McDonald's.

Paid out as follows upon his Account.[5]

Impr to Sanders Bain half yrs wages . . .	01 – 00 – 00
It to Rob Polson	01 – 00 – 00
It to John Polson[6]	00 – 16 – 08
It to Donald Stuart and his wife . . .	01 – 01 – 10
It to Sanders more Cameron . . .	00 – 14
It to Mary Bean Mary Rob and Isabel Shaw.	08
It paid to Hugh	00 – 16 – 08
It to Tamos Lee for two carts . . .	00 – 10 – 00

---

[1] Sub-tenants. [2] Servant.

[3] Scots currency, equal to £1 15s. 6d. sterling.

[4] It seems unlikely that this was a timepiece. It may have been his share
towards the watch on foxes(?). [5] I.e. Lachlan's account.

[6] He always signed his name Wilson ; he was at one time a private in
Lachlan's company.

It pd. for a small rough hide and ½ a hide
      tanned .   .   .   .   00 – 09 – 06
It pd. for a dozen hooks .   .   .   .   00 – 04 – 00
It for making shoes for your servants .   .   00 – 04 – 00
It six stone and three pound iron .   .   .   00 – 16 – 08
It pd the Kincardon woman [1] .   .   .   00 – 02 – 06
It to the men that cut his hay in the midow .   00 – 04 – 00
                                        ─────────────
                                        £08 – 10 – 06

Iron given Lachlan 8th jully 1771 22 pd.

[Page twenty-eight.   1771.]
      Ane account of White oats disposed of to different people of
Cropt and of peas.

Impr to Donald Robertson [2] for 20 sh: ready money	01 –	3 –	0
It to Johnathan Ross wright in Ruthven at five	00 –	2 –	0
It to McPhadruck I mean James his son [2] .	00 –	1 –	0
It to William Davidson in Ballinlon per bill .	00 –	2 –	0
It to Wm. Cameron in Ballinrish and his ffaryr in law	01 –	0 –	0
It to Sanders McIntosh [2] miller . . .	00 –	01 –	0
It to Donald Roy McDonall in Laggan [3] .	00 –	01 –	0
It to Sanders McKenzie Gardner [2] . .		1 –	0
It to Sanders mors son my servant [2] . .		1 –	0
It of peas sold at 15 pence per peck to John more [2]	00 –	01 –	0

                                        ─────────────
                                        06 – 03 – 0

It to Peter Robertson's wife [2]   .   .   . [4] 00 – 0 – 0½
It twixt David on Dunachton more [2] and
      Kennoth [5] .   .   .   .   .   .   00 – 0 – 1
It to James McPhadruck's wife [2] .   .   .   00 – 0 – 1
It to Alexr. McIntosh Miller [2]   .   .   .   00 – 0 – 1
It to William Campboll's wife [2] .   .   .   00 – 0 – 1
It to John Roy Campboll's wife [2]   .   .   00 – 0 – 0½
It to Alexr. McDonall in Dun: beg [2] .   .   00 – 0 – 1
All the above is charged on the oyr side first page.
      [The entries on this page are evidently incomplete.]

      [1] A place-name farther down the river.
      [2] People on Dunachton and Kincraig.
      [3] A district higher up the river.
      [4] The measures in this column are evidently bolls, firlots, and pecks ; they
refer to purchases of peas.   [5] Kenneth McPhail.

[Page twenty-nine.]

Ane Account of what oats I disposed of Cropt 1770

I bought nine bolls victuall of which six from my son Lachlan, five firlots from the smith and seven from old McPhadruck

(There follows a list of the names upon the first part of page twenty-eight.)

The above is at the ten Pd[1] Marts payt.

It of peas at 15 pence ready money or sixteen to such as will not pay in May.

(There follows the list of persons given on the second half of page twenty-eight with the amounts purchased.)

[Page thirty. 1770–1771.]

Ane account of small oats disposed of Cropt 1770

Impr to Sanders McIntosh Miller[2] . . .	03 – 2 – 0[3]	
It to William McDonald in Achnabochin[2] .	02 – 1 – 0	
It to John McIntosh in Dun : more[2] . .	1 – 1 – 0	
It to one McDonald in Galvie[4] of my own oats and five firlots of what I had from McGlash: for which he pd ready money money at eight sh: per boll . . .	01 – 0 – 0	
	08 – 0 – 0	
Given John McIntosh[2] in Kincraig upon Acctt of Dun: McIntosh Servant to Captain Grant in the Regt. . . .	00 – 6 – 8[5]	
Jully given him to buy bear meal for my use .	02 – 4	
Sepr 1771 then given a hide to Samuel Davidson[2] in Croft payable Whitsunday at 9 sh: str.[6]	9 – 0	
It one half hide given John McIntosh shoe maker in Dunachton more[2] . . .	5 – 6	
It to Donald Dow Shoe maker in Pitchurn a large half hide at	10 – 6	

Donald McQueen[2] payed the half hide he got

Samuel paid the nine shillings for the hide

[1] Scots currency.
[2] People on the Davoch.
[3] Bolls, firlots, and pecks.
[4] Gallavie, a place-name.
[5] Evidently £ s. d. sterling.
[6] The Samuel Davidson mentioned on this page was a member of a very large family which is constantly mentioned in the Account Book. They have died out in Badenoch, but there are descendants in Strathdearn, tenants on the land of old Balnespick's great-great-grandson.

[1771.]

It to the Gardner in cash April 18th six sh: str..When going to take instrument agt Borllum a shilling

It to the Gardner to be given Pitchurn 3 and sixpence and two more the day Mrs Stuart was buried to buy meal

It when going Ins: after Lachie 11th Jully   5 sh:

[Page thirty-one. 1771.]

Ane Account of my sowing April the 4th by the blessing of God I began sowing peas on the Gardiners Croft 1771 . . .   1 – 0 – 0 [1]

It of hinderon peas on the 2 rigs next the Kitchen . . . . . .   0 – 0 – 2½

It of Captain Leslie's oats in Laginamore and the part next the road till the old stack in the east end . . . . .   1 – 0 – 0

It one the Side next the wood of my own white oats . . . . . .   0 – 0 – 2

It on the west end of Croftnacore within the Park . . . . . .   0 – 2 – 2

It on the east end of Do. of said white oats .   0 – 2 – 0

It in the Lands of Achnabochin of clean Rye   0 – 2 – 0

It of Rye and Hinderon white oats twixt said ground and Paul's yr was ten pecks of white oats and six of rye [2] . . .   1 – 0 – 0

It of clean white oats twixt said lands . .   1 – 0 – 0

It on Croft na core within the Dyke of small oats . . . .   12 – 2 – 2

It on Achnabochin of small oats with two pecks of birlie mixed   2   3

It on Paul's land of small oats . . .   2 – 2 – 0

It on Paul's land 4th May . . . .   0 – 3 – 0

It on said day of birlie which day by the blessing of God I had done my oat seed . .   1 – 2

   24 – 3 – 2

From the 13th April till friday 19th yr was no plowing nor sowing till the 22nd with snow and drift. Tuesday 16th being

---

[1] The measures are bolls, firlots, and pecks.

[2] Paul McPhail had died the year before, and Balnespick was evidently cultivating his share of Auchnabeuchin.

the coarsest day ever seen, nae beast would go out of doors, dry wind and frost nights from 22nd April till the 4th May.

The 9th May sown within the dyke	. .	00 –	2 – 2
It of bear twixt muck and tathing	. .	1 –	0 – 1½
It on Achnabochin in muck	. . .	0 –	0 – 0½
		1 –	3 – 0

By the blessing of God I had done 21st May.

[Page thirty-two. 1771.]

Ane account of what meal was sold of the 20 bolls bought of the farms of Dalcross[1] June and Jully 1771

	B.	f.	p.
Impr. to Alexr. McIntosh Prosnacalach[2] . .	2 –	0 –	0
It Peter Callum[2] in the new Possession by the Clune	1 –	0 –	0
It to John Dow McDonal in Tommuckach[2]	1 –	0 –	0
It to Sanders McKenzie Gardner[2] and Donald Roy Campboll[2] half boll each . .	1 –	0 –	0
It to John McPherson in Pitchurn of said meal	1 –	0 –	0
It to Samuel in Clonach[2]	1 –	0 –	0

[Page thirty-three. 1770.]

Ane Account of what victual I bought of Cropt 1770.

	B.	f.	p.
Impr. from McPhadruck	1 –	3 –	0[3]
It from Alexr. the Smith	1 –	1 –	0
It from Lachlan my son[4]	6 –	0 –	0
	9 –	0 –	0
It of oat meal from Lachlan preceeding the 4th May	3 –	0 –	0
It the 9th of bear skilling	0 –	3 –	0
It from Sanders more miller bear meal . .	3 –	0 –	2
It from Lachie May 29th of meal oats . .	1 –	0 –	0
It from the miller June 6th bear meal . .	0 –	3 –	2
It from Clury[5] the 12th of bear meal . .	2 –	0 –	0

[1] Dalcross, in the parish of Croy, on the Moray Firth. This estate is mentioned, in C. Fraser Mackintosh's *Letters of Two Centuries*, as valuable corn-producing land.   [2] People on the Davoch.

[3] Bolls, firlots, and pecks.   [4] See p. 29 of the Account Book.

[5] Clury in Strathspey rented by a relation of Balnespick's wife.

[All the people and places on this page are connected with the Davoch with the exception of the purchase of Dalcross corn, and that from Clury and from John McPherson in Pitchurn.]

It 20 bolls of meal bought of McIntoshes farms [1]
It carried home for the use of the family by
    Sanders McIntosh in Prosnacallich of
    Kincraig 27th June . . . . 2 – 0 – 0
It by John Dow in Tomnamuckach 2nd Jully 2 – 0 – 0
It by Peter McDonal in the new possession on
    my own horse . . . . . 1 – 0 – 0
Brought home by John McPherson in Pitchurn 2 – 0 – 0
It from Inverness of bear meal at ½ guinea each
    boll . . . . 4 – 0 – 0
            [Page torn here.]

[Page thirty-four.]
I have in the Glen 10th June 1771
Impr of three year old he stots 4
It she three year olds 7
It three cows the millers being one that is, so there's but
    2 cows sent to the bull one of them being with calf
    the other was all winter in the Park . . . 2
Four stirks 3 he and one she 4
The Bull and eight 2 yearolds he and she . . . 9
                          26

Theres 11 cows at home of which with the millers cow
    makes nine that is with calf and two ferry [2] cows . 11
Theres at home 2 year old she stirks at Kin: and one at
    Dunachton 3
                          40

Theres in the Glen June 28th of my cattle
Impr 4 three yearolds he 4
It of 3 year olds she 7
It of 2 yearolds he and she 6
It of year olds 4
It a bull and the cow that was in the Park . . . 2

Jully 25th all the cattle I have in the hill is of 3 yearold stots 4
It of three yearold queys 7
It of two year olds last May 6
It the young cow that was in the Park all winter and the
    bull and the Dollnavert ox not yet found . . 2
Theres at home 12 cows and the bull and six stirks and a 2
    yearold

[1] Referring to p. 32.   [2] A barren cow.

[Page thirty-five. 1770.]

Ane account of what lime stone[1] was carried out of the Quarry by Mr McLean.

At and preceeding the 3rd Jully 1771 of loads . . . 278
It Jully the 13th of Loads at 9 ston each load[2] . . 260

[Page thirty-six. 1771.]

Ane accot. of the number of people that I had peeling the oak bark having begun Thursday 4th Jully 1771

	Days	Pay
Impr William Campboll in Tomnamuckach .	1	8
It John McPherson in Pitchurn . . .	1	8
It friday the fifth ½ the day the rain having come one the fors and two making one day[3]	1	8
My servant Donold and Donald McEvan .	1	8
Alexr. McDonald in Aben and Wm. Mc-Pherson Dun:	1	8
Thomas McPherson in Pitchurn and Sanders more Lachlan's man	1	7
Alex. More McDonal and Peter Rob: in Dun: beg	1	6
Saturday 6th Sanders More and Sd Peter in D. beg	2	10
John McPherson and Pitchurn . . .	1	8
Alexr. McBean in Leold	1	7
Thomas McPherson in Pitchurn . . .	1	7
Donald McEvan in Achnabochin . .	1	6
Donald Kennedy my servant . . .	1	6
Donald Sanders mores son in Dun: beg . .	½	3
	14½	8 – 4

Tuesday the 9th I had ten at work
Both the Sanders McIntosh ½ day each . . 1   8
Kennoth McPhail 1   7

[All the men mentioned, with the exception of the McPhersons in Pitchurn, were on the Davoch.]

[1] Even when the *First Statistical Account* was written in 1792, lime was only used by the lairds and larger farmers.
[2] The load of stone that the carts now used in the Highlands would carry would be about 27 stone.
[3] Apparently the men worked in pairs for a half day, and each pair received wages for one man's full day's work.

	Days	Pay
McGlashan and Donald Roy my servant .	2	12
Peter Robertson and Angus Dow miller . .	2	12
John Roy and John Dow	2	14
Faryr in Leold and son.	2	13
	19	5 – 6[1]
	24	13 – 10

[Page thirty-seven. 1771.]
Carried from the oyr side of men and cash

	men	cash
18 men Wednesday the 10th		
The Sanders McIntosh	2	1 – 4
Sanders McDonald in Aben and his broyr peter .	2	1 – 4
Sanders nephew Sandy the cooper and ken: McPhail	2	1 – 2
Donald Roy Campboll and the miller Angus Don	2	1 – 0
McGlashan and Donald Roy my servant . .	2	1 – 0
Donald Gordon in ffarletter and Charls Campboll yr	2	1 – 4
John Roy and John Dun: kincraig . . .	2	1 – 2
Faryr McLean in Leold and John Don . .	2	1 – 0
Geo: McDonald servant to James Roy[2] James McP. Leold	2	1 – 0
	18	10 – 2

These 11 Sanders McIntosh Prosnacalich John
    Roy John Don Fr: and son Peter Robertson
    the miller James Angus Don and John Roy in
    D. beg Lach: Shaw James Roys servant Geo:
    Donald Gordon and Charles Campbell in
    ffarletter
The above people were only peeling the trees yt
    were cast the night before which was done
    with heavie rain for fear the bark would stick
10 Saturday of the above number to make out the
    deficance of Thursday

[All the men, with the exception of those from Farletter, were on the Davoch.]

1 Five shillings and sixpence.
2 The sub-tenant of the largest holding on Kincraig.

	men	cash
Donald Gordon in ffarletter	I	0 – 8
John Roy and John Don	2	1 – 4
James McPherson and Faryr and son . .	3	1 – 7
James Roy's man Geo: and Donald Roy Campboll	2	1 – 0
McGlashan and John Dow	2	1 – 1
Donald Roy my man	I	6

Thursday 18th Jully theres in the stable 2 short pieces and long piece iron and the anker of iron said day taken out 13 pound 7 once for shoeing the mare.

[Page thirty-eight.   1768–1769.]

Theres four hunder ston of hay sold to John Grant vintner in Aviemore at five pence per ston the best hay and three pence hay that was partly damaged of Cropt 1768

Impr delivered his servant by my gardner the 8th Novr.	39 stones
It delivered his servant by myself 19th Decr. .	37
It delivered to John Grant by myself . . .	80
It Janry 26th delivered by the Gardner . .	47
It ffebry 7th delivered by myself . . .	205
	408

To Alexr. McDonald [1] the smith of hay . .	4
To Alexr. McIntosh [1]	2
To Donald McGlash: [1]	2
To William McDonald in Achnabochin [1] . .	4
To Alexr. McKenzie Gardner Dunachton [1] . .	6
To Mr Scott's servant	5

Sold of the hay 1769

Impr to John Grant of Aviemore of the hay from the midow 12 August	105
It 20th Sepr. of sd hay	171
It of the hay of the parks said day not good .	133
It 3rd of Dito hay out of the Burn . . .	030

January 22nd 1773 Then received of James McBean Parks £2 : 19 as payt. of his bill he having kept a shilling that he payd the Smith in part of his bill.

---

[1] People upon the Davoch.

[Page thirty-nine.   1769 (?).]

Ane account of what money and meal was given to McGlashan [1] and Donald Roy [2]

Impr to McGlashan in part payt. of the month he
    served first   .   .   .   .   .   00 – 03 – 0
It for a firlote meal   .   .   .   .   .   00 – 04 – 6
It given him to buy shoes the day he went for
    Elgin with the Bark   .   .   .   .   00 – 01 – 6
It given him by William Callum to support
    his horse   .   .   .   .   .   .   00 – 00 – 6
It to Donald Roy to be given his ffaryr in spring
    last   .   .   .   .   00 – 02
It St Coms Day half guinea   .   .   .   00 – 10 – 6
It at Inverness over and above his expences   .   00 – 01
It when going to Elgin with the bark   .   .   00 – 00 – 6
It given McGlashan to buy meal for his wife
    and children   .   .   .   .   .   00 – 02 – 0
It the 20th Novr. to his wife   .   .   .   00 – 02 – 0
It given Margaret McBean John Dows
    daughter to be sent to buy shoes   .   .   00 – 01 – 0

[Page forty.   1771.]
DEBIT
    Ane account of what I am due Mr Shand [3]
Impr in the year 1769 for wine and oyr articles   .   £05 – 03 – 10
It to three dozen Port and Malaga in 1770   .   02 – 08 –
It to 4 dozen in April 1771   .   .   .   03 – 16
It of cash left in my hands in part payt. of the
    bargain of spars and deals [4] bought from
    McIn: [5]   .   .   .   .   .   .   20 – 00 –
                      £31 – 07 – 10

CREDIT
Impr advanced to James Bell upon Mr Shand's
    Acct.   .   .   .   .   01 – 10 – 00
It to John More Shaw for bringing in of deals
    and barks to 30 dozen .   .   .   .   00 – 12 – 06

---

[1] The McGlashans were servants to Balnespick for three years, but their names appear as subtenants during that time.   They paid rent for their holding.
[2] Farm servant.   [3] *I.e.* I owe Mr. Shand.
[4] The Spey timber trade was an important industry.   The York Company was still operating.   In *Memoirs of a Highland Lady* the descriptions of the floating of the timber read like an account of the backwoods of Canada.
[5] Mackintosh.

CREDIT

It for the Cross Cut Saw	00 – 12 – 00	
It to eight stone meall to your servants . .	00 – 13 – 00 [1]	
It for six firlots small oats sent to Kinrara for		
your horses	0 – 12 – 00	
It for six stone hay sent to Do. . . .	00 – 03 – 00	
It for eighteen bolls Bark as yrs a discount of		
2 bolls for eight sh: per boll . . .	07 – 04 – 00	
It to Wm.[2] my son for 100 Ston hay sent to		
McLean	02 – 10 – 00	
It to three men for one day binding it in ropes		
for carriage	00 – 02 – 00	
It for 20 bolls down wieght of Bark . .	08 – 00 – 00	
It to James Grant in Kinrara for making my		
spar wood	00 – 09 – 03	
It to Sanders Shaw on Kinrara for bringing in		
to Spey 31 Dozen Deals and 2 dozen		
Backs Sepr. 4th	08 – 00	

£22 – 15 – 09

[Page forty-one.   1771.]

The 22nd August 1771 I began by the blessing of God cutting my hay

Thursday the 8th Sepbr. Alexr. McKenzie[3] Alexr. Shaw[4] and John McGlash was cutting said day and Friday till four o'clock.

Thursday 12th said three were cutting as they were friday and saturday.

Sanders McKenzie and Sanders Shaw began to cut in the bushes[5] Thursday the 19th and continued till five o'clocke friday the 20th when the rain obliged them to give up at all those different times.

Saturday 21st they began in the morning but the water[6] and rain obliged them to give up in less than an hour as the water got under all they cut then and the day before and under the cocks of hay that was on the lower part of the meadow which obliged me to remove them to higher ground. The water was not so high since April as this day

The remaining part of the hay was cut by Mackenzie and
[Page torn here.]

[1] Duplicate entry, see p. 17 of the Account Book.
[2] Balnespick's second son, Colonel William Mackintosh.
[3] The gardener.   [4] Probably the cooper.
[5] This entry shows how primitive was the old Highland haymaking.
[6] They were probably cutting on the swampy meadows by the river and loch, which are now used for grazing.

[Page forty-two. 1771.]

Wednesday the 18th September was a fine fair day as was
    thursday so that Thursday I housed about 30 carts
    of hay in the barn but they were not so well filled
    so that I dare not judge them to be above 7 stone
    each 30
Tuesday 24th put in a stack 40 carts at 8 st: each which
    is 320 stone 40
Said day in a small cocke to be put in a stack . . 05
It 20 carts thereafter but so damaged that I will not
    make above 12 carts at 8 stone each . . . 12
It was only put together the 9th Novr. . . . 87

[Page forty-three. 1771.]

I began cutting down my bear in the Park by the blessing of
God upon Thursday 26th Sepbr. 1771. By reason of rain and
frost had only done cutting my bear 1st Octbr. and then the peas.
The rain and snow came on the 3rd so that I only cut five thrave
of small oats till the [breaks off here]

		Th.	st.	sh.
Impr of bear in the Park	43	– 00	– 07	
It of the row of bear	45	– 00	– 00	
It of white oats in Auchnabochin all lodged .	37	– 00	– 00	
White oats rush 17 and of Rye 12 . .	29	– 00	– 00	
It of small oats very bad mostly grass . .	72	– 00	– 00	

It of white oats rush and ten thrave rye in			
McPhails	27 – 00 – 00
It of white oats all lodged	19
It of birlie also lodged	15
It of small oats very bad mostly grass . .	30
It of rush and rye half and half . . .	24
It more of the small oats	18

It of the small oats from the Park put into the
    oats barn where the bear is . . . 30
It numbered in the Park of small oats after
    housing the above of which the greater
    part was put in the new barn . . 68
It of white oats the best I have partly damaged
    with wind and cattle and is in the side of a
    stack below very poor small oats . . 26
More of small oats twixt the barn and the stack 112

Th.

Twixt Carstan na Gowr and Lagnahull yrs of
    Captain lesslies oats mostly lodged and
    destroyed mostly with wind and cattle .   50
It is mostly in the stack that has the peas as is
    the rush partly 286

[Page forty-four.]
    Decr. 2nd 1771
    The which day my cattle was viewed by Sandy McDonald [1]
Impr 13 cows one of them from Dellnaverts roup . . 13
  It five threeyearolds last May one of them bought from
    Sanders mors son 05
  It seven queys last May 07
  It five she two year olds last May and two he two year
    olds of the same age 07
  It three she year olds last may and two he . . . 05
  It six stirks or calves and a bull 07

                    44

    Ane Accott. of what cattle I have Janry. 18th 1772
Impr in the buyer 10 load cows and a ferry cow . . 11
  It four she two year olds and 2 he 06
  It of stirks six half he and $\frac{1}{2}$ she 06
  It with John Dow [2] a she 3 year old 01
  It with Sanders McPhadruck 2 three year olds she . . 02
  It with Sanders more in Prosnacaloch a he three year old 1
  It in the Park 4 four yearolds stots 4
  It of queys fouryearolds 7
  It of she three year olds 1
  It of he 3 year olds 2
  It a five year old bull 1

                    42

[Page forty-five.   1771.]
    A list of the meal bought, used and home raised in 1771.
It is practically a duplicate of the list on page 59.

    [1] Probably the head herd of the community and the same individual as
' Sandy of the Straths.'
    [2] Wintering by the tenants was in many districts one of the service dues.

[Page forty-six. 1771 (?).]

James McPhadruck is due for money given him
    to buy whiskie 23rd ffebry. with four
    shillings and six pence given him to
    ballance of money he advanced to John
    McIntosh in Crathie[1] .   .   .   . £2 – 0 – 0
It to James Roy in Park the use of   . .   1 – 1 – 0
It to Samuele in Ballminsach of Crathie 13
    March the use of four Pd sterling to bring
    home a load of whiskie for himself . 4 – 0 – 0
To Sanders Mores son Donald April 12th a
    guinea of which I was due him 3 – 6

[Page forty-seven. 1771.]

    Ane account of what cattle I have March 14th 1772
Impr in the Buyer ten old cows and a ferry cow   . . 11
It of stirks four he and two she 6
It of two yearolds 3 she and 3 he   6
It in the Park 4 four yearold stots   .   .   . 4
It in the Park 2 three year olds one he and one she . 2
It of quies four yearolds 7
It one of the same age that is with old McPhadruck . 1
It with old McPhadruck 2 three yearold hes   . . 2
It with John Don one she 3 yearold .   .   . 1
It with Donald Roys relict 3 yearolds one of them he and
    one she 2
It with Sanders more on Prosnacalich 1 she three yearold 1
It with Wm. McIntosh in Long (?) of Perth four stots
    five and six year old[2] 4
It a bull five yearold in the Park in about the Doors . 1

                                              ————
                                            48
It of sheep[3] the eleven bought and the ram being included 51
It of year olds the 4 bought in Glen: included . . 31

    [1] A local place-name, not the Crathie in Aberdeenshire.
    [2] The age of these animals suggests great shortage in food to make them
so late for the market.
    [3] The earliest mention of sheep, but it is evident that Balnespick had a
few before this date.

[Page forty-eight.]

Ane accott. of money and rent due by the Smith after footing accounts with him Marts 1769

[All through the Account Book variations of this account appear. This one was evidently begun in 1769 and added to from time to time during the next two years, but fuller versions are given in other parts of the book.]

[Page forty-nine. Date uncertain. After 1771 (?).]

Ane account of what I advanced for Donald Robertson[1] and for his relict after his death   a stone meal.

Impr to two stone hay out of my own barn .	£0 - 1 - 0	
It to ten stone hay from ffarletter . .	0 - 5 - 0	
It after his death to his relict a boll barley .	1 - 0 - 0	
It to Donald Campboll's[1] relict on her act: for straw	0 - 2 - 6	
It to James Robertson[1] for the funeral expence	1 - 0 - 0	
It to Kennoth[1] for 2 stone hay . . .	0 - 1 - 0	
It to Lachlan to pay Angus Dow's[2] horse .	2 - 0 - 0	
It to James Roy[1] in Park the use of[3, 6] . .	1 - 1 - 0	
It to Peter McDonal in Garstain Crea of Kinrara[4]	1 - 0 - 0	
It to Alexr. Bain McIntosh in ffarletter to buy bear[5, 6]	0 - 11 - 6	
It to Angus Dow[1] miller Dun: beg . .	9 - 5 - 0	
It to Donald Bain McAlbea[1] in Tomnamuckach[5, 6]	0 - 9 - 0	
It to John McIntosh wright in part of the money I mean the £18 str from his broyr	2 - 0 - 0	
It due by James McPhadruck[1] as ballance of the money given him to buy whiskie .	0 - 3 - 0	
It to James Polson in Pitourie . . .	0 - 2 - 0	
It to Angus Bain in Pitourie to buy Widdes[7,5,6]	0 - 3 - 0	
It to Donald McQueen[1] the use of 20 sh: note[5]	1 - 0 - 0	
It to John Robertson[1] in Kylintuie[5, 6] .	1 - 1 - 0	

[1] People on the Davoch.
[2] The miller.
[3] A duplicate from p. 46.
[4] Duplicate on p. 23.
[5] These entries are duplicated on p. 50 of the Account Book.
[6] These entries are also duplicated on p. 51 of the Account Book.
[7] Part of the old wooden plough.

a stone meal.

It to Sanders more McIntosh[1] the day he set out for Glasgow[2]	£3 – 0 – 0
It to James McPhadruck the day that his wife set for Aberdeen[2]	0 – 2 – 0
It to Alexr. McDonald in Dolphour was given Wm. Campboll upon his account[3] .	1 – 1 – 0
It to PeterMcIntyre in Glenfeshie the use of[3, 4]	1
It to Archie Bain Robertson in Tanour of Kinrara[3, 4]	1 – 0 – 0
It to John Bain's wife Balldon[5] Jully 6th[3] .	3 – 0 – 0

[Page fifty. 1771 (?).]

Received from Donald Cruikshank the ½ guinea that he got in borrowing and 13 and six pence in part of his rent   He is still due the ballance and the ½ crown and the 20 pence for the yard.

[The whole of the rest of the page consists of entries that are duplicates with those on pages 49 or 51. The only difference is that Donald McQueen is said to owe 17s. instead of £1. He had probably repaid 3s.]

[Page fifty-one.]

August 16th given John Glass[1] the use of to buy harness and iron . . .	£2 – 1
It to Samuel McDonoll in Kylehuntly[6] to buy whiskie £4 – 2sh: of which he payd in whiskie	2 – 1
It to Samuele[1] in Clune to buy meal . .	1 – 0
It to Peter McDonoll in Kinrara[3] . .	1 – 2 – 6
It to John McIntosh in the Isle[3] . . .	1 – 0 – 0
It to John McIntosh[1] in Dunachton more[3] .	2 – 0 – 0
It to Donald Roy McDonoll in Laggan[3] .	1
To Alexr. McIntosh in ffarletter[3] . .	11 – 6
To Donald McIntosh[1] in Dunmore[3] . .	0 – 1 – 0

[1] People on the Davoch.

[2] Sanders more McIntosh was a farm servant and McPhadruck one of the sub-tenants.

[3] These entries are duplicated on p. 50 of the Account Book.

[4] These entries are also duplicated on p. 51 of the Account Book.

[5] A hamlet a few miles farther east. The school for which Balnespick collected the dues was there.

[6] A farm on the other side of the river.

To money advanced for the millston[1] all the above being
    cash given in borrowing

To Samuel Davidson	£0 – 1 – 10
To David his broyr	0 – 1 – 10
To the tenants of Clune	1 – 10
To the tenants of Caritnakyle James stuart etc	
To Angus Dow and McGlashan . . .	1 – 10
To John McIntosh and Kennoth . . .	
To the smith's Relict and McIntosh .	
To Samuel in Croft in Borrowing . .	£1 – 0 – 0
To Donald more in Craigan dow in Borrowing	0 – 2 – 0

[Page fifty-two.   Date uncertain.   1770 (?).]
    Ane account if meal given in borrowing

	B.	f.	p.
John McIntosh in the Isle	0 –	1 –	0
To Lachlan Tosh a stone			
Donald more[2] in Craigandow a stone			
James Polson in Pittourie a stone			
To McGlashan's[2] wife a stone			
To Donald Robertson's Relict a stone			
To Samuele[2] as he got home his meal a firlote pron		1 –	0
To Alexr. McIntosh[2] the day he got a stone			
To Lachlan McIntoshes funerals of meal 3 stone[3]			

To John Charles[4] Thursday 17th June being the
    day he began his work one stone meal
Monday the 22nd. of meal to John Charles 2 stone
To John Dow[2] and John Roy[2] two stone
John Charles 4 stone 3rd. Jully
John Charles got in whole of meal preceeding the
    6th Sepbr.[5] two bolls
To Petter McKay Smith in Reats with a ston in
    borrowing the boll is marked on account
    oyr side[5]
ffraser the wright got spars from Kinrara in payt.
    of his wages.   Harvest 1770
Petter Collie got some deal wood in summer 1771

[1] The provision of a new millstone when it was required was one of the
service dues that had to be performed by tenants thirlled to a mill. All the
names noted below were of sub-tenants on the Davoch of Dunachton.
    [2] Sub-tenants.   [3] One of Balnespick's farm servants.
    [4] John Charles Cameron lived at Balnespick. The account does not make
it clear in what capacity he was there.
    [5] The entries relating to these people on p. 59 are possibly duplicates.

[Page fifty-three.]

Ane accott. of money advanced to Petter McDonald mason and to his wife after his death [1]

Impr when she got acct. of her husband's death
in order to bear the expences of the buriall £02 – 16
To the wife to pay the funerall expences of her
sons . . . . 2 – 00
To her when here in Jully 1773 . . . 1 – 00
To her share of the contents of the bill she
accounting for the half of her moyrs . 4 – 03 – 4
_____
9 – 19 – 4 [2]

[1773.]

Having counted with Donald Robertsons Relict
7th ffebry. She is due me . . . £00 – 16 – 6
Jully 31st 1775 given Petter McDonald's relict 1 2
Sepbr. Sent the mason's wife by the blind
woman 1 2

[Page fifty-four. 1772.]

Jully 6th 1772 I began by the blessing of God peeling my bark.

[This page contains a list of names very similar to that on p. 37. He peeled bark three days. On Monday he employed. 7 men ; on Tuesday 22 men ; on Wednesday 20 men. The wages paid are not given. The list of names is given on p. 55.]

[Page fifty-five. 1772.]

By settlement with Mall [3] McPherson in Balnespick [4] for peeling a parcel of oak trees 12 sh: of which payed 4 and 2 at anoyer time.

[1] This page was evidently written at different times. The part down to £9 19s. 4d. was perhaps written at once, the latter part was evidently jotted down.

[2] This was probably partly a gift, not a loan. Balnespick evidently never expected to be repaid, for it does not appear among the list of sums due after his death.

[3] Probably contraction for Malcolm.

[4] This property belonged to Balnespick, who sold it some years before the commencement of the Account Book. He then rented the Davoch of Dunachton and Kincraig from Sir Eneas Mackintosh, but he was still always known as Balnespick. Balnespick lies on the other side of Loch Inch from Dunachton. It is now a small farm.

To Wm. Campboll[1] Donald more[1] in Craigandow and oyrs for
   peeling a large parcel £2 – 10 of which payt. six shillings
   and eight pence to Wm. Campboll.
Payed to those marked on the oyr side[2]
Impr Thomas McPherson Wm. Gow and Alexr. John Dow[1]
   payed Therse Donald More[1] Faryr[1] and the oyr Faryr[1]
   and John McAlister and James McPherson payed   Old
   John Dow[1] and McGlasnan[1] payed.

Ane account of Oak Bark sent to Aviemore for Mr Thom's
Accott.   Jully 10th.

Our six horses being weighed at sight of John Grant Aviemore each cart containing fifteen ston and $\frac{3}{4}$	7 – 3 – 0[3]
Said day on Mr. Grant's two horses . .	2 – 0 – 0
To six carts full	7 – 3 – 0
To 6 carts	7 – 3 – 0
To 6 carts	7 – 3 – 0
The 13th seven carts	8 – 3 – $3\frac{1}{2}$
	42 – 0 – $0\frac{1}{2}$
It sent Mr Duff first	6 – 1 – 1
It sent Sd Duff	8 – 1 – 2
It more to Duff the 12th Sepbr. . . .	ten bolls.

[Page fifty-six.   1772.]

Ane Accott. of what cattle I have Jully 30th 1772 in hill and Strath for the said day	32
It in the Strath over and above the calfs and the bull not mentioned above	22
	52

The different kinds are as follows :

Impr of four and five year old stots	11
It of three year old stots	4
It of two year old stots	3
It of yearold he	4
It of Large cows	13
It of four yearold queys McPhadruck's included . .	8

[1] Sub-tenants on Dunachton.
[2] See p. 54.
[3] Bolls, firlots, and pecks.

It of three yearold queys	6
It of 2 yearolds she	3
It of 1 yearolds she	2
It the Bull 5 years old	1
	—
	55

It Petter Lesslie's son demands 16 sh: and 6 pence for fox
  killing
Due by Donald More in Craigandow of borrowed money
  fourteen sh: and sixpence of the (? ? ?) over and above the
  ballance of the rent etc ffebry 13th 1773
1st of June therse only due of the borrowed money six pence [1]

[Page fifty-seven.   Date uncertain.]
    Ane Account of what money am due the Smith's relict as
per portion of the bond 1772

To her as her share being the 4th . . . £10 –	0 – 0
To Do: as her share of four Pd. discounted by	
Charles Gow in Inverflang in Athole	
where was married with the eldest sister	2 – 0 – 0
To Do: as her share of the four Pd. Str. payed	
by Peter McGlashan	2 – 0 – 0
To cash received from her to part payt. of the	
funeral expences	1 – 0 – 0
	————
	£15 – 0 – 0

[This page relates to the affairs of the widow of McDonald the smith.]

[Page fifty-eight.   1771–1772.]
    Ane account of what meal was made of cropt 1771

	B.	f.	p.
It of bear meal from Pethe [2] 1772 . .	6 –	0 –	3
It of bear meal	5 –	1 –	2½
It from different people at home of bear meal	5 –	1 –	1
It from Dunkeld	1 –	0 –	0
It from Mr Young	2 –	2 –	0
	————		
	20 –	1 –	2½

[Down to the part dealing with the detailed disposal of Cattonach's meal,
this page is a duplicate of p. 45, but is rather clearer.]

[1] A much later entry   [2] Perth.

	B.	f.	p.
It made of my own cropt of oat meal . .	8 –	1 –	0
It of oat meal from Pethe in March . .	4 –	0 –	0
It of the 13 bolls bought from Cattonach [1] .	7 –	0 –	0
It of Mr Young's 44 – 1 taken for the use of the family with what is marked above [2]	13 –	1 –	0
	32 –	2 –	0

Impr sold of Cattonach's meal to the following persons [1]

	B.	f.	p.
To John Dow McAlbea [5] and his son ffaryr [3][5]	1		
To John Don McDonal in Tomnamuckach [4][5]	0 –	1 –	0
To the Smiths relict [5]	1 –	1 –	0
To Samuel Davidson in Clunach [5] . .	1 –	1 –	0
To James McPhadruck [4] and John Rob: [4] in Kylin: [5]	1		
To John Forbes Gardener	1		
	6 –	0 –	0

Payed in whole for bought meal this year £61 – 5sh.

[Page fifty-nine. 1772 (?).]
    Sold of Mr Young's 44 bolls and a firlote as following payable Marts 1773 at 20sh: per boll.

	B.	f.	p.
To John Dow [5] and John Roy [5] in Kincraig .	04 –	0 –	0
To John McIntosh in Isle of Dellnavert .	2 –	0 –	0
To William Campbell [5] and his broyr in law McBean in Pitchurn	2 –	0 –	0
To James McPhadruck [5] and John Robertson [5] in Kylintuie	2 –	0 –	0
To James Stuart in Torraden and Alexr. McDonald [5] in Caritnakyle . .	2 –	0 –	0

[This account is very similar to the one on p. 67, but they refer to different years.]

[1] Apparently 13 bolls were bought from Cattonach. Seven of them were used and six were sold.
[2] On p. 45 this entry is 15 – 1. The same figure is reached if this entry is added to the entry of 2 – 2 – 0 of Mr. Young's meal a little higher up the page. By comparing the figures on p. 59 it is evident that only 11 – 1 bolls were eventually used.
[3] Probably half of the entry on p. 59.
[4] Repeated on p. 59.   [5] People on the Davoch.

	B.	f.	p.
To Donald McGlashan[1] and Sanders McIntosh[1] jointly	1	0	0
To Wm. Dow[1] and Duncan Shaw's relict .	1	0	0
To John McGillivrie[1] and his Aunt Ann .	1	2	0
To Faryr McBean[1] in Luald . . .	1	0	0
To John Dow McAlbea[1] and his son Faryr[1].	2	0	0
To Donald[1] and John More McAlbea[1] .	2	0	0
To Donald Bain McAlbea[1] and James McPherson in Luald and Tomnamuckach[1] .	2	0	0
To Donald McQueen[1] in Dunmore . .	1	0	0
To the Smith's wife[1] and Coll[1] a boll each .	2	0	0
To Peter McDonald[1] above Clunach and in the new land	1	0	0
To Peter McKay in Raits Smith . . .	1	0	1
To Angus Dows wife[1] a boll in whole . .	1	0	0
To John McIntosh wright a boll . . .	1	0	0

To John Charles 2 bolls and to those that cut out the gravil a filot and a firlot for the peeling of the oak bark.

[Page sixty. 1772.]

I began cuting my bear Tuesday 22nd September 1772. Said day cut down in Achnabochin by the blessing of God

	H:	St:	Sh:
Of After muck bear	33		
It on the row to the east of the house of muck and after muck bear as bad as ever was seen	96		
It more of barley and mixed Scots bear . .	10		
	139		
It of white oat rush on Lagnamore and the croft this side (of the road) . . .	35	0	7
It of abused rush and very small bind that was put on the Croft put in the stack above the hay	30	0	
It in said stack from Achnabochin of poor small oats and small bind	35		
It of small oats on Achnabochin part mixed with white oats	57		
It of bad small bind of Rye on said ground .	15		
It of white oats on said ground . . .	9	1	

[1] People on the Davoch.

H: St: Sh:

It of bear as marked above being the whole
    from Achnabochin . . . . 169 – 1
It cut in the West Park of good small oats . 190
It of good white oats yr 019
It of after growth poor put in the little stack 010
It of oats from the strath put in the said stack 030
It put in said stack of Sanders McIntoshes
    oats [1] under hay 13
It put in the bear barn of Sanders oats [1] . 25
Therse of straw and a stack of Rye out of the park.

[Page sixty-one. 1772.]

Theres of the oats marked on the oyr side of
    Sanders McIntoshes cropt of oats . . 038 – 0
It of bear that is put below part of his oats in
    the bear barn 31
From the Carit of bear 003

My whole cropt of bear for the year 1772 in-
    cluding Sanders McIntoshes . . 173 – 0 – 10
It of tiend bear . . . . . . 3 – 0 – 0

                    176 – 0 – 10

I had done cutting Friday the 16th Octbr
I had all housed Tuesday 20th by the blessing
    of God
The amount of Sanders McIntoshes corns as
    proof

                         B. f. p.
To bear . . . . 3 – 2 – 3½
To oats allowing ten firlots and two pecks to
    the boll . . . . . . 2 – 1

[Page sixty-two. 1772.]

Ane accott. of what meall was made of cropt 1772
                           B. f. p.

Novr. the 14th of bear meal . . . . 3 – 1 – 3
Janry. the 2nd of bear meal . . . . 3 – 2 – 2
March 13th of my own bear . . . 2 – 0 – 1
Malted . . . . 3 – 0 – 0
Thrave measured for seed . . . . 2 – 2 – 0

                   14 – 2 – 0

[1] See p. 61.

	B.	f.	p.
The above is all my own cropt of bear			
It of the Dollnavert bear made in meal the			
28th May 1773	2 –	0 –	0
It from Clerk Duff of bear meal . . .	16 –	2 –	2
It of oat meal Novr. 14th	1 –	3	
It of Oat meal Decr. 28th	3 –	1 –	2
It three firlots pron ½ meal at do: time . .	0 –	1 –	2
It put in the chist that is in the barn 16 Janry.			
four firlots of white oat rush [1] . .	3 –	2 –	0
Janry. 25th of heated oat meal . . .	1 –	3 –	0
It of clean oat meal 4 bolls in the chist in the			
outer house and one taken in . .	5 –	0 –	0
It three firlots and peck ½ meal . . .		3 –	2½
	16 –	0 –	2½
To a boll of meal bought from Forres 20th at			
14 sh: and four pence	1 –	0 –	0
It a boll from Knockan dow in Janry at			
fifteen sh:	1 –	0 –	0
It from Easter Elchies 13th March . .	1 –	0 –	0
It of my own cropt of rush sd. day . .	1 –	3 –	2
It of Duff's meal 22 May	2 –	0 –	0
It of Duffs meal 5th Jully	8 –	0 –	0
Of oat meal since the 14th Novr. . . .	31 –	0 –	1
It of bear meal since said time . . .	24 –	0 –	0
It from Mr. Duff's 2 bolls	1 –	0 –	0

[Page sixty-three. 1773.]

    Ane account of corn and straw bought in the spring 1773.

	B.	f.	p.
Impr from the widow in Caritnakile [2] . .	01 –	2 –	0
It from Sanders More McIntosh [2] in Kincraig	6 –	0 –	0
It from Brae Morray [3]	5 –	2 –	2
It from Captain Shaw out of Dalnavert .	04 –	2 –	0
	17 –	2 –	2

[1] Probably owing to the bad harvest the corn grown for ' rush ' was ground.
[2] People on the Davoch.
[3] In Laggan, higher up the river.

For two bolls birlie from Braemore 2 pd
    sterling the carriage eight sh: . . £02 – 8
The Brae Morray Victuall stands me carriage
    and servants meat included .   .   . 6 – 14 – 0
    over and above my carrying it from
    Strathspey .   .   .   .   . 7 – 0
Sanders McIntoshes Victuall [1] .   .   . 6 – 0 – 0
The widow's [1] .   .   .   .   . 1 – 00 – 0
The dalnavert Victuall of oats .   .   . 4 – 08
It of Bear from Dalnavert .   .   .   . 2 – 2 – 5½

[Page sixty-four.]

Ane Acct. of the money payed to the different people that sold to Liet. John McPherson yr cattle which was contained in the bill taken by me 1772 [2]

Impr to Donald McDonald in Dunachtonbeg
    seven pounds six shillings of which yr was
    only due .   .   .   .   . £06 – 0 – 0
Ballance of money formerly given him 16 sh:

Having counted with John McIntosh shoe maker upon the 15th Janry. 1773 for what shoes he made for my family amounting to 26 pair two of which are pumps which comes to four sh: and five pence so that he is still due me thirteen Pd [3] for the half hide he got last spring.

Dunachton 2nd Janry. 1774 John McIntosh is payed all preceeding shoes and the three small pairs made of the hide he had.

[Page sixty-five.]

Ane Account of what bear and oats I disposed of Cropt 1772.

[The first eleven entries on the page are duplicates of ones on p. 6 of the Account Book and are omitted. All the names in the list on this page are of people connected with the Davoch except the Boatman's wife.]

---

[1] People on the Davoch.

[2] Unfortunately there is only one entry under this heading. The entries relating to the shoemaker were evidently added afterwards. No doubt the sale of the cattle was to pay for grain bought in the scarcity of '70 and '71.

[3] Scots, i.e. 13s.

	B.	f.	p.
To Donald Sanders Mores son of the birlie from the South 2 pecks which stands me 20 pence each as it made at his own sight but 3½ .			2
To Coll of Birlie			1
To Samuol in Cluanach of bear . . .	1 —	0	
To Sanders McIntosh of small oats . . .	1 —	0	
To Angus Dows relict of small oats . . .	1		
To Dito of bear	1		
To Sanders McIntosh of bear	1 —	0	
To the boatman's wife in a present of bear .	0 —	0 —	2
To McGlashan			2
To Sanders McIntosh of bear	0 —	0 —	1
To Wm. Paul Buie's son of oats . . .	0 —	1 —	0

[Page sixty-six 1774.]

After counting with the McPhails 6th Janry. 1774 am due them six and sixpence but they have seven head of my cattle to winter which will amount to one pound one shilling if they winter them rightly and a shilling more if the brandered[1] quey is with calf in whole £1 – 8 – 6 So that they will be only due me eighteen pence of £1 – 10 that I agreed to take.[2]

[Page sixty-seven. 1772–1773.]

A particular account of what meall I sold of the fiftie bolls bought from Mr Young by Elgin in the year 1772 at eight stone to the boll, but those who got the above meall had nine stone delivered to them.

	B.	f.	p.
Impr to John Roy McIntosh and John Dow both in Kincraig	4		

[1] Brindled.

[2] These McPhails were the widow and sons of Paul Buie McPhail. Balnespick owes the McPhails :

	£	s.	d.
In debt perhaps for work . . .	0	6	6
For wintering the cattle . . .	1	1	0
Extra for the quey . . .	0	1	0
	£1	8	6

The McPhails owe Balnespick £1 10s. for something not stated—perhaps for their father's arrears of rent.

	B.	f.	p.
It John McIntosh in Isle of Dollnavert [1] .	2		
It William Campbell in Tomnamuckach and his broyr in Pitchurn [1]. . . .	2		
It to James McDonald and Jo. Robertson in Kylintuie	2		
James Stuarts relict and Sanders Buie in Carit .	2		
It Donald McGlashan and Sanders McIntosh	1		
Wm. Dow in Carit	0 –	2	
John McGilvrie and Ann Dow his aunt .	1 –	2	
Faryr in Leald	1 –	0	
John Dow McAlbea and his son Faryr . .	2 –	0	
Donald McAlbea and his broyr John Don .	2 –	0	
Donald Bain McAlbea and James Mcphers: Lealt	2 –	0	
Donald McQueen in Dun : more . . .	1		
Peter McDonal above Cluanach in the new land	1		
Peter McKay Smith in Reats [1] . . .	1		
Angus Dow late Miller his relict . . .	1		
	26		

The above is payable Marts 1773 at 20 sh: per boll.

Therse of Cattonachs meal still due [2]

To John Dow McDonol in Tomnamuckach .	0 –	2 –	0
To McPhadruck and John Glass [3] in Kylintuie	1 –	0 –	0

[Page sixty-eight.]

A particular account of one hunder bolls bought from Clerk Duff in May 1773 payable the eight October first at eighteen sh: the boll such as will pay before Martinmas 1773

B. f. p.		£	s.	d.[4]
2	To Meldrum [5] and Stuart [5] per bill .	1 –	18 –	0
2	To Donald McPherson in Kinabrock and John McLean . . .	1 –	18 –	0

[1] These three names are the only ones in the list belonging to people not living on the Davoch.
[2] P. 58 of the Account Book records these purchases.
[3] Gray John.
[4] This column was evidently added in from time to time as the people paid.
[5] People on the Davoch.

B. f	p.		£ s. d.[1]
3		To Petter McIntyre and oyrs in Glenfeshie [2]	2 – 17
2		To Wm. Campboll and Duncan Stuart in ffarletr	1 – 18
3		To Donald Robertson and Barbara Shaw in Auchna: [3]	2 – 17
2		To James Warrack and his son in Kylehuntly	1 – 18
2		To Cameron and McIntyre Chelsaman [4] in Glenfeshie	1 – 18
3		To James Robertson [3] and Janet Paul's relict [3]	2 – 17
3		To Patrick Murray turner and oyrs in Glenfeshie	2 – 17
1		To Elspet McDonold and her son [3] .	19
2		To Davidson and Gordon in ffarletr .	1 – 18
3		To McKay and Kennedy in Need [5] .	2 – 17
1		To McKay the Boatman and P. McKay	0 – 19
2		To Donald Kennedy in Knochanbuie .	1 – 18
3		To James McBean in Uper Lynvile and others	2 – 17
3		To McPherson and McIntosh in Dolnashulke	2 – 17
2		To Charles in Renberach . . .	1 – 18
1		To John Reoch McIntyre at Woodend of Inch	19
1		To Samuole in Cluanach [3] . . .	19
1		To William Campboll [3] and Sander's More's [3] son in Dun : beg . .	1 – 18
1		To Donol Roy McDonol in Lagan .	19
1		To Cruikshank in Craigandow [3] .	19
1		To McPherson Miller in Dun : beg [3] a boll at home	1
1		To Samuole Davidson [3] in Croft .	1

47 Bolls	£44 – 5

[1] This column was evidently added in from time to time as the people paid.
[2] A glen on the opposite side of the valley.
[3] People on the Davoch.
[4] An ex-soldier in receipt of a pension from Chelsea Hospital.
[5] I.e. Noed, a local farm.

[Page sixty-nine.   1773.]
47 Bolls of Clerk Duffs meall carried from the
        oyr side amounting in cash to   .   . £44 – 5
14½ bolls to Mr Gordon at   .   .   .   . 12 – 17
 8 bolls to Captain Shaw at Dito price   .   . 07 – 04
───   ─────────
69½   64 – 06

04¼ bolls to Chelsamen who have paid
03   to Paul Buie's [1] sons for services
 I   to John Robertson [1] in Kylin: payd Martinmas 1774
 0   to David Davidson for ready money
 ¼   to James McPherson in Leold [1]
 ¼   to James McAlister in Dolphour
1¼   to Alexr. McPherson [1] tayler in Dun : beg

August 16th given in borrowing
    To John Gow [2] in Kingussie   .   .   . £0 – 10 – 6
    To Donald McQueen commonly called
        McIntosh [1] in Dun: .   .   .   . £0 – 10 – 6
    To Angus Cameron Weaver in Dolbrady   . £0 – 5 – 0
    To John McPherson [1] Miller Septbr. in
        borrowing .   .   .   .   .   . £0 – 6 – 0

    More of Meall to different people out of Captain Shaw's meall.
    [Here there follow the names of eight of the sub-tenants on
the Davoch.   They each bought a peck of meal.]
    To the slater two stone and a lippie.

[Page seventy.   1773.]
    Ane account of what bear was cut down by the blessing of
God in the year 1773 Sepbr. 2nd.

	TH.	St.	SH.[3]
Impr in the Gardens of Auchnabochin . .	12 –	0 –	0
It on Drumstank of bear	18		
It in whole of the row of bear twixt the Rubage of the old house tathing and muck	58		
It on the new ground of small bind . .	12		
	100		

It on the row of small oats preceeding the 18th
    Sepbr.   .   .   .   .   .   . 48 – 0 – 6

───
[1] People living on the Davoch.   [2] A wright.
[3] The measures on this page are thraves, stooks, and shaves.

	TH.	St.	SH.
It of small oats on Dollinloch . . .	132	1	
Mown on the little crofts to the east of the burn of white and small oats mixed . .	12 –	1 –	4
It on the meadow ground formerly under hay [1]	74		
It to the west of the Duch [2] of small oats .	60		
	327 –	0 –	10
It on Drumstank of small oats . . .	70		
It of white oats on said ground . . .	41		
It of Birlie	08		
	119		
It on the row of white oats	20		
It of Rye	02 –	1 –	0
It on the ground to the east of the Chapel [3] of white oats	21		
It of birlie on the hay ground . . .	68 –	0 –	0
It of bad birlie before Wm. Dows Auchnabochin	4 –	1 –	0

[Page seventy-one. 1773.]

	TH.	St.	SH.
Carried from the oyr side twixt bear oats rye birlie etc.	662 –	0 –	10
It of the Rye cut some time ago and is the sole of the furthest stack	16 –	0 –	6
	678	1	4

I had done cutting by the blessing of God the 21st October New
Style From the end of Sepbr. till the 18th October never
one dry day and before then many showers.

I had all finished the 22nd Octbr. and housed by the blessing of
God. The season from the first or rather 3rd of Sepbr. was
very windy and so much rain that Spey was still over the
banks till the 2nd Novr. that year was little frost

[1] Probably natural hay-meadow ground taken in under permanent arable
cultivation.

[2] This ditch, so constantly alluded to, was probably one of the earliest
undertakings of its kind in the district. It was on the west side of the Chapel.
The piece of ground that it drained was for many years out of cultivation,
but it was broken up last year and the ditch was found. It was made of flat
stones beautifully fitted together, much as Sir John Sinclair advises in his
View of the Northern Counties (1793), p. 39.

[3] St. Drostan's Chapel was the burying-place of the Mackintoshes of
Balnespick. It dates from pre-reformation times and is now ruined. It
stands on the flat piece of ground below the house.

[Page seventy-two. 1773.]

Ane account of what meal is made of Cropt 1773.

	B.	f.	p.
Octbr. the 2nd of bear meall . . .	03 –	2 –	0
Decr. 2 of bear meall	3 –	0 –	1¼
Said day of fine bear meall		1 –	2
Janry. 29th of bear meall		3 –	3
Febry. 22nd of bear meall and Rye . .	2 –	1 –	1
March 3rd of bear meall and Rye . . .	3 –	2 –	0
	13 –	2 –	3¼
It of bear meall Saturday the 3rd June . .	04 –	1 –	1
	18 –	0 –	0½

[1774.]

It of bear and peas bought by Mr Collin Campbell which was kiln dryed and ground at lethen [1] and came home in meall 20th Jully (therse of my own meall in the house what will serve till the eight of August) [2] . . . . 11 – 2 – 1

29 – 2 – 1½

Ane account of what oat meal was made of my cropt said year.

Off birlie and white oats including what was left in the press Novr. 2nd . . .		3 –	3¼
Off the rush that was on the Row . . .	1 –	1 –	1
Decbr. the 2nd of small oat meall the pron included	3 –	0 –	2
Janry. 29th of oat meall		2 –	1
Febry. 22nd of small oat meall			
In the Press		2 –	0
It of rush meall Sd day	3 –	0 –	0½
More of said meall of which sent Invereshie in payment of the grain given Captain Shaw at my desire		2 –	2
March the 3rd of white oat meal . . .	4 –	0 –	0

[Some of the items on this page are evidently included in the totals on the following page. It is not clear how one of the totals is made up.]

[1] Lethen in Nairnshire.

[2] The sentence I have put in parenthesis was evidently added in after the entry was finished.

	B.	f.	p.
March the 18th of small oat meal of which sent to Kincraig a boll that was borrowed for Captain S.	10 –	0 –	3½
two bolls and 3 pecks pron ½ meal . . .	1 –	0 –	1½
	30 –	1 –	3
Of birlie meall made the 3rd June . . .	2 –	0 –	1

Saturday 11 June a sugar loaf was taken down.

[Page seventy-three. 1774.]

	Bolls
There was ffebry. 25th sent to the kiln to be dryed of white oats	6
There was left in the barn of Dito oats . .	5 – 2
It of hinderon white oats	1
It bought from Clury of Cropt . . .	10

Of which came to the family use . .	4
of Dito meall to the McPhails[1] . .	1
Of Dito meall to John Glass[1] and James McDonold[1] both in Kylintuie payable Martinmas 1775 at 17sh: per boll	2
Dito to Janet Kennedy a boll to the Capt's daughter	1
Dito to Samuol in Clune[1] . . .	1
Dito to Sanders McBean in Reats .	1
	10

The whole meall that spent in the family The two Oct. of our own bear made in meall Rye included was . . .	18
Bought from Mr Campboll six bolls bear meall and two of peas which made of meall	11 – 2 – 1½
	29 – 2 – 1½
Made in meall of our own oats the pron counted as half meall . . .	32 – 2
	62 – 0 – 1½

There was of oat meall in the house what served till the 20th Novr. 1773

[The previous page has a good many items that are included in the totals on this page.]

[1] People living on the Davoch.

[Page seventy-four.　1774.]

　　Dunachton 19th of March 1774. Then having counted with James Robertson in Kylintuie he is payd for any demand for accounts or oyrwise preceeding this date and he has payed me any money that I gave in borrowing of which I have given him credit for thirteen and six pence that I was due Sanders mores son.

March 22nd given James McPherson in Luald in
　　order to pay for the long carriage [1]　.　.　2
It　to ffaryr in Dun : more Sd day when going for
　　the porter the use of which shilling Faryr is to
　　have in case the quey he hass is with calf　.　1
Donald Bain is due a sixpence of the money he got to buy fish
James McPhadruck pd the money he got when going to Forres
　　all but ten sh: as 20 sh: given him when he paid his rents
　　Marts 1772
The above I received Jully the 2nd. 1774.

[Page seventy-five.　1774.]

　　Ane account of my sowing in the year 1774. By the blessing of God I began March 10th at Achnabochin on the stone of the old houses and Gardens of rye .　.　.　.　2 – 2 [2]

It　on Drumstank of Rye　.　.　.　.		0 – 2
It　of white oats on Dito ground　.　.　.		2 – 2½
It　of Birlie on the crofts between the gate and Dollinloch　.　.　.　.　.		2 – 2
It　the 20th of small oats mixed with birlie on Drumstank　.　.　.　.　.	1 –	2 – 2
April the first on the row of peas　.　.　.		1
A little white peas on the east after rig　.　.		¾
On Dito ground of Rye in Rush　.　.　.		2 – 0
On Dito ground of small oats with Rye .　.	3 –	1
It　of clean white oats on the row 1st of April		1
It　on the crofts this side of the road [3] of clean white oats .　.　.　.　.　.	1 –	1 – 0
It　on the row of Birlie mixed with bear .　.	0 –	2 – 2
	0 –	2 – 0

---

　　[1] It is not quite clear why Balnespick should pay his sub-tenant for this service due. Perhaps he had employed McPhadruck to perform one of the Long Carriages that Balnespick owed the minister as part of his teinds.

　　[2] The measures on this page are apparently bolls, firlots, and pecks.

　　[3] General Wade's Road, which runs through the wood below the house. Balnespick generally writes of it as the ' King's Road.'

To the east of the burn on Dol in Loch of small	7 –	0 –	2
One Dito ground of white oats mixed with the above small oats April the 4th . .	1 –	1 –	2
Sown in Craigandow of birlie . . .		1 –	3¾
It of small oats mixed with birlie being the 25th April which day I have finished .		1 –	2

19 –	2 –	3

My oat seed was not hindered one day since the first was sown; only Monday the eighteenth and Tuesday there was wind and some snow but did not stop plowing. We've had mostly frost every night till the 22nd April and snow and frost closs from the 15th December till the 22nd March.

[Page seventy-six. 1774.]

7th of April on the Culsern to the west of the barn of white oats		1 –	1
It on the rigs next the potato [1] of white oats .			3
It on the ground next the Culsern to the east of the Chapel of mixed white oats and small		2 –	3
It on the leys and new ground of Small mixed with birlie and two leys . . .	2 –	0 –	0
It of birlie mixed with the above two bolls .		2 –	2
It on the second leys of small oats . .	1 –	0 –	0
It of birlie		1 –	0
It on said ground of small oats . . .		3 –	0
It of birlie mixed with said oats . . .			3
It of clean birlie one the ground one which it was last year only a firlot one the ley furthest down of all		1 –	1
It of birlie with which bear is to be mixed to the west of the Chapell . . .			2

7 –	2 –	3
19 –	1 –	2

27 –	0 –	1

[1] The earliest mention of potatoes in the Account Book.

P

[Page seventy-seven. 1774.]

Ane account of what bear I have sown by the blessing of God in the year 1774.

Impr in the ground by the gate with barlie .	0 -	0 -	3
It one the row with birlie [1]		1 -	0½
It of bear on Drumstanke 2nd of May . .		1 -	2
It sown on the tathing behind the barns .		1 -	3
It on the affter muck on the new ground and in Park the 12th May . . .	0 -	0 -	3
It on the Gardners Croft 19th . . .		3 -	2½
	2 -	2 -	1

By the blessing of God I finished my bear seed friday 20th. There was little or no rain from the 3rd May till I had done. Cold north winds and frequent frosts so that grass and corn makes a poor appearance, and so continued only four days of very hot. From the first of June constant rain and cold winds till the 17th. The meadows still covered with water. Then came on fair fine weather Except the four days mentioned above we've had hardly one day without wind and rain till the 4th Jully O.S.[2]

[Page seventy-eight.]

Having counted with James McDonald in Kylin-tuie about the whyskie he brought from Ferintosh Decbr. 21st 1774—for two pints and a chapin whyskie brought for me	4 -	4½
for nails having payed a shilling . .	1 -	3
	5 -	7½

Theres due me by James the price of four gallon whiskie at 14sh: the gallon out of which the above sum is to be taken so that all in my favour is the ballance .	£2 - 10 - 3½

---

[1] Probably refers to the entry on p. 75.

[2] Old Style. This paragraph has evidently been added to from time to time.

APPENDICES

[Page seventy-nine. 1774.]

Ane account of what oats I disposed of April 1774 of cropt 1773.

	B.	f.	p.
To Charles Robertson [1] wife of small oats .	1 –	1	
To Samuel Davidson in Croft [1] of white oats .		2	
To James McDonald in Dolphour of white oats		2	
To John McIntosh in Isle of Dellnavert .		2	
To Alexr. McIntoshes [1] wife of birlie . .		–	1
To Coll [1] a boll of small oats . . .	1		
To William Davidson [1] in leald of small oats .	3		
To Petter McIntyre in Glenfeshie of birlie and his son in law Donald Bain jointly .		1	
To James Lee [1] of the birlie that was a little green		1	
To John More Shaw of said birlie . . .			2
To Petter McDonoll of birlie . . .			2
To said Petter of small oats		1	
To Breackachie [2] of birlie for ready cash .	1 –	2 –	0
To Mrs McIntosh at reats ready cash . .	2 –	1 –	0
To Donald Gordon Farletter of birlie . .	0 –	1 –	0
To Donald McWilliam's wife in Croft Cornoll of Birlie		1 –	0
To Cruikshank's [1] wife of Birlie . . .		1 –	0
To Sanders More McIntoshes [1] wife of Birlie .			2
To John Robertson in Kylintuie [1] . . .			3½
To Wm. McPhail also McBean [1] . . .			2
To McLean boatman		1 –	1
To McLean, boatman at Kinrara for crossing .			1

[Page eighty. 1774.]

	B.	f.	p.
To Samuel [1] in Cluanach of birlie . . .	0 –	0 –	2
To Dito of bear		1 –	0
To John Davidson [1] in Croft of Birlie . .		1 –	0
To John Roy [1] in Kincraig . . .			1
To John More McAlbea [1] for service . .			1
To Cruikshank's [1] wife more birlie . .			1

[1] People living on the Davoch.
[2] At that time held by an ancient family of the McPhersons, now extinct.

To be given John Dow in Crathie upon Sanders
    Mores [1] account of which John returned
    to him 3/6 . . . . . £1 – 1
To John Robertson [1] in Carit the use of nine
    shillings march the 6th . . . 9
To John Dow McIntosh in Crathie the use . 2 – 0
To Donald Stuart [1] in the Hight above the Carit 11
To William More Davidson [1] in Dunachton beg
    over and above paying £2 – 18 upon his
    acct. to Samuol in Cluanach.[1] The bill
    accepted by him to said Samuol is in my
    hands 16
To Robertson John [1] in the Carit 25th April
    to be paid in a fortnight and never to call
    again 1
Donald Stuart [1] is due as ballance of 40sh: . 9

[Page eighty-one. May 3rd, 1774.]
    Then counted with Alexr. McBean my servant.
He is due me a sh: since he went for the beast to
    Strathdearn a sh: given my wife when he
    bought the black cloth a sh: when he went
    to draw blood a sh: to be given Donald
    Stuart's wife [the last named was not
    given] [2] in whole . . . . 0 – 3 – 0
Ballance of the cloth . . . . . 4 – 0
It to him by McPhadruck's wife . . . 5 – 0
It a boll oat of which he gave his moyr . 9
Novr. the 30th having counted and cleared with
    Sanders Davidson my servant I am due
    to him of his years wages and shoes only. 13 – 4
It to James Tuesday the 29th to buy shoes . 1 – 6
To John McIntosh wright Novr. 14 . . 1 – 00 – 0
To Anne McGillican . . . . . 13 – 0
To James McIntosh my servant the 22nd June
    1775 of his years wages . . . 1 – 5
A shilling more as ballance of the money when
    he was at Nairn 1

[1] People living on the Davoch.
[2] The sentence I have enclosed in brackets was added afterwards.

payed James all the years wages of the last half
    year of farings . . . . .   3 – 4½
of cash the day he left this place . . .   2 – 6
                                                5 – 10½

[Page eighty-two. 1775.]
    The McPhails began cutting the Alles [1] in August.
Ane account of what money is due me in borrowing or for
hides without bills July 6th 1775
    To Donald Roy in Lagan March last [2] . . £1
    To Donald McIntosh in Achnabochin to be
        given the Smith's relict the use of [3] . £0 – 17
    By James McPhadruck having got the ten SH: [3] £0 – 11
    By Faryr McAlbea in Dun: more for hides [3] . £0 – 16
        am obliged to take half of the bulls hide when sufficiently
        tanned at 8sh: [2]

[Page eighty-three. 1775.]
    Ane account of what meal I disposed of payable Marts 1776.

	B.	f.	p.
Impr to James Robertson in Croft Carnoll per bill	2		
To Coll [3] a boll and ½ anoyer ½ to Wm. Dow [3]	2		
To Wm. Gow in Pitchurn per bill . .	1		
To James McPhadruck [3] and John Robertson [3] per bill	4		
To old John McAlbea [3] in Dun: more . .	1		
To Donald his son [3]	1		
To Donald McWilliam [3] in Auchnabochin .	1		
To Alexr. McDonald in Carit [3] and Petter McDonald [3] in the New Land jointly .	2		
To Donald [3] and David Stuart [3] per joint bill .	2		
To Donald McQueen alias McIntosh [3] in Dun:	1		

Of the above therse only due fifteen bolls at eleven pd. per
    boll the oyr two being payed £13 – 15

[The list of names on the first part of the page is repeated on p. 85, with
'payed' marked against the names, apparently as the money was paid.
The list of names below the 1775 is repeated on p. 86, with 'payed' marked
against each name.]

[1] Probably alders, which were often written of as 'allers'; they were
used for making carts and implements. See Miller's *Survey of Moray*, 1798,
p. 324.
  [2] These entries were also jotted down at the bottom of p. 80.
  [3] People on the Davoch.

[1775.]

Ane account of the 21 bolls bought from Dellnies and to whom sold payable as above at Martinmas 1776.

To Petter McIntyre in Glenfeshie . .	2
To Petter McDonald and his son . . .	3
To Faryr Davidson and Kel McDonald .	2
To Petter Murray turner	1
All the above is on one joint bill being eight bolls.	
To Patrick Murray turner upon his own bill .	1
To Donald Shaw and Robert his broyr in Runolen	3
To Malcolm McPherson and William his broyr	3
To McKay the Smith's relict for whom McLean has given his bill . . .	1
To James McLean boatman . . .	2
To Invereshie's servant	1
To Donald Roy in Laggan	2
There's of bills for Dellnies meall at 20 sh: per boll	21

[Page eighty-four. 1775.]

In case those who bought the 21 bolls of Dellnies meall will pay within eight days of Martinmas 1776 they are to have a discount of 1 sh: per boll

All the meall on the oyr side is bought with ready money.	
Therse a boll meall given the fiddler of Lachlan my son's meall of which his fayr in law got a firlote	1
To Cruikshank's relict of which Margery Don in Craigandow got a firlote of my son's meall	1
It bought from Clury ; such as are below pays 20 sh: Marts 1776 [1]	
To little Faryr in Dun: more [2] . . .	1
To Alexr. McIntosh at the Gate [2] . .	1
To Samuole in Cluanach of which ane for the little boy Sandy [2]	2
To Anne Cameron in Balnespick . . .	1

[1] All the purchasers of this meal are noted again on p. 87, with 'payed' added to their names.

[2] People living on the Davoch.

To Isabel Robertson spouse to James Gordon a
    boll at home of the ten I brought to the
    house   .   .   .   .   .   .
To John McIntyre at the wood end of Inch
    na (? ?)   I
To said John ane oyr of Clury's meall at home
    the 29th August both bolls at two pd. st:
    for which he has given bill   .   .   .   I
To McErish [1] the shoemakers wife a boll at
    home for 17 sh: Marts first   .   .   .   I
To the McPhails for services of sd. meall [1]   .   I
To Coll [1] Donald McWilliam [1] and John
    McIntosh in Crathie a boll jointly. A
    firlote each to the last two and the $\frac{1}{2}$ to
    Coll   I

[Page eighty-five.   1776.]
    A particular acct. of what meall I bought summer 1775
payable Martinmas 1776. All that was given my own tenants
of the meall bought by Mr Colin Campbell is at eleven pd. per
boll   There was seventeen of which 2 pd
    [Below follows the same list as that given on the upper part
of p. 83 with ' payd ' marked against the names.]

[Page eighty-six.   1775.]
    [The upper part of this page is a duplicate of part of p. 83,
except that ' payed ' is written against each name.]
    Of the nine bolls of Clury's meal that came to the house
Isabell Robertson having got a boll before then of the ten [2]

To James Toshach for cutting hay 1st August   .   2 stones
To Alexr Shaw the cupper in part for cutting hay   . $1\frac{1}{2}$
To Sanders Bain McIntosh at and preceeding the
    29th August for ditching [3]   7
More to the said Sanders the 14th   2
To Sanders the 19th Sepbr.   I
To Sanders the 27th   I
To Sanders the 25th October   I

[1] People living on the Davoch.
[2] The entries under this heading evidently are a continuation of the list
of sales of Clury's meal on p. 84. On that page 11 bolls were disposed of,
leaving 9 to be accounted for. Isabel Robertson's boll is evidently the same
as that mentioned in the fifth item under this heading on p. 84.
[3] For adding to the ' Dutch.' See p. 88.

[Page eighty-seven.   1775.]

20 bolls bought from Clury Jully 1775 of which was sold

[Then follows a list of the purchasers of the 11 bolls of this consignment of meal that were given on p. 84. They are all marked as paid. The following additional names are added at the end.]

To Campboll in Dolphour a firlote
To Wm. Dow in Auchnabochin a stone
To Anne McGillican preceeding the 15th Sepbr
To James McDonald in Dolphour for Rob
To Sanders Mores Wife
To Anne McLean

[Page eighty-eight.   1775.]

In whole given Alexr. McIntosh for the Dutch preceeding the 6th Novr. 1775 what is marked on the oyr side being included

	Stone
Off stons	13
Tuesday 19th Decbr.	1
Janry the 9th	1
Janry the 26th	1
	—
	16

To Anne McGilligan preceeding the above date what
    is marked on the oyr side being included .   .   7 Stones
To her of meall 24 Novr.   1

	£	s.	d.
To Buy widdes		3	6
June 24 to Sanders to buy shirts . . .		3	6
Given Sanders Bain I mean the above Sanders			
McIntosh a pair shoes . . .		1	6
To his wife by his orders		2	
Anna McGillican cash to buy shoes . .		2	
More to cash to her		2	
for the potatoes in the yard to Sanders Bain .		2	
To said Sanders wife Monday 11th Decbr .		2	
To his wife the 2nd of Janry. 1776 . .		7	

	£	s.	d.
To the price of a sheep sold by my wife . .		2 -	2
To his wife 27th Janry.		5	
To wool given his wife a peck pron . .		1 -	10
To a shilling given her when she preceeded Forrys		1 -	0
Given Sanders 10th Janry. to buy meal out of ffarlettr		3 -	4
The herd above the Gate his peese . .		1 -	3

[Page eighty-nine.]

Ane Accott. of the rent and stipends as also the schoolmr sallary payable Marts 1776.

The Account of such of the tenants as payd a sh: each to be given the fox-killer, 1777
   from Coll
   from John Fraser weaver at the Gate
   from James McPhadruck
   John Robertson in Carit
   Charles Robertson yr
   David Stuart
   Mary McIntosh
   Alexr. McDonell in Carit
   Samuel Davidson in Croft
   David Davidson in Dun: more
   Kennoth McPhail
   Donald McQueen
   John Dow McAlbea in Dun: more
   James McIntosh

[Page ninety. 1777.]

Dunachton 19th August N.S. 1777 sd. day by the blessing of God I began cutting my hay. That day I had the following persons :—
19th   Alexr. Shaw the cupper and Jo. McPherson the fidler
          the day and Donald Stuart in Craigandow after him   2⅔
20th   James McIntosh and Sanders Shaw the fidler till affter
          dinner   2 the whole day 2⅔

21   James McIntosh and Sanders Shaw till ten forenoon
        when the rain obliged me give it up   .   .   .
23   James McIntosh Sanders Shaw the fidler the whole
        and John bain after eight   4
29   James McIntosh affter ten which makes out the day
        of the above working for him   1
      said day Sanders Shaw and the fidler the whole day . 2
      John Bain said day affter eight   .   .   .   . ⅔
      Saturday the 30th the foresaid three   .   .   . 3
      Monday the first Sepbr. staid there till after dinner . 3
      Tuesday 9th Sepbr. the foresaid three and Faryr the
        weaver 4
      Monday the 15th the foresaid three and Allen
        Gordon's horse   3

    [Here follow several torn and damaged pages dealing with
the harvest 1778.]

[Page ninety-one.   1779.]

    I began cutting my hay by the blessing of God upon
Wednesday 11th August 1779.
    Said day only James McIntosh in Keepoch More   .   . 1
    Thursday 12th said James John Robertson the big weaver
        and Malcom McGilespick in Inveringlish   .   . 4
    It McGillespick James McIntosh and Fraser   .   . 3
    It the above three and Wm. the Grieve   .   .   . 4
    It Monday Wm. McPhail from Reats and Sanders
        McOlroy James McIntosh 3
                                            ———
                                             15

    Said day cutting for Lachlan in the meadow
    John Robertson ffraser the weaver Donald fferley and the
        grieve 4
    It On Monday 22nd Wm. McPhail and Fraser the weaver 2
    ffraser was here ane half day but did but little .   .   . ½
    Finly McDonold four days here   4
    James McIntosh 2 days
    There was 113 carts put in the first stack.

[Page ninety-two.   1779.]

I begin cutting down my bear by the blessing of God upon Wednesday 11th August 1779 in the New Style.   Said day of the bear that was behind the barns and the Byre including that was under potato which was muck taken from the door of the Byre

	Th.	St.	Sh.
Bad bear	28 –	5	
I cut no more until the 17th then cut of muck bear	41		
and of tathing and some muck . . .	35	5	
	104 – 10		

Of oats I mean small oats in the Red Park [1] .	148		
Of Birlie and bear all put in the South end of the oat barn	61 –	1	
Of clean Birlie which is put in the sole of the stacke next the killn	32		
It of white oats on seed stack clean from the Red park put in sd stack . . .	83		
More of white oats from said Park . .	17		
Of Mr McLean's white oats mostly shaken by the wind and the rain	13 –	1 –	5
It of the heasley [2] oats of which yrs a good deal of rye on said ground	45		
Of Rye one the row put on the Stack 9th .	14 –	1	
Of Rush on Tomvoid [3] the 11th Sepbr. . .	96		
	503 –	0 –	5

Which day by the blessing of God I had done shearing had nae rain to hinder but one day and was six days that was cut after the poor bear.   I had all housed upon the 15th.   There being some showers of rain prevented me till then

There was only 46 thrave of the white oats put into the east stack.

[1] This field is still cultivated as part of Dunachton-more.   It is generally called the Lodge field, but older people remember the other name.

[2] The meaning of this word is not clear.   Sir John Sinclair speaks of ' hazely ground,' meaning ' poor ground.'

[3] Still part of the arable of Dunachton-more.

[Page ninety-three. 1780.]

Dunachton 11th April N.S 1780 which day by the blessing
of God I began my sowing. The 11th Novr. till the end of
ffebry. Loch Inch was closs frozen then only it broke we had
yn a thaw with rain and wind for four days so that the river was
different times near the Chapel. From the 20th March till the
above day we had for most some snow and constant frost the
whole of the winter from the 11th Novr. till the end of ffebry.
there was constant snow on the ground and many days most
violent drift yet the snow was not very loose.

	B.	f.	p.
Tuesday 11th April sown of clean Rye behind the barns	00	1	2
Mixed with small oats for rush on the North side of the row next tenants rye	00	1	0½
Said day of white oats clean in the middle of the row	1	2	3
Of small oats 11th sown with above Rye on the row the north side next the tenants	1	2	0½

Twixt what was sown in the Red Park and the row I have in
sacks the 14th fourteen bolls of small oats

[Page ninety-four. 1780.]

[This page begins with an account of the weather and items
that are duplicates of those on the preceding page, with the exception of the last entry on that page, which is omitted. It then
continues.]

14th April of small oats in the Red Park	2	2	
Said day in the Red Park by James	1	1	
15th small oats	2	2	
17th of Small oats in Sd Park	3		
It of small oats in Sd Park	1	1	

| 18 April of small oats to the east of the chapel on the ley below to the east of the Dutch | 2 | 0 | 0 |
| 19   in said ground of small oats | 1 | 3 | |

| of birlie on said ground | 2 | | |
| In whole of small oats white oats and birllie sown clean preceding 19th of April | 22 | 1 | 2 |

[Page ninety-five.]

		B.	f.	p.
	Carried from the oyr side	22 –	1 –	2
24	sown of birllie with bear . . .	00 –	3 –	2
2 May	sown with birllie and bear . .		1 –	3½
6	sown in the tathing and muck . .	23 –	2 –	3½
8	of clean bear to the east of the chapel part was sown in muck . .		2 –	2
14	N.S. sown of bear on the row . .		2	

April 21	given george the grieve at Kininvey eleven pecks of clean rye with three pecks of birlie which makes in whole with a firlote white oat skilling .	1 –	2	
	To Mr McLean of birlie . . .	1 –	2	
	To Samuele in Croft [1] of Birlie . .	0 –	2	
	William his broyr [1]	0 –	1	
	John Dow McAlbea in Dun: beg [1] .	0 –	1	
	To Hellin [1] in Clune . . .	0 –	0 –	2
		4 –	0 –	2

[Page ninety-six. 1768 (?).]

A particular rental of the Lands of Dunachtune more, Dunachtune beg, Kincraig, the miln stipends included.

only meaning what is set to tenants at above date.

Impr to Alexr. McIntosh in Kincraig five
      Oxengets [2] . . . . . £46 – 18 – 04 [3]
It to John Roy McIntosh yr three oxengets at 28 – 03 – 00
It to John don McCay yr the same . . 28 – 03 – 00
It to John McBean in Ball don for the masdall 22 – 00 – 00

---

[1] People living on the Davoch.

[2] Oxgate or auchten part : on old church lands they consisted of 13 acres. Each oxengate was supposed to support an ox for the common plough. In the case of farms held in common the usual unit was the ploughgate, consisting of 8 oxgates and maintaining a common plough (Cosmo Innes, *Scotch Legal Antiquities*, p. 241). On Dunachton the oxgate seems to have consisted of 17 acres.

[3] All the sums mentioned on this page are in Scots money :

    £1 Scots = 1s. 8d. sterling.   1s. Scots = 1d. sterling.
For the value of the rents in sterling, see p. 97.

It James Roy McBean in the Park and for Park
        End .   .   .   . £37 – 00 – 00
It James Stuart in Prossadon for an Oxenget
        in Kin: .   .   .   .   .   . 10 – 13 – 04

It John Davidson and son in Leuld ane
        oxenget   .   .   .   .   .   . 36 – 05 – 04
It Faryr McBean yr for ane achteen part   . 36 – 05 – 04
It James McPherson yr for half Achteen part 18 – 02 – 08
It Wm. Campboll in Tomnamuckach the same 18 – 02 – 08
It Donald McBean yr the same .   .   . 18 – 02 – 08
It John Dow McDonald yr the same .   . 18 – 02 – 08

It John McBean in Dunachton beg ane
        auchteen part   .   .   .   .   . 37 – 00 – 00
It John Campboll yr .   .   .   .   . 18 – 10 – 00
It Petter Robertson yr   .   .   .   . 18 – 10 – 00
Alexr. McDonald yr and son   .   .   . 30 – 08 – 00
It John more McBain yr .   .   .   . 15 – 04 – 00
It Angus McDonoll miller the croft included 25 – 04 – 00

It John Davidson in Dun: more for above
        croft   .   .   .   .   .   . 52 – 08 – 00
It David Davidson in Dun: more   .   . 31 – 11 – 00
It Faryr McBean in dito   .   .   .   . 17 – 15 – 06
It John McIntosh yr .   .   .   .   . 17 – 15 – 06
It Kennoth McPhail yr   .   .   .   . 17 – 15 – 06
It Donald McQueen .   .   .   .   . 17 – 15 – 06
It Paul McPhail yr   .   .   .   .   . 32 – 11 – 00

[Page ninety-seven.]
Carried from the oyr side   .   .   . £632 – 18 – 04[1]
Petter McDonoll in Auchnabochin for ane
        auchteen part   .   .   .   .   . 39 – 12 – 08
It William McDonoll yr the same   .   . 39 – 12 – 08
It Alexr. McDonoll the Smith for Drumstanke
        and ane oxengate more of Achnabochin . 27 – 11 – 04
It Donald McGlashan for ½ Auchtenpart yr . 19 – 16 – 04
It Alexr. McQueen yr for ane half oxenget . 09 – 18 – 02

---

[1] Scots currency. (Footnote continued on next page.)

James McDonoll in Kylintuie Fallow is included at £4	45 – 01 – 04
Duncan Shaw in Carit na Kyle	40 – 00 – 00
Samuel and Lach: Shaw in Clune	30 – 00 – 00
The third of the meadow that is set to the tenants of Achnabochin and James McPhadruck	20 – 00 – 00
Donald McBean in Crainandow	25 – 05 – 00
The Miln when set	110 – 00 – 00
	155 – 01 – 00
	1059 – 11 – 00 [1]

(Footnote continued from p. 222.)

The Value of the Rental of Dunachton in Sterling.

	£ s. d.		£. s. d.
Kincraig :		Dunachton More :	
5 oxgates	3 – 18 – $2\frac{1}{3}$		4 – 7 – 4
3 ”	2 – 6 – 11		2 – 12 – 7
3 ”	2 – 6 – 11		1 – 9 – $7\frac{1}{2}$
masdeall	1 – 16 – 8		1 – 9 – $7\frac{1}{2}$
Park	3 – 1 – 8		1 – 9 – $7\frac{1}{2}$
1 oxgate	0 – 17 – $9\frac{1}{3}$		1 – 9 – $7\frac{1}{2}$
			2 – 14 – 3
	£14 – 8 – $1\frac{2}{3}$		
Luald :			£15 – 12 – 8
1 oxgate	3 – 0 – $5\frac{1}{3}$	Auchnabochin :	
1 ”	3 – 0 – $5\frac{1}{3}$	1 oxgate	3 – 6 – $0\frac{2}{3}$
$\frac{1}{2}$ ”	1 – 10 – $2\frac{2}{3}$	1 ”	3 – 6 – $0\frac{2}{3}$
$\frac{1}{2}$ ”	1 – 10 – $2\frac{2}{3}$	1 ”	2 – 5 – $11\frac{1}{3}$
$\frac{1}{2}$ ”	1 – 10 – $2\frac{2}{3}$	$\frac{1}{2}$ ”	1 – 11 – $0\frac{1}{3}$
$\frac{1}{2}$ ”	1 – 10 – $2\frac{2}{3}$	$\frac{1}{2}$ ”	0 – 16 – $6\frac{1}{6}$
	£12 – 1 – $9\frac{1}{3}$		£11 – 5 – $7\frac{1}{6}$
Dunachton Beg :		Kylintuie (present name	
1 oxgate	3 – 1 – 8	Cuillintuie)	3 – 15 – $1\frac{1}{3}$
1 ”	1 – 10 – 10	Carit	3 – 6 – 8
1 ”	1 – 10 – 10	Cluanach	2 – 10 – 0
1 ”	2 – 10 – 8	Craigandow	2 – 2 – 1
1 ”	1 – 5 – 4	The Meadow	1 – 9 – 4
1 ”	2 – 2 – 0	The mill	9 – 0 – 4
	£12 – 1 – 4		£22 – 3 – $6\frac{1}{3}$

Total rental, £87 – 13 – $0\frac{1}{6}$

[1] This total is not correct, but possibly the items may have slight mistakes.

[Page ninety-eight.   1769.]

Ane account of the rent payed by the tenants of Dunachton and Kincraig for Martinmas 1769.

Scoolmasters salary included.

cess charged for September and December last [1]

Impr Petter McDonald in Auchnabochin .	. £40 – 02 –	8 [2]
It Samuele Davidson in Clunach . .	. 15 – 00 –	0
It James McBean in Park . . .	. 35 – 05 –	0
It David Davidson in Dunachton more	. 32 – 00 –	0
It John Don McBain in Dun: beg .	. 38 – 14 –	4
It to Alexr. McQueen in Auchnabochin	. 10 – 00 –	8
It Paul McPhail in Dun: more . .	. 36 – 01 –	0
It to Kennoth McPhail by money from Dolnavert	. 18 – 00 –	6
	225 – 05 – 2	

It James McPherson in Luald . .	. 18 – 07 –	8
It from John Dow	. 18 – 07 –	8
It from John McIntosh . . .	. 18 – 00 –	6
It from John McQueen in Dun: more	. 18 – 00 –	6
It from John McIntosh in Kincraig .	. 37 – 10 –	8
It from Donald McBean in Craigend .	. 25 – 16 –	10
It from Faryr McBain in Dunmore .	. 18 – 00 –	6
It to Donald Davidson in Luald . .	. 36 – 15 –	4
It to James McDonal in Kylintuie .	. 25 – 11 –	4
It to John Campboll in Dunachton beg	. 18 – 15 –	8
It to John Davidson in Croft . .	. 42 – 18 –	2
It to Wm. McDonoll in Auchnabochin	. 40 – 2 –	8
It to Wm. Campboll in Tomnamuckach	. 18 – 07 –	8
It to John McCay in Kincraig . .	. 28 – 10 –	6
It to John McBean in Ball dow . .	. 22 – 00 –	0
It to ffaryr McBain in Luald . .	. 36 – 15 –	4
It to Peter Robertson in Dun: beg .	. 18 – 16 –	8
	472 – 09 – 6	

[The addition on this page and on the following ones is Balnespick's own.]

[1] Cess or Land Tax, a tax levied on the land rent of Scotland and fixed at £47,954 1s. 2d. per annum. On Dunachton it probably amounted to about 3d. sterling per annum on each oxgate of the better land. It seems to have been collected four times a year.

[2] Scots currency.

[Page ninety-nine.]

Carried from the oyr side	. . .	£632 – 18 – 04
It from Lachlan Shaw in Clunach	. .	015 – 00 – 00
It from Alexr. McIntosh in Kincraig .	.	039 – 04 – 08

751 – 19 – 06

It to Donald McGlashan . . . . 20 – 1 – 6

Donald McGlashan payed the cess for Sepr. and Decr.
The whole tenants of Dun: more payd the harvest and winter
cess except the Smith.
Received six and six pence out of Dun: beg
The miller nor John more has not yet counted with me nor
payd.

[Page one hundred.]

Ane accot. of the rent Stipends and Schoolmr Sallary payable
Martinmass 1770 for the Lands of Dunachton more the Carit
and Kylintuie. The Harvest and winter cess is what is here
mentioned.

Impr Duncan Shaw in Carit na Kyle	. .	£40 (Scots)
It John Davidson in Croft of Dun: more	.	52 – 18
It to David Davidson his son in Dito .	.	31 – 15 – 4
It to Donald more in Craig an dow	.	25 – 04
It to ffaryr McBean in Dun: more	.	17 – 17 – 6
It to John McIntosh in Do:	. .	17 – 17 – 6
It to Kennoth McPhail in Do:	.	17 – 17 – 6
It to Donald McQueen on Do: .	.	17 – 17 – 6
It Pauls land when set in Do:	. .	35 – 15 – 0

257 – 02 – 4

It the Lands of Auchnabochin		
Impr William McDonol yr	. . .	39 – 16 – 8
It McGlashan younger	. . .	19 – 18 – 4
It Alexr. McQueen in Do:	. .	09 – 19 – 2
It Sanders McDonald the Smith in Do:	.	27 – 12 – 4
It Petter McDonalds auchten part when set .		39 – 16 – 8
It of Kylintuie with what it has of midow and		
the Fallow	.	51 – 14 – 8

179 – 07 – 10

Q

Angus the Miller got the use of twenty pound scotts payable
  Martinmass next for wintering a cow and a crown for
  wintering a stirk.
Donald McGlashan got the same
Angus got the use of a crown in May 1772
The above 20 Pd. is all payed.

[Page one hundred and one.]
  The Harvest and winter cess is what I receive.
  Ane accout. of the payments made of the rent by the tenants
of Dunachtonmore for Marts 1771.
  The Stipend and Schoolmrs Sallary included.

(Scots)

Impr by John McIntosh yr rent and stipends . £17 – 14 – 4
  It from Alexr. McQueen in Auchnabochin
    rent and stipends . . . . 9 – 17 – 8
  The said Sanders pd six pence of cess.
  It David Davidson in Dun: more . . . 32 – 01
  It Donald Mc Queen in Dun: more . . 18 – 00
  It Samuell Davidson in Clune . . . 52 – 18
  It from Ken: McPhail in Cash £18
Donald more in Craigandow payed his cess pre-
    ceeding 25th June with his rent . . 25 – 06
Faryr payed his cess till June 25
Having counted with Donald McBean in Cragandow March
    10th 1773 after paying his rent and stypends till Whit-
    sunday the ballance due me is £21 – 02
    he is also due at the above date borrowed money £8 – 8

[1773.]
  Decr. 6th given John Robertson in borrowing fourteen sh: [1]

[Page one hundred and two.]
  [The first part of the page deals with the rent roll of Dolphour,
a neighbouring farm which Balnespick seems to have managed
during Captain Shaw's last illness.]
  The rent of half of Craigandow is due by Cruikshank as also
a shilling as ballance of the boll meall as also seven sh: payed
Sanders mores son upon his accott.
  Cruikshank's relict payed all the cess due for her part of
Craigandow.

    [1] This entry is probably English money, the other entries Scots.

[Page one hundred and three.]

Ane account of the rent received from the tenants of Dun: more for Marts: 1772 the stypends and cess being included

Faryr McBean in Dun: more . . .	£17 – 15 – 00
James Robertson for his broyrs land . .	35 – 15 – 00
David Davidson	31 – 07 – 04
Samuel Davidson in Dun: more . . .	52 – 08 – 00
From William dow in the Carit in part payt .	07 – 04 – 00
John McIntosh payd his rent Stypends and cess till Whitsunday	17 – 14 – 04
James McDonall and John Rob: payed yr rent stypends and cess at and preceeding the 25th Janry. and also the midow ten merks in whole	51 – 14 – 08
Alexr. McDonald in the Strathes payd his rent	13 – 06 – 08

[1773.]

22nd October Ken:s wife delivered in part of rent	12
5 Decbr. from Kennoth	6
23 Decbr. received from Paul Buie's relict to acct. of rent and oats	17 – 08
Donald McQueen payed his rent 1772 and all the cess till spring 1774 . . .	17 – 14 – 4
more from Paul Buie's relict	2 – 13

[Page one hundred and four.]

Ane account of what money I received Wednesday 24th Novr. 1773

	(£ sterling ?)
from Samuel in part of his rent and meall .	2 – 2
from Faryr McAlbea in Dunachton more .	2 – 0
from David Davidson	1 – 0
from Wm. Dow on Donald Bain McAlbea's Acctt.	1 – 0
Donald more McAlbea in payt. of his meall .	1 – 0

Therse 14 pence due David that he was overcharged and a shilling to Donald Bain.

[Page one hundred and five.   1773.]

Ane accott. of rent payed 1773 and stipends and cess.

(Scots)

John Robertson in Kylintuie and 8 pence of cess	£15 – 06
Faryr McAlbea	17 – 15
John McIntosh in Dun: more in part . .	12
More from the said John . . .	5 – 14 – 4
David Davidson	31 – 06
Ken: McPhail his cess pd. and all preceeding demands	17 – 14
James Robertson	35 – 07
James Robertson Keepochmore in part of his rent	14 – 06
Samuel Davidson	52 – 08
It from Alexr. McDonell in Carit na kyle .	13 – 06 – 8
Received from James McIntosh the ballance of his rent and payt. of the firlote oats .	2 – 7 – 4
It Donald McIntosh payed all his rent . .	17 – 14 – 00
he is to give a bill for 20sh: and a cautioner [1] to D. McD.	

[Page one hundred and six.]

(Scots)

James Lees rent payed	31 – 06 – 08
Sepbr. 14th 1774 it was then James McDonol in Kylintuie paid his rent and stipends being [2]	25 – 16 – 0

[Page one hundred and seven.]

Ane accot. of the rent received from the tenants of Dunachton for March 1774   Stipends included.

(Scots)

John McIntosh payed till the 25th Decbr. .	17 – 13 – 06
Coll	08
Charles Robertson in Carit . . .	21 – 13 – 04
David Davidson	31 – 06 – 08

[1] A letter warning a tenant that his stock would be taken and put up to sale to pay for his rent and arrears.

[2] This is probably his arrears for 1773.

(Scots)

John McAlbea in Dun: more	. . .	17 – 13 – 06
Samuel Davidson in Croft	. . .	52 – 08
Paul Buie's relict	. . .	13 – 06 – 08

183 – 15 – 00

Kenneth McPhail	. . .	17 – 13 – 06
Faryr McAlbea in Craigandow	. .	21 – 00 – 00
Faryr for his Lands in Dun: more	.	17 – 13 – 06
William Dow McPherson for arrears	.	25 – 04
Donald McQueen in Dunachton More	.	17 – 13 – 6
Donald more McAlbea in Dun: more	.	17 – 13 – 6
James McDonoll in Kylintuie	. .	25 – 03 – 06
John Robertson	. . .	15 – 17 – 10
Having counted with Donald McIntosh in Auchnabochin he is due twixt rent and stipends and cess	. . .	09 – 07 – 00
and his son	. . . .	2

[Page one hundred and eight.]

Ane account of rent 1775 stipends and schoolmrs sallary included and Decbr. cess

(Scots)

McQueen in Auchnabochin	. . .	09 – 11 – 8
Paul Buie's relict in Carit	. . .	13 – 06 – 8
David Davidson in Dun: more	. .	31 – 06
Donald McQueen in Dun: more	. .	17 – 18 – 6
Alexr. McDonell in Carit na Kyle	.	13 – 06 – 08
Faryr McAlbea	. . . .	17 – 16 – 06
Donald McIntosh in Drumstank	. .	17 – 03 – 04
John McIntosh Dunachtonmore	. .	17 – 18 – 06
John McAlbea there	. . .	17 – 18 – 06
James McDonell in Kylintuie	. .	25 – 10 – 2

191 – 18 – 8

Charles Robertson in Carit	. . .	21 – 13 – 04
Donald more McAlbea in Dun: more	.	17 – 18 – 06
John Robertson in Kylintuie	. .	16 – 01 – 2
Samuel Davidson in croft	. . .	32 – 18 – 00
James McIntosh in Keepoch more	.	16 – 13 – 4

(Scots)

John Robertson in Carit	21 – 13 – 04
James Stuart in Cragandow in part of his rent and cess	12

158 – 17 – 08

Kennoth McPhail in Dunachton in Payt of his rent stipends and cess as above and schoolmr sallary	18
Cruikshank's wife	9 – 12
Coll and Wm Don payed	26 – 00 – 00

[Page one hundred and nine.]

Ane accot. of the rent stipends and schoolmr Sallary at marts 1776.   (Scots)

Charles Robertson in Carit	21 – 13 – 04
John Robertson there	21 – 13 – 04
John McDonald yr	13 – 16 – 08
Paul Buie's relict	13 – 16 – 08
James Stuart's relict in Kylintuie . .	06 – 13 – 04
Mary McIntosh there	06 – 13 – 04
James McIntosh in Keepoch more . .	16 – 13 – 04
Donald Stuart in Craigandow . .	12 – 02
Cruikshank's relict in the same . .	12 – 02
Samuel in the croft	52 – 18
David Davidson in Dunachton more .	31 – 18 – 04
Faryr McAlbea there	17 – 00 – 00
John McIntosh yr	17 – 17 – 06
Kennoth McPhail yr	17 – 18 – 04
Donald McQueen yr	17 – 00 – 6
John Dow McAlbea	17 – 00 – 06
Donald more his son	17 – 00 – 06
There's ane half penie to be discounted out of each of the six half aughteen parts	
Donald McIntosh in Drumstank . .	16 – 04
McIntosh yr	09 – 10
Coll McIntosh in Auchnabochin . .	15
Wm. Dow McPherson yr . . .	11
James McDonoll in Kylintuie . .	25 – 10 – 02
John Robertson there . . .	16 – 01 – 02

392 – 09 – 04

[Page one hundred and ten.]
The rent payable by the tenats of Dunachton more and the Carit for Marts 1777 Stipends and cess included till the 25th Decbr. also the Schoolmrs Sallary.

Fraser the weaver at the gate	£10 (Scots)
John Robertson in Kylintuie	21 – 19 – 08
James McDonol yr the son	21 – 19 – 08
James McIntosh in Keepochmore	13 – 06 – 08
Charles Robertson in the Carit	14 – 00
John Robertson yr	29 – 06 – 08
Alexr. McDonoll	31 – 06 – 08
Paul Buie's relict	13 – 06 – 08
Samuel Davidson in Croft	35 – 06 – 06
David Davidson Dunachton more	34 – 03 – 00
John McIntosh shoe maker in Dun: more	38 – 05 – 00
Donald McQueen yr	19 – 02 – 00
Ken: McPhail his grassum [1]	19 – 02 – 00
old John McAlbea	19 – 02 – 00
Donald more his son	19 – 02 – 00
Donald McIntosh in Auchnabochin	30 – 02 – 00
Coll McIntosh yr	27 – 00 – 00
William Fraser	10
James McDonoll and John Rob: for yr share of the midow	06 – 13 – 04
	416 – 15 – 04

Donald Stuart in Cragandow payd only six sh: of his rent.
After deducting the stipends and cess I shall have five pound str to pay as the whole is now included. I have also to pay the schoolmr's sallary which amounts to £1 – 1 – 3½
David Davidson payed his rent stypends and cess.

[Page one hundred and eleven.]
A particular acct. of the rent payable at Martinmas 1778 The stypends and cess in included.

John Campboll at the Gate	£12 (Scots)
James McIntosh at Keepochmore	15 – 06 – 08
Charles Robertson in Carit	14

[1] A preliminary payment not unlike the modern premium.

(Scots)

John Robertson yr	31 – 16 – 08
James McDonoll in Kylintuie	21 – 14 – 08
John Robertson yr	21 – 14 – 08
Samuel Davidson in Croft of Dun: more	35 – 10
David Davidson in Dun: more	34 – 02 – 04
John McIntosh yr	37 – 18 – 04
Kennoth McPhail yr	18 – 17 – 01
Donald McQueen yr	18 – 19 – 01
John Dow McAlbea yr	18 – 19 – 01
Donald McAlbea yr	18 – 19 – 01
Donald Stuart in Craigandow	13 – 10
Donald McIntosh in Drumstank	31 – 00 – 06
Coll McIntosh in Auchnabochin	29 – 08
John Fraser yr	29 – 08
Lachlan McIntosh yr	29 – 08
for the Midow by the tenants of Kyle and Achnabochin on the east side of the burn	6 – 13 – 04
	468 – 00 – 04
Alexander McDonol	13 – 06 – 08
Paul Buie's Relict	13 – 06 – 08
	494 – 13 – 08

There is ower and above due by the whole tenants of the barony a half year sallary to the Schoolmr which I payed at Whitsunday.

[Page one hundred and twelve.]

Ane accot. of the funds belonging to Capt George McIntosh [1] at his death and how settled by his will and testament upon the 5th of March 1780 having died the 8th said month

[1] Captain George Mackintosh, who made this will, was the brother of William Mackintosh of Balnespick. He served in the 60th Regiment and died unmarried. His tomb is built into the wall of St. Drostan's Chapel at Dunachton. His epitaph is ' Honest and Brave.'

Captain Lachlan, to whose children he left so much of his money, was the ' Lachie ' of the Account Book. He married Anne Mackintosh, the sister of the Chief, and bought the estate of Clune in 1780. William Mackintosh, to whom the legacy of £300 was left, was his eldest son, and succeeded him. He married the niece of The Chisholm, of whom it was said that but three ' the's ' were spoken of in Scotland : the Pope, the Devil, and the Chisholm.

Aneas or Eneas Mackintosh, William's brother, died comparatively young

Mr Ross of Cromarty his bond for £2000
    sterling with a years interest payable
    17th Jully 1780 . . . . . £2100
By Mr Lachlan McIntosh late mercht. in
    Giberalta now at London by his acct. currt.
    with the said Captain George McIntosh
    1st Janry 1780 . . . . . £0240 – 14
                                  £2340 – 14

    Of which legate as follows—
To Wm. McIntosh eldest lawful son to his
    nephew Capt. Lachlan McIntosh of
    Balnespick £300
To Aneas McIntosh 2 lawful son to above said
    Capt McIntosh £300
To Molly Shackleton in London . . . 100
To Annie McIntosh Eldest daughter to forsd.
    Capt. 100
To Margaret his second Daughter . . 100
To Jannet his third Daughter . . . 100
To a catechist in the Parish of Alvie . . 100
To be life rented by the Capts Broyr Coll . 100

and unmarried. The following list of his services was copied from a memorandum in his own handwriting :

   'Lt Colonel Eneas Mackintosh.
     Joined the 85th at Gibralta 1796
     Left it 1797
     Went to Helder three times wounded . . . 1799
     Went to Madiera 1801
     Later part of same year Jamaica where I was until . . 1807
     Walcheren 1809
     Portugal (early) 1811

When promoted to the rank of Lieut. Col. by the recommendation of the
Duke of Wellington on account of my conduct in the battle of 5th May 1811
Fuentes de Honor near Cuidad Rodrigo. Volunteered the month following
to storm and launched the storming party at Fort San Christobal, Badajos.
Was the first British officer who volunteered such a service in the Peninsular.'

    There is a story that after the Peninsular War Colonel Mackintosh accom-
panied his uncle, Sir Eneas Mackintosh of Mackintosh, to a levée. The King
took especial notice of the young soldier because of his gallant conduct, to the
surprise and annoyance of the older gentleman, who could not understand how
the King could take more notice of any young relative, however distinguished,
than of himself, the Captain of Clan Chattan.

To Mr McIntosh in London to buy mourning £010
To his nephew Wm. Bain's son . . . 040
To Donald Shaw and his wife in Doldowny . 030
To be laid out in building a tomb . . . 030
To Mrs Shaw and Miss Annie McIntosh at
    Kincraig to buy mourning . . . 010

                           £1320

             To Ballance . . 0920 – 14 – 6
To his nephew William . . . 200

                     720 – 14 – 6

The neat ballance in favour of the execr. and son as marked
    above the funeral expences with what is due the executor
    and doctors.

[Page one hundred and thirteen.]

    Ane exact Rental of Dunachton more, Kylintuie and the
Carit as is payable at Marts 1779. The stipends and cess is
included.

John Campboll at the Gate . . . . £10 (Scots)
James McIntosh in Keepochmore . . . 16
Charles Robertson in Carit 14
John Robertson yr . . . . . 31 – 06 – 08
Alexr. McDonol yr . . . . . 13 – 06 – 08
Alexr. McBain yr . . . . . 13 – 06 – 08
James McDonol in Kylintuie . . . 21 – 12 – 4
John Robertson yr . . . . . 21 – 12 – 11
Samuel Davidson in the croft of Dunmore . 34 – 16 – 00
William Davidson in Dunmore . . . 37 – 16 – 04
John McIntosh yr . . . . . 37 – 13
Kenneth McPhail there . . . . 18 – 16 – 6
Donald McQueen yr . . . . . 18 – 16 – 6
Donald Don McAlbea . . . . 18 – 16 – 6
Donald McAlbea . . . . . 18 – 16 – 6
Donald Stuart in Craigan Dow . . . 14 – 17 – 00
David Stuart yr . . . . . . 27 – 07

(Scots)

Coll McIntosh in Auchnabochin . . . £35 – 08
Lachlan McIntosh . . . . . 35 – 08
Donald McIntosh . . . . . 36 – 00 – 00

504 – 06 – 00

The half years sallary to the schoolmr. which I payed.
The Midow since last year not payd.
Peter McDonol in Clune payed me the 9 sh: for the hide.
The Midow is payd.

[Page one hundred and fourteen.]
[*Draft of a Letter.*]
DUNACHTON, 1*st* *Janry* 1781.
DEAR SIR,
I should have acknowledged the receipt of yours with the
ten pound sterling with the two years interest before now, but as
Miss Peggy's trunk arrived some time ago I meant to write by
her servant. I can't understand what could prevent her as the
post informs that she is in health. I presume as you keep the
new Christmas and have generally a number of your friends and
neighbours upon that occasion she did not incline being absent. It
has happened very well and we shall expect to have the pleasure
of her company at our honest old Christmas which we observe
as not wishing to be singular in our country. Mrs McIntosh is
very apprehensive that she will never have the pleasure of seeing
your ho: and I am partly of that opinion in respect to myself.
She joins me in aff. compliments to you and daughters

[Page one hundred and fifteen.]
[*Draft of a Letter.*]
DEAR SIR.
I shall be glad if this finds you and family in good health
and spirits. I presume as this is the first day of the new year it will
be agreeable if I give you handsel as none can wish more heartily
to your prosperity and long life. Inclosed you have your broyrs
draft for £30 and notes which with a small anker butter I presume
clears the last sh: I am due. When so large ane acct. is payed
within the 12 month, Mrs. McIntosh thinks yr should be some
consideration. She unites with me in wishing you, your sister and
your little miss all happiness in this and succeeding new years

[Page one hundred and sixteen.]

A note of the comprising of Paul McPhails Bigging in Dun-achton more by Alexr. McDonald and Alexr. McIntosh both sworn birlie men

His Barn	£9 – 10
His fire house	2 – 00
The little room without said house . .	1 –
The stable	15
His Byre	1 – 10
A little Barn	3
Two sheep coops	1
The stone work of the whole . . .	1

$$£19 – 15\ ^1$$

The ground comprising	£24 – 16
	19 – 15

$$5 – 1$$

(*Signed*) Alexr. McDonell [2]
Alexr. McIntosh [3]

[Page one hundred and seventeen.   1772.]

I began my sowing by the blessing of God Saturday the 14th of April.   I sowed rye in the croft eight days before then to make rush.   But the frost and snow was so very intense that little was sown before the 4th.   Wee had snow and frost since the 23rd Decbr. till this day being the sixth that yrs some appearance of a thaw.

Impr of white oats on the croft behind the Kitchen with some rye 4th April . .	01 – 00 – 02
It on the two wester crofts of white oats with rye the 6th April	01 – 00 – 02
It within the Park 2½ pecks rye clean . .	2½
It of clean white oats	00 – 03 – 00
It of rye in rush	00 – 02 – 00
It of small oats within the Park at and preceeding the 16th April	07 – 03 – 00

[1] Scots money.   The value of the buildings = £1 10s. 2d. sterling.
[2] Probably the Smith.
[3] This name is mentioned several times as belonging to Dunachton but it does not appear on the rent roll, and he was probably a cotter.

It at and preceeding 30th April of small oats 03 – 02 – 00
It sown in Carit na Kyle the 4th May which
      day by the blessing of God I had done of
      my oat seed sowing .   .   .   . 01 – 02 – 00½
It of clean white oats in Achnabochin the 18th
      April .   .   .   .   .   . 01 – 01
It of white oats mixed with small oats .   . 03 – 0
It of clean rye .   .   .   .   .   . 01 – 01
It of small oats at and preceeding the 29th
      April which day I have done in Achna-
      bochin .   .   .   .   .   . 05 – 02 – 00
It was dry cold wind and some frost since the
      thaw of the 6th April till wee had a
      few showers of rain upon the 11th May
The whole sown twixt Rye white oats and small
      is .   .   .   . 25 – 01 – 02½

[Page one hundred and eighteen. 1772.]

    Ane account of what bear was sown 1772 by Gods blessing

                                                  B.   f.   p.
Impr in Achnabochin in affter muck at and pre-
      ceeding the 6th may .   .   .   . 00 – 02 – 03
In Dunachton in affter muck 7th and eighth
      May .   .   .   .   .   . 01 – 00 – 03
In tathing the 12th and 13th May .   .   . 00 – 02 – 00½
Measured to be sown in much   .   .   . 00 – 02 – 03½

                                                 03 – 00 – 02

It sown in Carit 3 lippies 23rd. May which day by the blessing
      of God I had finished my sowing
I sowed in the end next the croft of [? ? ?] Barley about a lippie
      was obliged to sow of the bear from nairn part in the
      midle of the end rigg. The whole of the rye that comes
      to the cropt was sown of that barley except the half
      rigg next the Leys. The ½ rigg next the affter muck
      was sown of the Nairn barly and next to it is the Lipie
      from Invereshie
The season was now very cold, dry wind and some frost since
      the thaw came on being the 4th April till the 25th May
      when there came cold wind and rain from the North.
There were two or three light showers upon the 6th May
      that had noe impression on the ground but was warm.

[Page one hundred and nineteen.   1774 (?).]

Ane acct. of what money I advanced to my servants.

To Alexr. Davidson for cloth   .   .   . £00 – 5 – 0
To cash to pay for shoes in Jully   .   .   .   2 – 0
To James McIntosh to pay for shoes Jully   .   5 – 0
To Alexr. Davidson when going to Ruthven
     market 15th Novr. 1774   .   .   .   5 – 0
payed all that was due to the above servants.

To Mcphadruck's wife for whiskie that money I bought for Alexr. McIntoshes funeralls four pints a chopin and ½ mutchkin at eighteen pence per pint 3 pence for the mutchkin

[Page one hundred and twenty.   1773.]

Dunachton 15th March 1773 by the blessing of God I began my sowing 1773

Impr Monday 15th Sown in the row of the
     Dollnavert small oats mixed with rye   .   01 – 2 – 0
It sown to the east of the burn within the Park
     all but ½ boll that was sown about the
     Chapell of the Dollnavert oats   .   .   8 – 1 – 0
It in Achnabochin of said oats   .   .   .   0 – 2 – 0
                                                  ─────────
                                                 10 – 1 – 0

The above was all sown preceeding the 23rd
Sown in the hay ground below the Chapell of
     the Morry oats mixed with white oats   .   1 – 1
On the Row with Rye   .   .   .   .   00 – 2
It more on the hay ground .   .   .   .   00 – 2
It more of small oats mixed with white oats
     on the hay ground   .   .   .   .   00 – 2
It On the New Ground and the Rigg next the
     Gate mixed with white oats of the 4 bolls   1
Of the said oats on Drumstank   .   .   .   2 – 0
On the Wester Park of Sd oats 15th April   .   3 – 1
                                                  ─────────
The whole sown of oats   .   .   .   . 18 – 2
The whole of white oats sown clean on the row 00 – 3 – 0
It this side of the burn of hinderon white oats   3 – 0
It on Drumstank clean   .   .   .   .   3 – 2

It mixed with small oats to the east of the burn and to the west of as also in Drumstank	I –	0 –	I
Sown of clean rye that came from Strathspey .	00 –	2	
It of my own rye mixed with small oats .	00 –	2 –	2

04 –	2 –	I

23 –	0 –	I

[Page one hundred and twenty-one. 1773.]

It of Birlie in Drumstank Clean and mixed the 15th April	00 –	I –	0
It on the hay ground which day by the blessing of God I finished my oats . . .	01 –	I –	0
more sown of the birlie before William Dow's door the 7th May and by the moss .	00 –	0 –	2½

I –	2 –	2½

B.	f.	p.
I began sowing my bear in the lymed ground and tathing the 23rd April before the 29th I had sown more in said ground .	3 –	1½
The 10th May sown on the ley with the muck and on the large rig of the gardners croft	1 –	3½
The 11th May sown on Drumstank in muck .	1 –	0½
In the Gardens the 18th May which day by the blessing of God I finished my bear seed .		2½
The season being very cold with wind from the north and some rain We had last week very fine weather and a great fall of rain upon Sunday night the 16th May		
There was sown not marked of bear in the ground in the Park a lippy of the two pecks		2

[Page one hundred and twenty-two. 1774.]

	Th.	St.	Sh.
Ane account of my cropt having begun cutting by the blessing of God Tuesday 27th September 1774 Said day the tathing bear was cut down behind the barn .	15 –	I	

	Th.	St.	Sh.
One the Gardners croft only finished the 5th Octbr. the former days being rainy .	44 –	1 –	0
on the ground taken in this year of which a thrave was thrashen for the horses .	08 –	1 –	0
On the ground taken in last year . . .	07 –	1 –	0
One Drumstank ower and above the teen [1] .	20 –	0 –	0
	96 –	0 –	0
Of Birlie and Bear cut about the Chapel .	30 –	0 –	0
One the row of bear and birlie . . .	06 –	0 –	0
More on the row of bear and birlie . .	19 –	0 –	0
The whole small oats on Dollinloch the last of which was cut down the 11th Ocbr. .	112 –	0 –	0
Of indiferent birlie by the east side of the ground below the bridge	011 –	1	
One the row of rush, the rye bad, the above was small oats	54	0 –	0
One the ground twixt the Dutch and the burn of clean birlie Small bind 20th Octbr. .	40 –	4	
Of small oats on said ground . . .	108 –	0 –	0
One the crofts above the Kings Road . .	24		
One the row of white oats	42 –	1	
It of white oats to the east of the chapell .	24		
	548 –	1 –	4[2]

[Page one hundred and twenty-three. 1774.]

	Th.	St.	Sh.
Carried ower	546 –	1 –	4
One Drumstank of white oats not very good .	32 –	0 –	10
It of Birlie very bad	8 –	6	
It of sm: oats on said ground . . .	39 –	10	
It of rye twixt Achnabochin and Drumstank more than payed the teen . . .	20 –	00	
	100 –	01	

[1] Teind, probably used here as meaning payment for the sub-tenant's cultivation of part of the farm. See p. 144.
[2] It is not clear how this total is made up.

	Th.	St.	Sh.
Of Birlie in Craigandow cut down the 27th Ocbr.	20 –	0 –	8
Of Brocked oats on said ground	9 –	0 –	0

The above to be left for the teen [entry not completed].

I had done cutting friday the 28th of Octbr. before day and sent so many of my servants to Kincraig where four of them were three fine days. Monday 31st by the blessing of God I had all my cropt put together.

The rains were so frequent from the time I began cutting till I had done I had not one whole fine days but two.

[Page one hundred and twenty-four. 1774.]

	Th.	St.	Sh.
1. In the stacke next the kiln of rye	20 –	0 –	0
It all the small oats of Doll in Loch	12		
	132		
There was more put in said stack of small oats			
2. In the stack next the above of the white oats from Drumstank	32 –	0 –	0
It of the small oats from the said ground and some birlie mixed out of which the teen was paid	39		
From the east side of the Chapell of small oats	09		
More in the stack of the small oats about the Chapell	20		
	100		
3. The third stack next the above of birlie from Craigandow not very clean	18 –	0 –	6
Of the clean Birlie in the Park twixt the Dutch and the burn	38		
	56 –	0 –	6
4. Stack of Birlie clean	09 –	0 –	0
Of Birlie mixed with bear	25 –	0 –	0
Of clean white oats with a little hay twixt them	24 –	0 –	0
	58 –	0 –	0

R

	Th.	St.	Sh.
Put in the Barn of clean white oats from the row and the crofts above the Kings Road the peas above	06 –	1	
The whole small oats rush form the row	54		
As also the 30 thrave of birlie that was about the Chapel	30		
From Craigandow of green oats put in the barn by mistake	08 –	0 –	0
It of small oats from the Park	50 –	0 –	0
	142		

[Page one hundred and twenty-five.   1774–1775.]

Ane account of what meal is made of the Cropt 1774

	Th.	St.	Sh.
Decbr. 22nd therse in the house of the bear and peas meall from Morray	0 –	3 –	0
It of our own oat meall said day	2 –	1 –	0
Said 22nd the first of our cropt of bear meall	4 –	1 –	2
Said day of birlie and bear meall	4 –	0 –	3
	11 –	2 –	1
Decbr. 30th of small oat meall	7 –	2 –	0
It in the press yr being about seven firlots	1 –	0 –	0
	8 –	2 –	0
The first ffebry. of Clean oat meall thought to be a little heated	7 –	2	
It of pron two bolls which is acknowledged to have of meall	01 –	2 –	0
It of clean oat meall Saturday 11th ffebry	1 –	3 –	2
In the press of said meall	0 –	1 –	0½
Said day of Rye mixed with a little bear	1 –	3 –	3
22nd ffebry of Birlie and bear meall	4 –	2 –	0
In the Press		1 –	2½
	18 –	0 –	0
Of heated oat meall made 1st April	3 –	3 –	0
In Press said day	0 –	1 –	0
	22 –	0 –	0
24th May It of small oat meal	2 –	0 –	3
It in the Press		3 –	3
The whole of the above meall bear and oats	45 –	0 –	3

[Page one hundred and twenty-six. 1775.]
Ane account of pease and bear bought from Mr Matthews
at ffort George and from Mr Campboll in Nairn 1775

	B.	f.	p.
Impr old peas from Mr Matthews . . .	12		
It of bear from Mr Campboll . . .	1 –	2	
of said pease given Mr Blair at 15sh: martinmas payment	2 –	2	
To Mr Gordon Dito at said price . . .	2 –	2	
The oyr seven bolls is made in meall for the family	7 –	0 –	0
It of bear meall and some Rye . . .	1 –	3	
It of very fine small bear meall . . .		3 –	1
	09 –	2 –	1

Of the above sent to Kincraig 3 August eight stone of the
bear meall as yr came the same weight here from yr
There is six bolls of the Clury meall taken for our own use.
Oyr four to be given out for work. Isobell Robertsons
boll was of the said four bolls
So yr will be in white oats, bear and pease for the use of the
family since the 22nd Decr. 1774   .   60 – 3 – 0

[Page one hundred and twenty-seven. 1775.]
Ane account of my sowing in the year 1775.
        By the blessing of God I began Tuesday
        14th of March New Style said day of Rye
        that I had from the Mrs of Lynvile on
        the Row . . . .   0 – 2 – 2½
It of Rye with small oats on the east side of
        the burn on Dollinloch   . . .   1 – 1½

                                            1 – 0 – 0
It to the east of the burn of small oats . .   8 – 0 – 0
        Of said eight bolls yrs five bolls next the
        burn on the long riggs of oats that was a
        little dryed in the kiln. On the east
        side is 2½ bolls of the same oats that was
        not dryed and ½ boll by the Gate

On the leys of the mixed small that had some
birllie only the head riggs next the stryp
at the end of the bear ground a boll of
the dryed oats

In whole 22nd March	9	0	0
One the row of rye the 6th April. The season was so stormie sine the 22nd March with snow, wind and rain that yr was little plowing and sowing. The above rye in rush		1	1
It of white oats in sd rush			1
It of small oats in sd. rush mixed . . .		3	1

1 — 1 — 2

Sown of peas one the Row a peck bad half of it was sown by the Chapell . . .	0	2	0
Sown of Birlie on the Crofts this side of the Kings Road	0	2	0
It of white oats on the row		2	2

[Page one hundred and twenty-eight. 1775.]

To the west side of the burn to the east of the Chapell of small oats brocked . .	1	0	3
It on said ground 13th April . . .	1	0	$3\frac{1}{2}$
It on the low part of the wood of brocked small oats that I think not sound . . .	1	0	0
Of Small oats and birrlie mixd on the ground next the plain	2	0	$1\frac{1}{2}$
Twixt the Ditch and the burn of Clean birllie .		3	3
22nd April of brocked birllie . . .		2	3

7 — 0 — 1

Of small oats on the North of the rye upon Tuesday the 18th April on the row .	1	2	2
The whole of my sowing twixt pease, rye, small oats and Birlie Having done the 22nd April is	29	3	0 [1]
Thereafter by the pese on the row . .			1

[1] It is not clear how this total was arrived at.

More of Birlie in the sd muck of the new
    ground by the Ditch   3
Sown by Gods blessing Tuesday the 2nd may in
    Drumvore of bear all preceeding the 5th   1 – 2 – 0½
It on the Gardners Croft and after the peas
    on bear on the after tathing .   .   .   1 – 1 – 3¼
It on the after muck by the Dich   .   .   0 – 2¼

[Page one hundred and twenty-nine. 1775.]

    Ane account of what oats, bear etc was sold of Cropt 1774 the price £10 or £9 – 12 ready money (Scots currency)

	B.	f.	p.
To James Roy in Park of white oats[1] . .		1 – 00	
To Thomas Cattonach Smith in Reats . .	1 –	0 –	0
To James Lee Carit rright yr[1] . . .		3 –	0
To James Glass[1]		1 –	0
To Coll of white oats[1]		1 –	2
To Donol in Auchnabochin[1] . . .		1 –	0
To Capt Shaw in Ovie	2 –	0 –	0
To the Miller of Birllie[1]	0 –	1 –	0
To Wm. McLean of Birllie . . .	2 --	1	
To Mr Gordon of Birllie of which paid a guinea	1 –	1	
To Samuel in Croft[1] of Birllie 2 a firlot white oats		3	
To Charles Rob:[1] in Carit of Birllie . .		2	
To both the McIntoshes[1] a peck each . .	0 –	0 –	2
To my son Lach: of birllie[1]		3 –	0
To Mr McLean of bear	3 –	0 –	0
	13 –	3 –	0
To Mr Robertson at Dalwhinie of white oats .	7 –	2 –	0
To Samuel in Cluanach of bear[1] . . .		1	
To John more Shaw in Kinrara of small oats .	1 –	0 –	0
To John Polson to be given his ffaryr[2] . .		2	
To Faryrs wife in Luald of Brocked birllie[1] .			2
To Shaw the Cuppers wife of said oats . .			1

All the above is paid[3]

---

[1] People living on the Davoch.
[2] A servant.   [3] Evidently added later.

[Page one hundred and thirty.   1775.]

Ane account of my cropt as cut down having begun by the blessing of God Tuesday the 24th August 1775

Th.   St.   Sh.

There were several showers of rain so that little was cut down before the 29th when the bear on the Gardners croft was all sheared being	48 – 00 – 00	
The 29 There was shorn on the new ground of bear	8 – 00 – 00	
The 18th there was cut down of the affter Tathing of bear behind the barn . .	16 – 0 – 09	
Of Bear on the row affter the peas . .	11 – 00 – 00	
It of bear on the tathing and muck Tomvote of poor bear	86 – 00 – 00	

169 – 00 – 09

Of Rye on the Row	19
Of small oats on the North side of the Row .	24
On the Row of poor thin Rush . . .	19 – 01
It of white oats on the row very good . .	22 – 1
It of Birrlie on the two Crofts this side of the road below the Town	18 – 1

103 – 1

[Page one hundred and thirty-one.   1775.]

All to the east of the Brn of brocked small oats and some Birrlie	100 – 00 – 00
Twixt the burn and the ditch of brocked poor oats	11 – 00 – 00
On the ground next the wood above the chapell of small oats partly brocked . . .	15 – 01
On the ground this side the chapel of birlie .	13
More of Birlie in diferent places by the Ditch and the Chapell	52 – 00 – 00
It of small brocked oats	82 – 01 – 00

174 – 00 – 00

I have by the blessing of God Done cutting my cropt Thirsday afternoon 28th Sepbr. Till the 20th yr was frequent rains. Since most agreeable till Monday 2nd

October. Then the rain began most
severe and continued till the 24th so that
I had most of the corns twixt the Ditch
and the Burn out till the 27th Octbr.

One Tomvote of Small oats 123
From the oyr side of the Row and the two crofts
   above the road of oats and rye . . 103 – 01
_____

The whole of my oats, rye etc of cropt 1775 . 581 – 00 – 09
Of bear sd. year some not good . . . 169 – 00 – 09

[The description of the sowings and harvests for this year show some discrepancies.]

[Page one hundred and thirty-two. 1775.]
   Dunachton friday the eighth Decbr. 1775
I brought the first meall out of the milln at
   which time yr is in the house of last

	B.	f.	p.
years meal			
Of Oat meal	5 –	0 –	0
Of pease meall	1 –	0 –	0
It from the milln of oat meall sd. day . .	7 –	0 –	2½
It of pron 5 firlots and two pecks at half meal		3 –	0
It a peck and a half			1½
	8 –	0 –	0
Of pron 7 firlots better than		3 –	2½
	9 –	1 –	0
ffebry 21st of small oat meal	5 –	2 –	0
of bear meall	1 –	2 –	2½
of pron sd. day a boll and a peck . . .	0 –	2 –	0½
	7 –	2 –	3
March 14th of white oat meall taken out of the			
milln	4 –	2 –	0
It one half boll pron to make a firlot meall .		1 –	0
	4 –	3 –	0
The whole meall made of cropt 1775 . .	21 –	2 –	3

[Some of the items on this page do not seem to be correct.]

[Page one hundred and thirty-three.]

Ane acct. of what bear meall was made cropt 1775

	B.	f.	p.
22nd Decr. of bear meal and a firlot peas .	3 –	0 –	2½
Said day of small bear meall for the table .	1 –	0 –	0
March 14th brought out of the milln of bear meall which with six pecks of the bear meall that was made in March is put in the chest below the window in the corner	10 –	3 –	1
Therse also in the end of the chist next the door the foresaid day	2 –	3	
It was taken out of the mill some time before. At which time yr was ten pecks of the March meall that was taken out of the chist in the corner but above said meall	0 –	2 –	2½
	18 –	1 –	2

From the 3rd Janry in the Old Style till the 3rd March in the Old Style Loch Inch was frozen only a little of what is next the midow. Opened the 20th of febry. in the new style.

[Page one hundred and thirty-four.   1776.]

I began my sowing by the blessing of God the 25th March New Style 1776

	B.	f.	p.
Said day sown of small oats one the leys behind the coats	2 –	2 –	0
One Dollin Loch 28th March of small oats .	4 –	1	
More on Doll in Loch of small oats . .	4 –	0 –	0
one the ground next the easter gate and the oyr two crofts		3 –	0
Tuesday the 2nd. Sown in Tomvote of small oats	2 –	2 –	0
more put in sacks to be sown on said ground .	5 –	0 –	0
On the row of small oats April 17th . .	2 –	0 –	2
On the row with which bear is to be sown the 18th April	1 –	1 –	1
one the ground twixt the ditch and the burn of small oats mixed with birllie of which 3 firlots birllie	3 –	3	
More on said ground of which two pecks birllie	1 –	0 –	1

	B.	f.	p.
More of small oats and birllie mixed . .	1 –	1 –	2
It of clean birllie	1 –	0 –	2½
One Tomvote 26th March of clean white oats	2 –	2 –	0
It on said ground of white oats on the head			
riggs next the Dutch		1 –	3
It of white oats with rye on the row . .		1 –	3

	B.	f.	p.
The whole of my sowing of oats rye and pease.	35 –	1	
It of rye on the crofts by the road the 26th			
March	0 –	2 –	3
It on the row of clean rye		2 –	3
It of rye in rush with white oats on the above			
row			2
Of peas of which taken out of the kiln two			
pecks		2 –	1½

By the blessing of God I have done my oat seed 26th April.

[Page one hundred and thirty-five. 1776.]

	B.	f.	p.
Sown with birllie one the gardners croft and			
behind the bear barn	0 –	1 –	3
The season was so cold with snow and frosty			
wind still from the North tho I had done			
of plowing the muck ground and Tathing.			
The 28th April I sowed bear till the 10th			
May at which time I sowed in the			
miding and tathing only . . .	1 –	1 –	2¼
It on the new ground below the Chappell			
where bear was sown the two preceeding			
years	0 –	0 –	3
	2 –	0 –	0¼

The season was not agreeable with north winds till the end of
May. Then the wind turned from the South with some
little rain. On the 14 June very great rain.

[Page one hundred and thirty-six. 1776.]

Ane accot. of what oats and rye I sold of Cropt 1775.

To James McDonald in Kylintuie of white oats	0 –	1
To James Roy in Park of Dito oats . .		2
To Samuel in Croft 3 firlots 2 to be payed .		2

To John Robertson in Kylintuie . . .	I
To Donald Stuart in Cragandow of Birllie .	I
To Kennoth's wife 17th April of Birllie .	I
Sold John Roy in Kincraig of Rye payed .	I
To John McGillivrie in Luald of Rye . .	I
To Alexr. McIntosh in Crathie of rye . .	2
To Alexr. in Luald of rye	I
John Dow in Tomnamuckach of rye . .	I
To Wm Campboll yr Rye	0 – 3
To Donald Bain McAlbea yr rye . . .	2
To John McPherson miller in Dun: beg of rye	I – 0
To Coll a firlot for damage done his corns .	I – 0
To old John Dow McAlbea a firlot birllie .	I
To John McIntosh shoemaker of birllie .	I
To Robertson in Dollwhinie of birlie . .	2 – 2

[All but two of the sales upon this page were to people living on the Davoch.]

[Page one hundred and thirty-seven.]

What pease I sold.

[This page gives a list of twenty-four sales of a peck each to almost the same people as those on the preceding page. A peck was also given to Polson Sanders Bain's wife for spinning.]

[Page one hundred and thirty-eight. 1775–6.]

Ane account of what small oats I bought of cropt 1775

Impr to my son Lachlan for seed[1] . . .	2 – 00 – 00
It from John Roy McIntosh in Kincraig[1] .	I – 00 – 00
It from Sanders McAlbea in Luald and moyr[1]	2 – 00 – 00
It from William more Davidson in Dun: beg[1]	0 – 01
	5 – 01

Ane accot of what bear I sold of said cropt

To Lachlan my son[1]	2 – 00 – 00
To Alexr. McIntosh in Crathie . . .	0 – 02 – 02
To said Alexr. from Wm. More two pecks malt	
To James Stuarts relict[1]	2
To Mary and Jannet her neighbours[1] . .	3

[1] People living on the Davoch.

[Page one hundred and thirty-nine.   1776.]

By the blessing of God I began cutting down my bear upon the 10th Sepbr. but finding it not ripe turned to the oats of Dollinloch after cutting of the bear on the Tathing got non cut but half days with dew and frost.

	Th.	St.	Sh.
	34		
Sepbr. the 21st on the foresaid ground which day prayed never to see worse bear .	53		
By the Dutch not very good being frosted .	08		
	95		

	Th.	St.	Sh.
Of bear and barley on the Gardners croft and behind the barns 24th Sepbr. . .	68	01	
It of rye on the crofts above the road . .	15	01	06
It on the row of rye 30th Sepbr. . . .	13	00	00
It of white oats and rye on the row first Octbr. The foresaid day I mean the 1st began cutting on Dollinloch all the east of the barn was only done the 18th with ½ days	128	03	
It of small oats on the row first octbr. . .	34		
Of white oat rush	16	01	
It of small oats behind the coats of white 14 thrave very poor all small bind . .	34		
On Drumvore of white oats 3rd Octbr. . .	102		
On said ground of small oats 4th and 5th .	126		
It of birllie that was twixt the chapell and the Duch	60		
It of small oats twixt the Duch and the burn .	129		

I had done cuting by the blessing of God Thursday 17th of October 1776.   Since we began shearing till we had done got but five days from morning till night there being rain, fogs and frost.

The remaining part of the season was very agreeable only some frost in the night.

[Page one hundred and forty.   1776.]

Ane account of what meal was made of cropt 1776

	B.	f.	p.
At and preceeding the 11th Janry put in the chest in the room in the cross house below the window in the end next the door therse 2½ bolls of small oats The whole in that chest is.	8	0	0

	B.	f.	p.
Taken into the house of the said birllie at the said date	5 –	0 –	0
Therse taken out of the returns of the eight bolls which made meall . . .	5 –	2 –	2½
Nine pecks pron which is allowed to have of meall		1 –	1
March the 3rd taken out of the milln of small oat meal of which put in the chist of the Tifall [1]	5 –	0 –	0
A boll pron at ½ meall		2	
March the 27th yrs birllie and small oat meall	7 –	3 –	2½
and three firlots pron to make . . .		1 –	2
It of small oat meall 28th of which is given to different people and to the gardner McKenzie five pecks only to the house 3 firlots and 3 pecks	4 –	1	
of oat meal 24th May	1 –	1	
	43 –	0 –	2
Therse the said 11th Janury. of bear meall of cropt 1776		3 –	3
There was a boll of rye meall			
It Janry 27th 1777			2
It of small bear meall sd day . . .			2
It of bear meall 29th April	4 –	3 –	2
Said day there was in a sack of the first bear meall that was marked above 3 firlots and 2 pecks			
May 24th of bear meall	1 –	1 –	2
More of small bear meall		2 –	3
	11 –	2 –	3½

[Page one hundred and forty-one. 1777.]
   ffriday the 28th march 1777 by the blessing of God I began sowing. Said day sown on the Gardners Croft of rye . . .   0 – 2 – 2½

[1] A lean-to shed.

The whole winter was close snow and frost but from the 8th Janry there was tollerable weather till the first ffebry. Then snow and frost till the 15th. Then tollerable weather till the first march. Thereafter snow and frost till the 28th it became tollerable but very cold so that I sowed non more till the first April which day sown in the gardners croft 3 firlots clean peas and 3 pecks on the east side of .   3 − 3

of rye said day on the east side of the croft .   3½

     1 − 3 − 0½

Said day sown on Drumvore on the side next the gate of my own white oats . . .   1 − 3

It one sd. ground mixed with white oats .   1

It below the milln next the Ditch Mr Gordons white oats . . . . . .   3 − 0 − 0

It of white oats mixed with small oats next the Drum . . . . . .   2 − 1 − 2

It on the after muck and after tathing of Drumvote of white oats with rye ½ boll rye . . . .   2 − 2 − 3

of small oats mixed with white oats on the Drummore sd first of April . . .   1 − 0 − 0

Of small oats all mixed on the Drummore .   9 − 2

I had done sowing the Drummore 4th April

It of small oats behind the coats . . .   2 − 2 − 3

It upon the Drumvote at and preceeding the friday 18th . . . . .   7 − 2 − 0

It on the said ground the 19th of small oats .   3 − 2 − 0

It on the said ground that was tathed and mucked . . . . . .   3 − 0 − 1

Of the best small oats and ½ boll birlie mixed .   0 − 2 − 0

On the ley of Laganamore of small oats mixed . . . . . .   0 − 3 − 2

With birllie   1

     I had finished my oat seed by the blessing of God Tuesday 22 of April. Never did see colder weather than from the 1st March.

[Page one hundred and forty-two.   1777.]

Tuesday 23rd September the see [1] of peats was broke

May Saturday the 4th given Donald McIntosh [2] to buy hay for his cown two sh: sterling

Ane account of what oats I disposed of crop 1776

To Donald McIntosh on Auchnabochin [2] of birllie	0 – 2 – 0	
To Coll McIntosh yr [2]	0 – 0 – 2	
To Alexr. McAlbea [2] in Luald of white oats	1	
To Wm. Davidson Dun: beg of white oats [2]	2	
To Donald Sanders mores son [2] in Dun: beg for sowing	1	
To James Roy [2] in part payt of his widers [3]	1	
To Samuel in Clune [2]	2½	

[Page one hundred and forty-three.   1777.]

ffriday 28th March by the blessing of God I begin my sowing

	B.	f.	p.
Said day in the Gardners croft of rye		3 –	2
It peas in said croft		3 –	3
The first of April sown of my own white oats next the gate on the Drummore clean	1 –	3 –	0
Below the killn one sd. Drum of Aberlour's oats	5 –	2 –	2
It on the affter muck and after tathing this side of Tomvote of white oats and half boll rye	2	2	3
It on Lagnamer of clean barlie		1	
On said ground mixed with small oats		1	
On Tomvote mixed with small oats the north side of birllie Inchdoing the whole rye		2	
Pease, Birllie and White oats sown 1777	12 –	3 –	2
The whole small oats sown on Drummore the last being sown the 4th April	10 –	2	
Sown of small oats behind the coats	2 –	2 –	3
The whole sown on Drumvoate having done the 21st April	14 –	0 –	1
Before then sown of small oats in Lagnamore		3 –	2
	28 –	0 –	2

[1] Probably an obsolete word for a stack.

[2] People living on the Davoch.

[3] Probably ' tred widders,' a part of the old Scots plough.

B. f. p.

I began sowing my bear upon Saturday the third
    May in the miding and what I put out of
    horse muck without mixing on the South
    Side and the sheeps muck 3 rigs and a
    part of the fourth   .   .   .   .   1 – 1 – 1
In the yard behind the house ½ peck and ½ on
    the ground taken in for potatoes on
    Tomvote .   .   .   .   .   •   1

    I had done by the blessing of God Wednesday the seventh,
but the half peck on Tomvote. From the middle of March
till the first of May tho it did not prevent plowing after the 28th
but one day or two. After the first May it became more mild.
Very little rain but constant cold wind from the north.

[Page one hundred and forty-four. 1777.]
    Dunachton 24th Sepbr. 1777. By the blessing
    of God I began cutting my bear on the
    row that afternoon and the next day I cut
    the whole being muck bear .   .   .   70 – 00 – 00
More of the bear in the garden and by the
    Dutch not ripe bad bear .   .   .   05 – 00 – 00
Cut on the ground given Coll and Donald more
    of brocked corn 63 thrave of which they
    got 6 thraw and 7 shaves The remain-
    ing 57 Thraw and 34 Thraw of the
    heighth is put in the furthest east small
    stack and three thraw of small oats from
    Tomvote in whole .   .   .   . 94 – 00 – 00
        [The rest of this page has been torn out.]

[Page one hundred and forty-five. 1778.]
    The season was very cold with frost and high
    winds till the first and second of April
    1778. Said day sown behind the barns
    of rye by the blessing of God . . 00 – 3 – 01
It of pease the 7th of April .   .   .   2 – 01
Sown at and preceeding the 7th April of rye in
    the third muck and Tathing this side of
    Tomvote   3
With the said rye of white oats .   .   , 1 – 3 – 2

It on the croft this side of Lagnamer of the oats from Dollinchappel . . .	2	—	3
Ane other peck on the head rig on the right hand at the end of the Dutch of Dunmore			I
On Drummore of Mr Gordons white oats .	5 — 1 —	0
Of brocked small oats	4 — 1	
The season after the 12th turned very cold with frost snow and wind till the 17th when yr was sown of small oats behind the coats	2 — 3 — 2	
The season still continuing cold tho' the snow was mostly off the rigs sown on Drumwode. On the south side of brocked oats 18th April	2 — 0 — 0	
There was no more sown of oats till the 25th there being snow and frost with high winds	3 — 0 — 0	
Therse more measured in the barn the 30th April	4 — 3 — 0	
Of which sown before then 2 bolls the remaining 2 bolls and a half was sown the 4 May a firlot was returned to the barn. More sown said day	3 — 2 — 2	

Which finishes my labouring as to oats	30 — 2 — 0

Till yesterday we had most disagreeable weather. Wind snow frost and rain for 22 days past so that last week I did not sow any. The firlot returned as marked sown which was not John Bain gave it the horses.

[Page one hundred and forty-six. 1778.]

I began sowing my bear by Gods blessing upon Thursday the 7th May. Sown in the after muck	1 — 0 — 0
In the muck of the miding	0 — 3 — 0
In the Tathing	1 — 0 — 2
	2 — 3 — 2

Ane account of what hay I sold 1778	£ s. d.
To Duncan Robertson in Dollbrady 20 st. .	5 — 0 — 0
To our Doy: [1] four st:	1

[1] Contraction of daughter.

To the chamberlain in Rothiemurchus [1] of hay
 18 st. . . . . . . 0 – 15 – 0
To Donald McIntosh in Auchnabochin 3 st: [2]
To James McDonald in Dollphour 4 st: . 1 – 0 – 0
To his son in law Wm. Davidson the taylor
 3 ston . . . . . . 15 – 0
More to Donald McIntosh [2] in Auchnabochin
 4 st: 1
To Coll there 4 stone [2] 1
To John McPherson late miller 3 stone at . 15
To John McIntosh in Dun: more 2 ston [2] . 10
To John Fraser Weaver 2 ston and one to his
 wife [2] 15

[Page one hundred and forty-seven. 1778.]

Ane accot. of what meall was made of cropt 1777
The whole made of bear and rye in meall . 07
Decr. the 20th then made of oat meall . . 08 – 1 – 1
Said day of pron a boll at half meall . . 00 – 2 – 1
Of white oat rush meall 30th Janry . . 08 – 2 – 0$\frac{1}{2}$
Of pron $\frac{1}{2}$ boll 1
Of small oat meall the 7th ffebry . . . 06 – 2 – 2
Of pron five firlots . . . . . 2 – 2
Of white oat meall the 19th March . . 09 – 1 – 2$\frac{1}{2}$
Of pron a boll and $\frac{1}{2}$ . . . . . 3 – 0
Of white oat meall the 29th April 1778 . . 04 – 0 – 3
Of pron $\frac{1}{2}$ boll 3 pecks . . . . 1 – 1$\frac{1}{2}$
Of small oatmeall 14th May . . . 08 – 3 – 2
Of pron 6 firlots 3

36 – 0 – 2$\frac{1}{2}$

The 20th December the first of bear and oat
 meall was come from the milln of cropt
 1777
Said day there was in the house of Cropt 76 . 08

In whole . . . . 54 – 0 – 2$\frac{1}{2}$

---

[1] Factor at Rothiemurchus.
[2] People living on the Davoch.

[Page one hundred and forty-eight.   1778.]

Ane accot. of what meall I sold of crop 1777.

	B.	f.	p.
To John Dow McIntosh in Crathie . .	1 –	0 –	0
To Coll in Auchnabochin [1]	2 –	0 –	0
To John McIntoshes relict there [1] . .	1 –	0 –	0
To Coll upon account of Sanders Bains wife [1]	1 –	0½	
To John McPherson the fidler [1] . . .	2 –	0	
To Alexr. Shaw the cupper	1		
To a man from the Braes	2		
To James Gordons relict	1		
To John Campboll at the gateside [1] . .	1 –	0 –	0
To Donald more McIntosh [1] . . .	1 –	0 –	0
To Wm. McPherson in Coraldy . . .	2 –	2	
To white oats to Sanders Grant the Chamber-lain [2]	1 –	0 –	0
To Mrs McIntosh of Borllum of white oats [3] .	2 –	0 –	0
To John McIntosh in Carit [1] of small oats .	1 –	0 –	0
To Alexr. more weaver [1] of small . . .	1		
To Bain my servant of small oats [1] . .	1		
To the relict of John McIntosh in Kincraig of Rye [1]	1		

To Sanders Bains [1] wife or he entered my service a firlot of meall and only 2 sh: that she acknowledged.

Since he entered my service a stone of meall about the end of Jully and a stone the 12th August 1778

[Page one hundred and forty-nine.   1778.]

Ane accot. of what meall was made of Crop 1778

	B.	f.	p.
Impr of Clean bear meall made 29th Octbr. N.S.	2		
It of rush oats, rye and oats 12th Dito meal .	4		
It of bear meall and pease Janry. 11th . .	4 –	0 –	1½
April the 30th of bear meall	4 –	1 –	2
It of very small bear meall		3 –	3
It Jully 7th of bear meall from the miln .	2 –	2 –	0
	17 –	3 –	2½

The 11 Decr. there was of clean white oat
meall in the house of crop 1777 . . 6 – 0 – 0

---

[1] People living on the Davoch.   [2] Factor to Grant of Rothiemurchus.
[3] The family name of the owners of Raits, who were Balnespick's neighbours on the west.

	B.	f.	p.
Of clean small oats the 12th December . .	3 –	3 –	0½
Of the pron		1 –	2
It of small oat meall 11th Janry. . . .	4 –	0 –	0
It of pron 9 pecks	0 –	1 –	1
Janry the 29th of clean white oat meall put in the chist next the bed	4 –	2 –	0½
In the pron nine pecks	0 –	1 –	1
It of small oat meall sd day in the end next the window	4 –	0 –	2
In the press	0 –	1 –	1
In the chest next the bed	1 –	1	
In the chest next the end of the cross house .	2 –	0 –	0
Taken into the house	1 –	2	
In the press ffebry the 11th	0 –	1 –	0
Of rush meall ffebry. 11th in the cross house .	3 –	2 –	0
It into the house	2 –	1 –	2
In the press		0 –	3
	28 –	3 –	1
April 30th of oat meall	5 –	1 –	3
It of pron eleven pecks making . . .		1 –	2
	34 –	2 –	2
The whole of my cropt including bear and oats	52 –	2 –	0½

[Page one hundred and fifty. 1779 (?).]

	B.	f.	p.
Of bear mixed with the birlie that is marked on the oyr side which was sown the 10th April		2 –	2
The season was so cold with rain, snow and wind from the 6th April till the 7th May that I did not sow any more bear. Said day sown in muck from the Door of the byers and the stable behind the byer and the barns		2 –	2
Sown in the miding the 12th May . .		3 –	0
Sown one the tathing		2 –	2
		2 – 2 –	2

By the blessing of God I began cutting my bear upon Wednesday the 11th August New Style 1779 Behind the Kitchen

[Page one hundred and fifty-one.   1779 (?).]

March 8th New Style by the blessing of God I began my
sowing said day of the oats that I bought with the straw from
Donald Davidson the remaining part not being sowed.

	B.	f.	p.
Sown of said oats in the Red Park . . .	6 –	0 –	0
More small oats of my own oats . . .	3 –	2 –	0
To small oats this side Drumvote March 19th.	3 –	2 –	2
The above was mixed with three firlots white oats and three firlots rye in whole . .	1 –	2 –	0
	14 –	2 –	2
Of white oats next the gate and on the west end of said park and a little one the end next the park	1 –	3 –	0
Of white oats from Mr. McLean in exchange of the oats last year from Dollchapel .	1 –	2 –	0
Of clean rye		1 –	1
Of pease		1 –	1
Of clean barlie by the waterside in the Red Park		1 –	1
Of barlie with which bear is to be mixed sown the first April N.S.		3 –	2
	5 –	2 –	2
	20 –	1 –	0

I finished by the blessing of God my oat seed
sowing the foresaid day.
Never did see finer season than we had all the
spring and most of the winter except ten
days in Janry.
I brought home three bolls birlie and only
sowed in whole of it .   .   .   .   01 – 3 – 0

[Page one hundred and fifty-two.]

Sold of white oats of Cropt 1778 payable Martinmas

	B.	f.	p.
To Mrs McIntosh Borllum	2		
To Donald Kinloch at Gordon Hall . .	3		
To Mrs McPherson Lynwile . . .	1		
To the Mrs of pittourie	0 –	1	
	06 –	1	

To Petter Grant a firlot of white oats
To Samuel in the Croft
                        All below is birllie
To Donald More McAlbea in Dun: more
To Alexr. McAlbea in Leuald
John Roys relict and Lachlan
John McIntosh in Dunmore and Lach: his son
to Donald the Captain's servant
This above birllie is to be 4 sh: per firlot if payed agt St. Coms
        market.
To Donald Davidsons wife in Croft Carnol
Of small oats to Fraser the weaver in Auchna-
        bochin the oats is mixed with a little
        birlie so am to charge a sh: more than for
        the small oats
Sown of said oats in William mores land in
        Dun: beg .   .   .   .   .   .   2 – 0 – 0
John McIntosh the shoe maker in Dun: more
        of the small oats that I bought from Don
        Davidson with the straw   .   .   .   0 – 1 – 0
Of said crop to Mrs. McIntosh in Auchna-
        bochin of good meal   .   .   .   .   1 – 0 – 0
To Campboll the weaver at the Gate   .   .   1 – 0 – 0
Campboll is due June 2nd 1779 four and sixpence ower and
        above the boll meal.

[Page one hundred and fifty-three.]

    Ane acct. of what meal was made of Cropt 1779.   I housed
all my cattle 12th Novr. N. St: 1779.   Snow and frost.
  . The first was bear meall brought from the
        milln the first Novr. foresd. for servant
        meal in which yr was five firlots rye six
        firlots small oats in whole   .   .   .   03 – 1 – 1½
Said day of fine bear for the table .   .   .   00 – 1 – 0
ffebry the 18th there was of clean bear meall .   08 – 0 – 2
Oct 17th yr was of the old bear come from the
        miln of which five pecks small for the
        table   .   .   .   .   .   .   03 – 3 – 1
There was of bear malted   .   .   .   .   02 – 1 – 0
To the tayler and hens of bear meall   .   .   01 – 2 – 2
                                                      _____
                                                      19 – 2 – 2½

Its to be remembered that it was of cropt 78 that all the oat
meall was made use till the 10th ffebry and that then yr
was three bolls and a firlot remaining

ffebry 10th there was brought out of the milln
of birllie and bear mixed . . . 07 – 2 – 0
of which 4 – 2 was put in the chist below the
window of the cross house of the pron . 1 – 1
At ye above date yr is of the old white oat meall
in the house six firlots and seven firlots
that Mrs McLean has in borrowing . 3 – 1 – 0
ffebry 28th brought out of the milln of Rush
meall of small oats and rye of which put
in the chist next the bed six bolls four
and a half in the end next the fire of sd.
meall and seven pecks brought into the
house in whole . . . . . 10 – 3 – 3
In the pron of meall . . . . . 3 – 0
It of said oat and rye March 28th . . 1 – 3 – 3
Of small oats said day both put in the chist at
the end of the bed . . . . 02 – 2 – 2
Of pron ½ boll . . . . . . 00 – 1 – 0
12th April put in said chist of the white oat meall   00 – 2 – 0½

27 – 3 – 3½

[Page one hundred and fifty-four.   1777.]

Ane acct. of what cattle I have the 4th June 1777.

Of cows that have or is with calf 11
Of fory cows two and Capt Shaws big cow . . . 3
One yal [1] cow that had a calf 1
Two 4 year old queys last may 3

17

Of three year old queys last may 7
Of two year old queys last may which are given Annie . 2
Of year olds she. 4

30

Of stots 3 year olds last may 5
of two yearolds last may 5
Of year olds last may 4
A five year old bull 1

15

[1] A barren cow.

Ane acct. of what sheeps I had at said time
Impr of three yearold wedders from Ja: Roy . . .	10
from Sanders Buie [1] in Carit	04
A five year old of my own	01
of rams 2 one four and the oyr 2 year old . . .	02
Of two yearold wedders of my own	16
A three year old wedder with John Robertson in the Carit and a two yearold with D. Davidson . . .	2
It of milk sheeps young and old	35
The whole	88
Sold of the 10 bought from James Roy eight There are lost of my own wedders and six made use of in the house	17 [2]
	71

[Page one hundred and fifty-five. 1778.]
Ane Accot. of what cattle I have upon the 17th May 1778
Off milk cows calfed and to calf	15
It one forrie cow and one that had a calf formerly . .	2
It of four year olds at this time 3 very trifling . .	7
It of two yearolds	4
It of year olds	4
The above are all she	32
It off four year old stots	5
It of three yearolds at this time	8
It of two yearolds	4
It of year olds	4
	21
The bull	1
	54
Of the above number sent to the Glen sd. day .	35

[1] Yellow Alexander.
[2] The loss of one sheep in eight would be considered extraordinarily poor sheep-farming nowadays in such good sheep country.

There is a stot and two small she beasts at Ovie. Two of them
are at home to be sent to the Glen and the trifling beast
that I had with Capt. Shaws cow is returned with the
wife at Ovie. She is to keep her till Whitsunday next.
She being due me eight sh: as the ballance of 13 given
her in May 1777.

All the cattle John Bain delivered to George 8th June is thirty
and Donald mors 3 yearold is with Donald's which
makes 31. of the above number yrs four stirks the oyr
four and the bull being at home and the 2 Quies thats
brought home from the roup [1] as also one of two yearolds
is brought home.

[Page one hundred and fifty-six. 1775, 1776, 1777.]

The 11th Decbr. 1775 given Donald Stuart
to buy shoes for the half year as they are
due . . . . £00 – 04

To John McDonald from the middle of March
till Martinmas the shoes are paid [2]

John McDonald for his half years shoes 8th
Janry 04

To David Stuart a pair of good single shoes at . 1 – 2

with the use of a guinea on May 26th of which he will expect
ten or twelve pd. as the ½ years fee [3]

In Decbr. 1776 eight shillings given to John Bain and David
Stuart to buy shoes to them

Payed John Bain of the wages due him preceeding marts 1776
only 13 sh:. Therse seven sh: still due him

Seven Sh: is pd. John Bain the day of St Coms market and
2 sh: given him to pay one pair shoes

David is payed of his wages and a sh: more by a guinea given
his broyr to assist in keeping a horse at his desire

In March 1777 I sold two hides the 9th Jully to John Bain
and to Lach: McIntosh both my servants at £1 – 05
payable at Christmas which will pay so much of yr wages.

I am due John Bain the last ½ years wages

Given John Bain the 18th October 2 sh: which pays him ½ years
shoes

[The three individuals mentioned on this page were all servants.]

[1] Sale.
[2] Shoes were always given as part of a farm servant's wages.
[3] Scots money.

Payed John Bain my servant all the wages due him preceeding
marts last and his shoes till Whitsunday 1778.
as also to Bain payt of his shoes till Whitsunday and 10 sh:
since his going to Fort George ten more due as marked
on the oyr side
Payed Sanders Bain all that was due him when he went South
after Martinmas.
Payed journeymans fee to his moyr being 20 sh:.

[Page one hundred and fifty-seven. 1771.]

Janry 31st 1771 Then having counted and cleared with
John McPherson in Lynallan of Phoness[1] and Petter Campbell
son to Alexr. Campboll some time in Elrish for a joint bill drawn
by me upon and accepted by the sd. John Mcpherson and the
foresd. deceased Alexr. Campbel for behalf of Donald Campboll
fidler after they had payed Johnathan Ross[2] for the board and
cloathing of the sd. Donald Campboll's broyr by his broyrs orders
the contents of the bill being fifteen pd. and a sh: all which was
pd. me at the above date but four pd. str. for which I gave bill.

At that very time I paid Johnathan Ross of sd.
   sum £3
At an oyr time by my orders from John in
   Lynallen 1
To the tayler that is married with Campbells
   sister . . . . . . 3 – 1
To him by John McPherson by my orders . 2 – 0
To his wife Campbells sister 14th Janry 1775 . 1 – 1
To his moyr to buy shoes, linnens etc when the
   boy was sent for Lond:[3] . . . 8 – 8
For a whole suit of clothes at said time and for
   making . . . . . . 11 – 4
To his broyr to buy goods March 1775 . . 15 – 0
                         11 – 17 – 0

[1] A very ancient family of McPhersons lived at Phoness. They died out
a little later than Balnespick's time. The last survivor described himself
as 'the seventeenth heritor who had sat in Phoness.' The John McPherson
mentioned on this page was evidently a sub-tenant of Macpherson of Phoness.
[2] Johnathan Ross is mentioned several times. He was a tradesman in
Ruthven.
[3] London [?].

[Page one hundred and fifty-eight.]

Carried from the oyr side.

To Geo McIntosh with Campbell in part of
    Prentice fee . . . . . 01 – 01
More to his wife being the whole due him . 01 – 01

[Page one hundred and fifty-nine. 1774 and 1777.]

Ane accott. of what cattle I have the 10th Sepbr. 1774.

Impr. of cows that had calfs, the cow bought at John David-
    sons roup being included 19
Dito of three yearold queys Jo: Davidsons quey is one . 03
Dito of three yearold stots 04
Dito of two yearold stots 02
Dito of two yearold she 05
Dito of yearold she 04
Dito he 02
                                —
                               39

Of the above number sold 12 and killed on . . . 13
                                —
                               26

I have stirks seven she and two he 09
                                —
                             35

It of three year old wedders sent to the Clune . . 10
It of year old wedders sent to the Clune 10th Sepbr. one
    of them being a ram 17
It of sheeps at home 60
It of lambs from the South 20 of which one was killed
    before this date 19
One more died before Marts
It at home of rams 02
                              —
                            108

26th June 1777 all the sheep that is at Dunachton . . 53
There is two rams and 10 wedders 12
Theres 4 three yearolds from the [? ? ?] and sixteen two
    yearolds of our own and a 5 yearold wedder . . 21
One with John Robertson in Carit a three yearold and a two
    yearold with David Davidson and a year old with
    William Dow's relict 03
Theres of lambs 12 he and 18 she 30
There was 20 sold at 18 pence each of the worst.

[Page one hundred and sixty. 1775 and 1776.]

Ane accot. of what cattle I have the 8th Decbr. 1775.

Off cows that had calves	13
Off four yearolds 8th May that is bulled . . .	04
Off three yearolds Agt may she	04
Off two yearolds agt May	07
Off she stirks	04
	32
Off three yearolds agt may she	4
Off two year olds agt may	2
Off year olds agt May	2
A bull four years old	1
	41
The number of sheep that we have at said time . .	64
four wedders two at home and two in the Cluanach . .	4
The Ram	1
Off year olds agt May if they live	40
	109
June 12th 1776. The number of sheep is only . .	51
It of she yearolds	17
It of he yearolds	19
It a wedder at home and 3 in the Clune . . .	04
The Ram	01
	92

Of lambs 42 tolerable and seven very bad not worth 8 pence each.

[Page one hundred and sixty-one. 1774-5.]

Ane accot. of my debt and funds made out the 12th May 1774 with intrest till Marts included.

Impr by Lord Adam Gordon pr. bond .	£1075 – 00 – 00
Sir James Grants bond with the intrest .	. 605 – 00 – 00
Corriebrough by bond with the intrest .	. ˉ105 – 00 – 00
Invereshie pr. bill with the intrest till Cands	

[The middle part of this page has been damaged. The entries evidently deal with the affairs of one of the sub-tenants against whom Balnespick had threatened to take legal proceedings for arrears of rent. The later part of the entry continues :]

Not a sh: of debt this she declares Theres 4 new plaids in
her chist and her moyrs plaid in the chist that the smiths
wife had.   Four gowns and four coats.   Three cloaks
on the two beds.
The settlement made with Coll about his land.   He pays just
now seven merks which is pd.   He pays at Martinmas
12 merks for that which he formerly possessed at fourteen
in whole 26 merks [1]

[For fuller details, see p. 167.]

[Page one hundred and sixty-two.   1774.]

Ane accott. of what money I expended on my family or
oyrwise in the year 1774.   Monthly accots not included.

	£	s.	d.
To three firlots malt from James Stuart Knock		12	09
The boll came at the said time . . .		4	03
For the new Town [2] for a pd. Tea ffebry 9th .		7	06
for a pd. more tea from the newtown . .		7	06
To Bisket from yr [3]		1	06
To corks six dozen		0	07
To Inverness for fish [4] at different times .		3	00
To the Newton for Three pair shoes one for my wife one for Grace, one for Christe and ane oyr pair for myself march the 23rd		16	
For a firlote peas from Forres . . .		04	
For whiskie from Ferintosh and oyr places preceeding the 26th March at which time not above four pints in the house .		02	
It for barley from Elgin being eight pd. .		1	
It of cash for half pd. Breakfast tea from Ins:		02	03
May the 8th for three pints Glenlivate whiskie		05	06
Jully 21st to Wm More Davidson for whiskie		03	06
To McPhadruck for whiskie . . .		03	06
To a Forress mercht. for a pd. Tea . .		03	08

[1] Merk was at that date equal to 1s. 3⅓d. sterling.
[2] Perhaps Newtonmore, but more probably Kingussie, which was founded
about this time.
[3] A few years later Lachlan's widow constantly ordered sugar biscuits
and ' plumb cake ' from Inverness.
[4] Probably salted herrings and haddocks.   In another old account book
there are many entries recording the purchase of such fish.

[Page one hundred and sixty-three.   1780.]
    [This page contains a list of Balnespick's sheep and cattle, but it is useless for purposes of comparison.]

[Page one hundred and sixty-four.]
    [This page contains a list of small sums of money expended for Captain Shaw, probably of Dellnavert, and is of little interest as very few details are given.]

[Page one hundred and sixty-five.]
    The 9th August 1777 taken out of sope in whole 14 bolls.

[Page one hundred and sixty-six.   1773.]
    Ane accot. of bills left with me the 2nd Decbr. 1773.

	£	s.	d.
[? ? ?] belonging to Sanders more McIntosh in Glasgow	19	–	8
To a bill due by Alexander Cattonach and Donald McIntosh the one in Gartain and the oyr in Lagan	1	– 10 –	9
To a bill due by James McDonoll in Ballchroan	0	– 12 –	0
To James McPherson in Cruden beg's bill .	2	– 02	
To a bill due by Alexr. McPherson Kylehuntly	2	– 00	
To a bill due by John McPherson in Prosnacalach [1] of Kincraig and James McBain in Park [1]	1	– 13 –	0½
To a bill due by Wm. Campboll in Tomnamuckach and Donald Bain yr [1] jointly .	0	– 07 –	6
For a bill due by John McIntosh in Kincraig [1] and his sister jointly	0	– 10	
To a bill due by Donald Robertson in Auchnachile and James McLean jointly . .	0	– 10	
I have also in my hands of Sanders [2] money for all which he has my receipt promessing to deliver said bills on cash . . .	3	– 01 – 00	
	13	– 05 – 11½	

Eight and 2 pence was the money I received of Donald Robertsons bill.
Received from John McIntosh in Kincraig and his sister upon actt. of said Sanders 10 – 06.

----

[1] Sub-tenants.   [2] Probably Sanders McIntosh or Sanders McAlbea.

[Page one hundred and sixty-seven. 1773.]

Ane accott. of my situation agt Mart 1773.

Lord A. G.[1] Debiter with Intrest agt

Marts	£1025
Sir L. G.[2]	0645
Corrie [3]	0115
Lurie	0086
Invereshie [4]	0102
Lachie [5]	0035
ffor Bark, butter and cheese . . .	0022
ffor wood, Lach: Roy wright . .	0004 – 8
ffor meall	0075
ffor rent	0017
ffor lent money and seed oats and bear .	0005
	2031 – 8

Ballance due Mr. Lach: London [6] .	019 – 4
Due Mr Shaw	166 – 13 – 4
Andrew Gows children . . .	060
To the children of the late Dellnavert [7] .	044
To John Fergusson and son . . .	042
To Different people upon Willes account [8]	026
To William McKenzies children . .	010
To John McIntosh his relict and children	015
To James Robertson for three queys .	003 – 19
To Sanders at Nairn	02 – 4
To Fraser that is with Cruikshank. .	003
To Servants Merchts	022

[The entries on this page are connected with those on p. 161.]

[1] Lord Adam Gordon.
[2] Sir Ludovic Grant of Dalvey.
[3] McQueen of Corriebrough.
[4] Macpherson of Invereshie.
[5] His son, probably for his share of the rent.
[6] Probably a Mr. Lachlan Mackintosh, merchant of London, with whom many transactions seem to have taken place.
[7] Captain Shaw, who rented Dellnavert.
[8] His second son William.

[Page one hundred and sixty-eight.]

Ane accott. of what the Smith[1] was due at the time of his decease.

The Ballance due me at Marts 1768 . .	00 – 17 – 07
To his bill for money paid John Davidson in croft for a cow payable Martinmas 1769 with two year intrest at Marts 1771 .	03 – 12 – 05
To cash given him in June 70 . . .	0 – 05 – 00
To his wife said year	0 – 05 – 00
To the ballance of three bolls meall payd Clury having received only 20 sh: . . .	01 – 10 – 00
To rent Schoolmrs sallary and stipends for three oxengets of Land Martinmas 70 and cess	02 – 11 – 09½
To rent of said lands for marts 71 cess included	02 – 11 – 09½
To the rent stipends etc for Marts 72, only Drumstank	01 – 12 – 01¼
To the widow in Pitoure for ½ hide leather .	0 – 06 – 0
To cash given the Smith in ffebry last to buy some necessaries before he went to Ross to buy meall	0 – 09 – 00
½ guinea for which he payed 18 pence To one half boll for his funerals from John Davidson in Leald	00 – 10 – 00
To a firlot meall when puting out the muck .	00 – 05 – 00
To David Davidson for a peck bear . .	00 – 01 – 06
To two bolls meal last summer . . .	02 – 00 – 00
To the Smith when going to Ross to buy meall	02 – 00 – 00
To Sanders McQueen for cloath to Sandy .	00 – 03 – 00
To cash given the wife that went with the children	00 – 01 – 00
To be sent the children's uncles . . .	00 – 02 – 00

[1] Alexander McDonald the smith is mentioned several times in the Account Book. This page and the next one give the most complete record of the borrowings of himself and his wife, but it varies in a few respects from the scattered entries of these transactions that occur in other parts of the book. A complete summary occurs in Chap. VIII., p. 138, of the Introduction.

[Page one hundred and sixty-nine.]

Of the debt carried from the oyr side . .	£20 – 14 – 02
To John McBain in Balldon for Whiskie he having given credit for ten sh: as the price of a boll oats given him by the Smith	00 – 15 – 03
It of cash payed for a cow and a calf . .	02 – 07 – 06
	22 – 16 – 11¼
To her share of 4 pd str: recovered from Petter McGlashan	02 – 00 – 00
To twenty sh: str: got from the relict . .	01 – 00 – 00
To seven firlots victual from the smith in Janry. 70	01 – 15 – 00
To her share of the 100 pd. scotts the half falling to her	04 – 03 – 04
To ane accott. of some work done by the smith in the year 69, 70 and 71 . . .	00 – 19 – 02
To the value of four quies sold to Lieut McPherson	6 – 06 – 00
	14 – 03 – 06

[Page one hundred and seventy.]

ffebry 24th 1772 sd. day all the night shirts I have is only 20 and one useless.

All the fine shirts are only 6

Wednesday 19th June I have of tolerable fine shirts ten and twenty two of coarse

There is three shirts a missing two in June 1776 and one in 1777

[Page one hundred and seventy-one.]

The men proper for proving the marches twixt McIntosh and Borllum

Donald Davidson commonly called McIntyre
John Davidson in Dunachton at croft
Donald McGlashan
Petter Shaw son to Allen Shaw now at the White milln
Duncan more Shaw in Kinrara
Alexr. McDonoll and Wm Davidson both in Caritnakyle
Donald Roy in Laggan poinded fforbes sheep, as did James McPhadruck and Donald McQueen each made them pay as did Donald Roy from Glengarrie then tenant in Auchnabochin the Smith etc.

Donald Davidson alias McIntyre told Donald McQueen last spring that he was in the knowledge that the tenants of Croft Carnoch [1] and the tenants of Dunachton did eat promiscuousely after they had taken the first eight or ten days of yr stiple [2] and so do continue until the bear appeared but never did hear that those tenants or Borllum pretended any right to pasture.

When the late Borllum called for this man to examine him about the marches he was displeased as he pointed out the marches as he pleased.

[Page one hundred and seventy-two.   1771.]

Ane Account of what money I advanced for Dear Geordie.

In money and cloaths having set out from here for Glasgow, Thursday the 25th April 1771.

Impr Mr George McIntosh mercht in Glasgow to be employed upon his behoof . .	25 – 00 – 00
It given to George ower and above what his moyr and broyr gave him . . .	03 – 00 – 00
It for a suite cloaths I had from Mr McIntosh Ins:	05 – 00 – 00
It for linnen from Perth and two shirts made of the linnen at home	03 – 15 – 00
It more sent to Mr George McIntosh to pay part of the accotts due for Geordie .	23 – 00 – 00
It sent him to pay the ballance by my son Wm for which Mr McIntosh sent a draft to a friend at Ed: to whom Wm payed the money	32
	91 – 15
Advanced for him while in Perth being only four months and ten days . . .	23 – 17 – 6
Advanced to buy negroes for him 23d Decbr. 1773	150
	274 – 17 – 06
To 12 pints and a chopen whiskie at 18 pence preceeding the 13th April 1776 [3] . .	18 – 09

[1] This farm is now owned by the same proprietor as Dunachton, but Balnespick does not seem to have held it as part of the Davoch, as the name does not appear in his rent roll of sub-lets. The farm lies between Belleville (Raits) and Cuillintuie (Kylintuie).   [2] The meaning of this word is not clear.

[3] This entry was entered long afterwards at the bottom of the page.

[Page one hundred and seventy-three.   1773.]

Tuesday 14th ffebry 1773 given the South Country ffox killer	. . . .	£00 – 02
Given old McGlashan in Janry 1773 of his sons money	. . . .	1 – 01
To his wife in ffebry at the milln	. . .	00 – 01
To his son Sandy the soldier to relieve a bill due Cameron in the parish of Alvie	. .	01 – 13 – 01
To his wife 10th March	. . . .	00 – 01 – 06
To his wife 24th March	. . . .	00 – 02 – 00
To his wife the 7th April	. . . .	00 – 02 – 00
To a shilling by Mrs McIntosh some time ago		00 – 01 – 00

[At the bottom of the page there are notes on his thirty-four shirts like the list on p. 170.]

[Page one hundred and seventy-four.   1770.]

Dunachton 10th ffebry 1770

	Dozens
Therse delivered Christie of Servits and Handtualls .	05 – 09
It two dozen and one covers I mean pillow cases .	02 – 01
Of sheets twenty two pair	
It of table cloaths twenty one	

[1771.]

Therse at Kincraig 26th March of sheets 25 pr. .	02 – 01
Therse of table cloaths 14	01 – 02
It of pillow cases	00 – 11
It of servits of different kinds coarse and fine . .	07 – 02

A note of such of the tenants as did not the long carriage.

Alexr. McIntosh in Prosnacalich, John McIntosh in Kincraig, Paul McPhail in Dunachtune, The Smith, McIntosh and McGlashan, Wm Callum all in Auchnabochin.

John McIntosh and Donald McIntosh and Faryr all in Dunachtune more, John Dow McAlbea, Alexr McDonoll and son, John More McAlbea all in Dunachton beg, Wm Camboll in Tommuckach all prom: ye double carriage this next season in the year 1770.

[Page one hundred and seventy-five.   1773.]

    Tuesday the 14th Decbr. 1773

Therse of night shirts 21
It of day shirts 10
All the shirts I have the 9th of Jully 1777
Off night shirts mostly a good deal worn . . . 19
Said day I got home of linnen my wife sent to Strathspey of
    good new shirts 06
Of fine shirts mostly a good deal worn but still good . 10
                                        —
                                      35

All the shirts I have Tuesday the 14th Sept 1779 is . 32
And six new shirts 06
                                        —
                                      38

June 14 1780

My number of shirts that Mary Clark delivered said day
    being in whole of which yr was eight of the former
    washing 38
There is two of the above shirts taken out being useless
    August 24th 1780
All the shirts course or fine that I have Thursday 9th
    Novr. 1780, of this number yrs. to be mended and
    not counted till that be done. 32

[Page one hundred and seventy-six.   1768.]

    Ane accot. of money consigned in my hands upon the 13th Decbr. 1768 at the desire of the Gentlemen of the Parish of Alvie in order to be applied as follows :

    To every man that brings here a large fox that is recently killed twixt the bounds of Dunachtunemore and the east end of Lynwilge five shillings str: and for every young fox killed and shown as above twixt the first of August two and six pence Str: and after the first August Old Style for every fox that will be delivered as afor sd. five sh: str: The same consigned in my hands is £10 – 03 – 8

    On the oyr side will be marked what ever is given out of said sum and to whom

[Page one hundred and seventy-seven.]

[This page contains a list of the names of those who killed foxes. In one year £5 – 4 – 10 was expended in rewards, and twenty-six foxes were killed; they were classified as 'large,' 'tolerably large,' and 'very small.']

[Copy of a leaf of paper found loose in the book. One side.]

A just calcule of each Auchten part of four in Dunaghton more as comprised by birley men. The sowing being computed to sow seventeen bolls each. The above computed to sow 15 bolls of which Discounted for the difference of Soile 3f 3p which leaves the sowing of it 14b. 2p. The rent of the Auchten part being £19 – 12 – 8 which brings it to £2 – 6 – 8 each bolls sowing which leaves the 14b 2p at £32 – 13 – 4.

The half of which £16 – 6 – 8 which leaves £2 – 00 – 10 to be Discounted of each ½ Aughten part.'

[The other side.]

	B.	f.	p.
A memorandum of what the half aughten part of land now possessed by John McIntosh in Dunachtown more will sow according to mens comprising	8 –	2 –	0
The sowing of the lands east by the brunt house is comprised to be . . .	18 –	0 –	0
The Difference of the Soile is looked upon to be	00 –	3 –	2
The grase inside the Burn be east the brunt house is comprised at	four shill: str:		
The rent which each Achtenpart pays . .	£19 – 16 –		4
The rent of each boll when equally divided of the sowing of the half auchtenpart above mentioned is come to	£2 – 6 –		8

[This 'just calcule' was written in a very neat copperplate hand—probably by the schoolmaster.]

[Scribbled note on flyleaf.]

Due for Ed: Journal from the 18th May 1765
 to the 10th May 1768 . . . 2 – 2 – 0
Invereshie pd the Journall 1st ffebry 1770.

APPENDIX II

Charts showing the Distribution of Balnespick's Sub-tenants and their Interrelation with him

The following signs are used :—

| | | | Figures on the rent roll as a sub-tenant.

= = Is mentioned in the account book, but does not appear
= = on the rent roll.

⊗ Balnespick gives employment.

⊞ Balnespick sells corn, etc., that year.

⊠ Balnespick purchases corn that year.

▽ Balnespick lends money.

KYLINTUIE. 50–60 acres. Now under partial cultivation. Distinctly less good land than the rest of the arable land of Dunachton-more.

	JAMES MᶜDONALD.	JOHN GLASS ROBERTSON.
1769	*Sole Tenant.* Paid very variable rent, perhaps to cover arrears.	*Cottar.*
1770		
1771	Became *Joint Tenant* with John Glass Robertson at an average rent of £8, 8s. 4d.	Became *Joint Tenant* with MᶜDonald. Rent £1, 10s. 7d.
1772		
1773		
1774		
1775		
1776		Rent raised to £1, 16s.
1777		
1778		
1779	Total of meal, 62 b. 1 p. He cleared off his debts in 1775, but borrowed again in 1776.	Balnespick sold him 6 b. 2 p. altogether.